# Israeli Identities

# Israeli Identities

## *Jews and Arabs Facing the Self and the Other*

Yair Auron

Translated by Geremy Forman

berghahn
NEW YORK • OXFORD
www.berghahnbooks.com

Published in 2012 by

Berghahn Books

www.berghahnbooks.com


First paperback edition published in 2015



**Library of Congress Cataloging-in-Publication Data**

Auron, Yair.
[Zehuyot Yisre'eliyot. English]
Israeli identities : Jews and Arabs facing the self and the other / Yair Auron ; translated by Geremy Forman. — 1st ed.
p. cm.
Includes bibliographical references and index.
ISBN 978-0-85745-305-1 (hardcover : alk. paper) — ISBN 978-1-78238-795-4 (paperback : alk. paper) — ISBN 978-0-85745-306-8 (ebook)
1. National characteristics, Israeli. 2. Palestinian Arabs—Israel—Ethnic identity. 3. Jews—Israel—Identity. 4. Cultural pluralism—Israel. 5. Group identity—Israel. 6. Israel—Ethnic relations. I. Title.
DS113.3.A94713 2012
956.94—dc23

2011037631

**British Library Cataloguing in Publication Data**

A catalogue record for this book is available from the British Library

Printed on acid-free paper

ISBN: 978-0-85745-305-1 hardback
ISBN: 978-1-78238-795-4 paperback
ISBN: 978-0-85745-306-8 ebook

For Ayelet,
For Naama, Yuval, and Yonatan,
With Love.

# Contents

# TABLES

# Preface

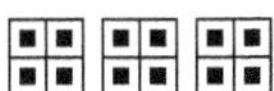

I was born and raised in Israel after the Holocaust. My parents immigrated to Palestine from Poland during the 1930s, before the Holocaust. For many years, I was unaware, or at least unable to grasp and internalize the fact that my close relatives, my aunts and uncles (whose number I still do not know), and my grandmother were killed in the Holocaust. Even when I was in my 30s and working at "Yad Vashem," I used to say that my interest in the Holocaust had nothing to do with my personal history or the history of my family, which did not appear to have been directly affected by the Holocaust. That is what I thought at the time.

I later came to realize that as an Israeli, I was raised and educated to believe in Zionist ideals and the (primarily socialist) social views associated with them: that is to say, the preference—if not superiority—of Israelis over "exilic Jews." It was then that I realized that consciously, and perhaps more importantly subconsciously, the Holocaust played a decisive role in my upbringing and the upbringing of my entire generation. I was raised on the miraculous bravery of the active Jewish resistance in the ghettos of Europe. The Holocaust was always linked with bravery, and bravery was always highlighted. I also came to realize that I knew nothing about the atrocities suffered by other non-Jewish groups at the hands of the Nazis or about other acts of genocide perpetrated before and after the Holocaust. In those days, the Holocaust was perceived as something that happened "to them" (the "exilic" Jews) "there" (in Europe).

The Six Days War marked a turning point and, in many ways, a rupture. As it did for many other Israelis, this war, in which I took part, raised in me fundamental questions regarding our very existence here in Israel; our attitude toward "the other," Arabs and Palestinians in particular, but also other non-Jewish groups; and of course, our attitude toward the Holocaust, which since then has come to be understood as something that befell us "here." Only then did I begin to recognize the suffering of the Palestinians and to understand that the physical ruins and remains I have seen in many parts of the country were actually the remains of Palestinian villages (in those days, we tended to refer to them as "Arab"). Since then, I have been attempting to clarify—with myself, with other Jews, and with the Palestinians—our attitudes toward and conflict with the Palestinians. For the past eight years, my family and I have lived in the Jewish-Arab locality of *Neve Shalom* (Hebrew) or *Wahat al-Salam* (Arabic), attempting to live a life of coexistence and to struggle against injustice.

I have spent years researching the tension between the particular and universal human components of Jewish and Israeli identity and the tension between the particular and the universal in general—these are tensions that divide Israeli society. I began by researching the causes for our actions with respect to the Armenian genocide, and I have been engaged with the subject of genocide for approximately two decades. I had difficulty understanding and accepting the Israeli government's long-term policy of denying the Armenian genocide carried out by Turkey. My research led me to many unexpected places and events and showed me a reality which, I must admit, I had not anticipated. I had hoped to find a greater sense of identification with and greater empathy for the suffering of the Armenian people, as well as more attempts to extend support in the few ways at the disposal of the Jewish people. Instead, I found considerable indifference and an attitude emphasizing the particular over the universal. The conclusions of the first phase of that project were published in my book *The Banality of Indifference: Zionism and the Armenian Genocide.*

In 1993, I published another book, titled *Jewish-Israeli Identity,* in which I explore the primary sub-identities within Jewish-Israeli society: secular identity, traditional identity, national-religious identity, and ultra-orthodox religious identity. These sub-identities, I discovered, had very few points of commonality and were separated by considerable tension. One point of commonality was the Holocaust, which, as I will show, plays a major unifying role in Jewish-Israeli identity. However, over the past two decades the memory of the Holocaust has also sparked a number of disagreements and debates, stemming primarily from tension between the unique aspects of the Holocaust and the universality of genocide (similar tensions exist between national and religious elements of identity and their universal counterparts). These tensions threaten the democratic, tolerant, and pluralistic nature of Israel society. Some sub-identities (or sectors) find it difficult to recognize the legitimacy of other sub-identities, and this results in considerable tension between the state's "democratic character" and the state's "Jewish character."

Later, I wrote a book titled *We Are All German Jews: Jewish Radicals in France during the Sixties and Seventies.* I found myself drawn to the hidden and often repressed elements of Jewish identity among members of this generation, who were deeply influenced by the Holocaust. This study focused not on the history of the new left but rather on the personal Jewish identity of its militants as radical Jews. It was the fascinating story of the Jewish identity of these radicals that provided the plot of the book. For me, this was another example of the relationship between the particular and the universal.

My next book, *Denial: Israel and the Armenian Genocide,* was a complex intellectual undertaking. Looking inward into my own consciousness and subconscious, and that of the society in which I live, was a difficult and painful experience. In many ways, it is not a book about the Armenian genocide but rather a book about what we sometimes refer to (justifiably or not) as the actualization of "Jewish values." It is a book about the nature and character of the state of Israel, and writing it, for me as an individual, was a fulfillment of my responsibility to my people and my society, and to the Armenian people. I believe that when we deny that a genocide was perpetrated against another people, we are actually defiling the legacy of our own Holocaust.

Over the years, I have been troubled by a disturbing sense of discomfort which has obligated me to criticize generations of Israeli governments for their evasive policies regarding the memory of the Armenian genocide. These policies border on genocide denial. The sense of discomfort caused me to explore both the observable factors and the deeper, more complex factors underlying these policies—policies that I cannot accept, particularly because we, as Jews, were victims of the Holocaust.

In recent years, I have invested much time and effort in researching and teaching about genocide. I am proud to be the director of a unique Open University project that has published twelve books on various aspects of genocide and that enrolls approximately 1000 students each year.

The future of and relationship between the different models of Jewish-Israeli identity appears to be largely, and perhaps entirely dependent on the future of the Israeli-Palestinian conflict. The same is true for Arab-Israeli (or Palestinian-Israeli) identity, and its relationship with the different models of Jewish-Israeli identity. In my view, the continuation of Israeli occupation and Israeli rule over another people will lead to the gradual but unavoidable end of the state of Israel as conceived by the original Zionist visionaries and the movement's founding principles. In one way or another, Israel will become a variation of an apartheid state, if it is not one already, at least in the occupied territories. We will increasingly come to be tainted with racism and a sense of absolute rule and paralyzing fear. At the same time, we will almost certainly refuse to acknowledge how racist we have become. This reality will undoubtedly strengthen religious identities in Israel, as well as the nationalist tendencies among religious and non-religious Jews alike. It will weaken the non-religious identities even further, and the humanist and liberal voices struggling against injustice and moral destruction will grow increasingly faint.

Although this prospect in itself is sufficiently depressing, we must also consider the likely deterioration in Israel's relations with the Diaspora and the international community. The intensification and radicalization of orthodox religious tendencies in Israeli society will undoubtedly lead to a rupture in relations with a large portion of world Jewry and most Jews in the United States, who believe strongly in the legitimacy of a number of religious models, such as reform, conservative, and re-constructionist Judaism.

This situation is unacceptable from a moral and humanitarian standpoint, and from the perspective of Jewish heritage, and the Holocaust in particular, it is shocking. However, as we will see, most young people in Israel do not identify with Yehuda Elkana's appeal that the Holocaust should "never happen again," which is by now more than twenty years old ("The Need to Forget," *Haaretz*, 2 March 1988). Instead, they identify with the Zionist lesson of the Holocaust—it "should never happen to us again."

In contrast, a compromise solution between Israel and the Palestinians will undoubtedly open up new horizons and lead to new developments. Still, neither of the two suffering peoples appears to have the strength, the ability, or the moral resolve to reach a compromise or a peaceful solution on its own. For this reason, external intervention, with all its drawbacks, may be the only thing that can save us and the Palestinians from suicide and mutual destruction.

A solution of compromise and withdrawal from most of the occupied territories will almost certainly involve a violent struggle with Jews with extreme nationalist-religious identities. Even if the state of Israel emerges victoriously, such a struggle will result in serious identity crises among some of the settlers and supporters of Jewish messianic ideas.

Without a doubt, determining the future of the occupied territories is the most significant political decision that stands to be made since the establishment of the state. It is, however, a decision that cannot be made as a result of mental and emotional exhaustion, fear, lack of leadership, and the inability to adopt decisive policy on the matter. In the meantime, as a result of the actions we have taken for the past forty-five years, we continue living out the seventh day of the Six Days War.

This book examines the question of Jewish-Israeli identity from both theoretical and empirical perspectives and integrates a comparative element by considering relevant, recently acquired data collected in a study undertaken in 1990. It also examines sub-groups within Arab (Palestinian)-Israeli society. This foundation of data, which endows the study with a broad horizontal and vertical comparative background, plays a crucial role in shedding light on phenomena taking place deep within Israeli society.

I would like to thank all my friends and colleagues at the Open University and Neve Shalom/Wahat al-Salam who have helped me at various points during this project. In particular, I would like to thank Relly Brickner and Adi Kliffer of the Open University's Evaluation Department, who were members of the research team and who assisted in the production and processing of questionnaires, and whose analysis was critical for the success of the study. I would also like to extend a special acknowledgement to Vered Funk, who with great professionalism and dedication typed the manuscript at its various stages of development. This research was supported by the Open University of Israel's Research Fund, and I would like to thank its staff for their ongoing assistance and support.

It is my distinct hope that this book will bring people closer together by increasing mutual understanding among Jewish and Arab citizens of Israel with their different identities.

# INTRODUCTION

## EXPRESSIONS OF JEWISH IDENTITY IN THE MODERN ERA IN THE DIASPORA AND IN ISRAEL

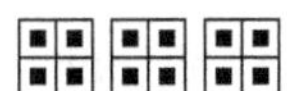

"To the Jews as a nation, nothing;
to the Jews as individuals, everything."
—Antoine Clermont-Tonnere

"To the Jews as a nation, nothing; to the Jews as individuals, everything ... [T]hey must be citizens individually." These words have been quoted many times since they were first articulated in December 1789 by Antoine Clermont-Tonnere, in an effort to convince his colleagues in the French National Assembly to support the provision of equal rights to Jews. This short, concise sentence illustrates the complex and problematic situation in which Jews found themselves during the modern era as well. It contains three fundamental concepts that are extremely relevant to the topic at hand: nation, individual, and citizen. The condition which Clermont-Tonnere proposed for providing Jews with equal rights—negation of their existence as a nation—was never clearly defined. In practice, it could never have been formulated in a precise manner in any event.

For example, when a Jewish person attending synagogue in Paris (the modern French state had already guaranteed the right to freedom of religion to all citizens, including Jews) faces east and prays for "next year in Jerusalem," is this merely a religious act or is it also a reflection of a national inclination?

The immanent lack of clarity in this definition has cast a shadow upon Jewish existence for more than two centuries and continues to do so. The new constitutional status enjoyed by the Jews after becoming equal citizens, and the resulting differences and similarities between them and other citizens of the state, was one factor in the emergence of modern anti-Semitism. Moreover, Emancipation and its implications undoubtedly resulted in major changes with long-term, far-reaching impact on Jewish life during the past two centuries. Many historians regard these two historical processes as the beginning of the modern era of Jewish history.

The fundamental meaning of Emancipation was the majority's provision of equal rights under the law—or full civil equality—to all Jews as individual people and citizens. This resulted in dynamic changes within Jewish society, which made efforts to adapt itself to the changing reality and to take part in shaping it. It is common to understand the *Haskala* as beginning with Moses Mendelssohn (1729–1786) and his associates in the *me'asfim* circle in 1880s Germany. The *Haskala* was aimed at bringing about changes in Jewish society in the realms of social activity, occupation, education, dress, language and religion. It stemmed from internal and external processes and questioned the essence of Judaism and its reason for existing. During the *Haskala,* historical processes that began in the sixteenth and seventeenth century erupted in full force, impacting most parts of the Jewish world during the nineteenth century. The nations that struggled for their right for self-determination in the modern era based their rights on common identity. The Jews first needed to clarify what their identity was.

## At a Crossroads

Herein lies the origin of the mysterious rupture at the foundation of Jewish existence. The Jews now stood at a crossroads. To a large degree, despite the great changes that have taken place since then, the Jews of Israel and the Diaspora are still standing at the same juncture, which, as a result of the *Haskala* and Emancipation, requires them to choose a path and define their identity. This has resulted in an opening up of the question of Jewish identity. The differences between the major streams of contemporary Judaism reflect the different responses to the process of Emancipation: Jewish identity prior to the Emancipation appears to be uniform, while Jewish identity after the Emancipation appears divided.

The new situation put the fused national-religious concept of Judaism (which regards Judaism as simultaneously a community, a religion, and a nation) to the test. Jews had to make a fundamental decision between accepting and rejecting Emancipation, between openness and closedness toward the surrounding non-Jewish society and culture. Next, they had to determine their conditions for openness and closedness.

Jews needed to provide answers, first and foremost to themselves, regarding how to relate to the state and the society that granted them equal rights, and how to relate to the price of equality and integration. They faced difficult questions, such as: How should they practice and preserve Judaism as citizens of new nation states? What was the nature of their relationship with the new democracy and the secular state that, in addition to civil equality, was supposed to ensure them religious freedom as well? Moreover, Jews now had to delineate their attitude toward the new nation state, which was trying to equate citizenship with nationality. When a Jew became a French citizen with equal rights, what was his or her nationality: French or Jewish?

Until the *Haskala* and Emancipation, the Jews were constantly being discriminated against and humiliated. Paradoxically, however, Jews' inferior status enabled them to worship god as they wished. The circumstances and conditions of the traditional Jewish suffering provided them with the ability to preserve their Jewish identity. As long as they were not requested or required to convert to another religion, they could maintain their Jewish identity, including its religious and national-ethnic differentiation from the surrounding population. During the period of Jewish seclusion (whether willing or coerced) that preceded the Emancipation, Judaism cultivated the motif of being a chosen and unique group of people as the foundation of their differences and isolation from non-Jews (*goyim*). The Emancipation also created a future-oriented perspective toward exile and redemption. Messianic redemption, it was thought, would redeem the Jews from their exile.

Over the past two centuries, Jews' answers regarding their Judaism and Jewishness have of course undergone many changes. However, we can nonetheless identify a number of the characteristics that are extremely significant to the discussion here. The immanent, unbreakable connection between religion and nationality was no longer shared by all Jews. The clarifications offered by some Jews with regard to their Jewish identity in its modern sense included some that highlighted the dominance or the exclusivity of the national component, others that highlighted the dominance or the exclusivity of the religious component, and still others that maintained a combination of the two. This process resulted in the emergence of a number of collective national and religious alternatives, alongside the quest for individual solutions.

The Israeli public, which has no experience with pluralism, often needs to be reminded that orthodox Judaism is only one religious alternative and that Zionism was only one national alternative. As a result of the *Haskala* and the Emancipation and based on a desire to solve the emerging problem of Jewish identity, a number of religious streams have been evolving in Judaism since the first half of the 1900s. These streams—the most prominent of which are Orthodox, Conservative, and Reform Judaism—differ from one another on many issues, including: the meaning, substance, and rituals of religion; the relationship between religion and nationalism, faith and ritual, and continuity, change and innovation; and the essence of Jewish-non-Jewish relations. Jews choose to practice different forms of Judaism in accordance with its religious significance for them.

Furthermore, the linkage between religion and nationality, or the concept that the Jewish religion is a national religion espoused by members of the Jewish nation alone, does not imply linkage in the opposite direction. That is to say, Jewish national identity during the modern period is not necessarily religious nationalism. In contrast to the linkage between religion and national identity, the link in the other direction—between national identity and religion—has ceased to be immanent and self-evident.[1] Many Jews minimize the significance of their religious belonging to Judaism and in some cases deny its very essence. This has introduced non-religious Jews to the stage of Jewish history. Non-religious Jews are secular Jews who do not regard their Judaism as religious in nature and who, to an even greater extent, do not regard religion as an authority for their Judaism. The process of secularization throughout human society in general and Jewish society in particular remains one of the most significant phenomena underway in Jewish society during the nineteenth and twentieth century.

It was against this background that Zionism came into existence, in addition to a number of other movements that emerged at the time. For this reason, it is simply impossible to understand the emergence of Zionism without understanding secularization. Again, it is important to emphasize that Zionism has been only one expression of Jewish national sentiment during the modern era of Jewish history. Others have included Autonomism, the Bund, and Territorialism. The attraction of universalist and cosmopolitan solutions, including communist revolutionary dogma, is also noteworthy. Jews who were attracted to these ideas, who sometimes had an extremely strong Jewish identity, hoped that the Jews' integration into the surrounding society, and their struggle to change it from its very foundations, would solve the problems of the Jews and create a new international reality in which no fundamental difference existed between the nations. These movements completely rejected religion in general, and Judaism was no exception.

All in all, I can say that Jews chose different ways of addressing the important challenge they faced, which is first and foremost a challenge of self-identity. Some completely rejected integration, opposed all changes, and held fast to the religion of their ancestors. Others saw integration as a necessity and attempted to negate their religious and national uniqueness by means of conversion or assimilation. Still others, as we have seen, attempted to integrate into society by joining broader movements that would work to erase all national and religious uniqueness. However, what appears to have been a large majority chose neither unconditional integration nor unconditional closedness, but rather embraced various forms of the more moderate approach of integrating into society while maintaining their unique Jewish identity.

During the nineteenth century, Jews underwent a process by which the elements differentiating them from non-Jews diminished. Some refer to this process as assimilation. Others refer to it as acculturation, modernization, or cultural adaptation to the surrounding environment. However, regardless of the terminology used, Jews during this period faced difficult questions of identity which they solved in various ways.

The *Haskala* generation of the early nineteenth century answered these questions with the formula: "Be a Jew in your tent and a man when you go out." These words point to a duality and a divided spirit, and illustrate the position of Jews during the Emancipation period as well. The formula envisioning "a Frenchman or German of the religion of Moses" points to a similar duality. During the nineteenth century, some French Jews tried to see themselves as Jewish by religion and French by nationality (like their co-religionists in other European countries), even if some of them had ceased performing religious rituals or believing in religious precepts altogether. At the same time, during the first half of the nineteenth century, the different religious streams of Judaism began to crystallize. These responses were expressions of the great hopes and expectations that Jews had for the Emancipation.

During the second half of the nineteenth century, almost 100 years after the beginning of the Emancipation, often bitter disappointment with the solution it offered and the price Jews had to pay for it had started to emerge. The nineteenth century was not only the era of liberalism but the era of nationalism as well. Jews encountered a chaotic entanglement of national contradictions and the tensions of other nations, and often found it difficult to find themselves. Then, and only then, did the Jews begin developing unique modern national solutions to the question of identity. One of these unique national collective solutions was Zionism—the only one not destroyed by the brutal history of the twentieth century. Fascism and Communism struck the Eastern European human reserve of these movements with a lethal blow. In a very different way, the success of Zionism—which rivaled these movements—also contributed to the disappearance of the non-Zionist national movements. Universalist solutions also met with great failure and disappointment.

In contrast, the different streams of Judaism—which are based on Jewish identity, belonging, and religious practice—still constitute a meaningful expression of Judaism in the West, and particularly in the United States. During the twentieth century, the non-orthodox streams underwent significant changes in their self-consciousness. Rejection of Zionism and the national component of Judaism as a widespread, essential element of the outlook of Reform Judaism declined and subsequently almost disappeared altogether. All the streams contain a hard core that rejects the formula "American in nationality and Jewish in religion." Some Jews express a desire to understand their nationality as Jewish as well, or at least to understand it as a mixed Jewish-American nationality, with varying degrees of emphasis placed on each of the different components.

Individual solutions also still remain. According to a number of assessments, few have chosen the path of conversion. Some, apparently without ideological motivation, have chosen the path of distancing themselves from Jewish identity in a way that makes Jewish identity irrelevant to their lives and devoid of meaning. This approach is commonly referred to as assimilation.

## Zionism as Revolution

The question of Jewish identity is undoubtedly one of the most challenging, fundamental questions facing the Jewish world outside of Israel today, at the beginning of the twenty-first century. In this context, the question of how to pass on Jewish identity to future generations has become more significant, and, directly or indirectly, the crystallization of the Jewish-Israeli identity found in Israel may end up being of great and perhaps decisive importance. This is because in some respects, the Jewish reality found in Israel is completely different than that found elsewhere. In other respects, there are many similarities. Zionism, the practical and ideological progenitor of the state of Israel, was and remains an active effort to solve the national problems of the Jewish people and to change its character and culture on the basis of national sovereignty.

Zionist ideology is based on the premise that the Jewish people are a nation like all other nations, aspiring to sovereign self-determination in *Eretz Israel.* As stated in the resolutions of the First Zionist Congress, Zionism aspires to establish a national home for the Jewish people in Eretz Israel. Zionism holds that the Jews are a nation and that Zionism is the Jewish nation's movement of national liberation. First and foremost, this stems from the fact that at least some Jews wish to see themselves as a people. Zionism's object of reference is the Jewish people, whose future existence Zionism is supposed to ensure. The various streams within Zionism that stressed "the suffering of Judaism" instead of "Jewish suffering" (such as spiritual Zionism), also did not relate to Judaism as a religion. Secular Zionist thinkers saw Judaism as a culture.

The "culture question" was already on the agenda during the first Zionist Congresses. To a large extent, this question went unanswered due to pragmatic considerations and the desire to prevent division in the ranks of the still nascent Zionist movement. Over the years, and during its struggles for actualization, which were actually struggles for survival, Zionism refocused its emphasis by moving in political and practical directions and neglecting moral and ideological aspects. The "culture question," which to a large extent is actually a question of Jewish identity, was left unresolved.

According to the historiosophic approach espoused by many, Zionism is a product of world secularization and secularization of a large percentage of the Jews themselves. Zionism also incorporates the profound impact of the nationalist movements of modern Europe and the ideas of modern secular nationalism. Nonetheless, the complex relationship between religion and nationality in the Jewish context has yet to be sufficiently clarified and remains unresolved today, both within the Zionist movement and within the state of Israel.

It is also important to note that, in contrast to all other national and religious responses to the new Jewish post-Emancipation reality, Zionism regarded the continued existence of Jews among other peoples as a negative phenomenon. This position, known as "negation of the Diaspora," really meant "negation of exile." Other national solutions embraced by Jews regarded the existence of Jews among other nations in a positive light. Without a doubt, the importance of the Land of Israel as a concrete concept, not to mention a target for Jewish political sovereignty, has decreased among the non-orthodox religious streams. Reform Jews in the United States voiced phrases such as "America is our Zion, and Washington our Jerusalem." Although religious Jews forged the connection between "exile and redemption" and messianic faith linked the vision of redemption with the Land of Israel, none of these social expressions brought the Jews to Eretz Israel. Redemption was conceived of as a divine act and as a vision for the distant future and the end of days. Many of the ultra-orthodox conceptualizations regarded Zionism as "climbing a wall," and opposed and struggled against it. At the same time, reform Jews opposed Zionism due to its central Jewish-national component.

Zionism's struggle against the other streams further accentuated the differences among them. Zionism emphasized negation of the exile, which at times drifted into negation of the "exilic Jew" sometimes associated with religious Jews. Instead, Zionism emphasized the "new Jew" of the Land of Israel who differed from the "exilic Jew." In this way, Zionism must be understood as a revolution.[2]

## The Ability to Remember and the Ability to Forget

The tension between change and revolution that exists within every revolutionary movement has been clearly manifested in Zionism since its inception. In 1934, Berl Katznelson, a central ideologue of the socialist Zionist movement, wrote the following words:

> Some understand our rebellion according to its simple aim, which is an extremely primitive revolutionary understanding: complete destruction of the old world, the setting ablaze of all the possession that have accumulated over the generations, and starting completely over—like newborn babies! This is a statement with strength and protest power. And a few revolutionaries, in fact, described the anarchistic days of the messiah in such terms. However, it is doubtful that this conceptualization, which naively renounces the entire heritage of so many generations and desires to start building the world from square-one, is progressive and revolutionary. Instead it may seen as profoundly and terribly reactionary.

Katznelson reminds us that "we have been given two abilities: the ability to remember and the ability to forget," and that "we can do nothing without both of them." He also stresses that:

> A rejuvenating, productive generation does not throw the heritage of so many generations onto the trash heap. It examines and checks it, distances it and brings it closer. Some grasp on to an existing tradition and build upon it. Others go down to the trash heap, find things that have been forgotten, polish away the rust, and revive ancient traditions capable of sustaining the soul of the rejuvenating generation.[3]

I am of the opinion that the Zionist revolution placed a greater emphasis on our ability to forget by emphasizing the negation of the Jewish past as opposed to renewal, the rebellion, and the present and future revolution in the Land of Israel. While doing so, the Zionist movement intentionally or unintentionally imbued the youth of the Land of Israel with an ambiguous if not completely negative attitude toward the exilic Jews and the Jewish people, the vast majority of whom did not live in the Land of Israel. Understanding the deep significance of this process is of critical importance for the discussion here, as it alienated and disengaged the youth of the Land of Israel from the greater Jewish people: the point of origin of Zionist ideology, and the object of its vision.

The effort to move "toward normalcy" and the revolutionary component of Zionism produced a stereotypical image and a black-and-white dichotomy of the "exilic Jew" as opposed to the "new Jew" of the Land of Israel. In this way, it disregarded the complexity, the anguish, and the internal contradictions of the modern Jewish experience.

## "When a Man Can No Longer Be A Jew, He Becomes A Zionist," and Vice-Versa

Yudka, the hero of Haim Hazaz's story "The Sermon" (*Hadrasha*) clearly articulates this point:

> To my mind, if I am right, Zionism and Judaism are not at all the same, but two things quite different from each other, and maybe even two things directly opposite to each other! At any rate, far from the same. When a man can no longer be a Jew, he becomes a Zionist. I am not exaggerating … Zionism begins with the wreckage of Judaism, from the point where the strength of the people fails. That's a fact!
>
> Please note that: not new or restored, but different … I believe that this Land of Israel already is no longer Jewish. Even now, let alone in the future. Time will tell, as they say.[4]

Yudka speaks these words, which were well-known in their time and which for years were studied in schools, before the secretariat of his kibbutz: "All clean cut and positive, like captains and heroes in council." In a later edition in which Hazaz inserted no substantial changes, the "chairman of the Committee" explicitly becomes the "head of the Hagana."[5] In any case, Yudka's words reflect an authentic element in Israelis' sentiments toward Jews and Jewish history.

"The Sermon" was published in many editions. Very few people have noticed that the story first appeared in *Luach Haaretz* in the autumn of 1942, at the height of the Holocaust, when extermination was proceeding in high gear and reports to this effect were already appearing in the print media in Palestine.[6] Hazaz was considered an important author, and the newspaper was highly regarded.

## From the Hebrew to the Canaanite

The borderline anti-Semitic character of the writings of the Canaanites during and following the war is hard to believe. In 1943, when the Jewish community in Palestine was aware of the fact that tens of thousands of Jews were being slaughtered each day, Yonatan Ratosh labeled the murdered and fleeing Jews "a mixed multitude of refugees and pilgrims" and called on the Hebrew youth "to be aware of the depth of the chasm and the alienation separating you … from those in the Jewish Diaspora who insisted on this Diaspora, with all its faces, roots, and adaptations, the impact of which remains indelibly imprinted on their thoughts and spirit."[7]

The Canaanite movement was a small organization which encompassed only a small minority of the Jewish youth in Palestine even at its height in the 1940s and early 1950s. Here, I am interested in the extent to which this group constituted an extreme expression of a more moderate phenomenon that existed on a much wider scale. To what degree were large numbers of Jewish youth in Palestine in one way or another Canaanites? Our understanding of the Yishuv's attitude toward the Holocaust as it was taking place, which is still incomplete but which is gradually being clarified from a number of angles.

It is also important to consider whether the Israeli youth of the 1990s have retained some of the more moderate elements of the Canaanite world-view. For the most part, these young people know nothing about the Canaanite movement and are therefore unable to attribute these components of their outlook to this group. In any event, we can identify a tendency toward "post-Canaanite liberalism" in Israeli thought of the 1980s.[8]

## "Are We Still Jews?"

Two important essays written in the early 1950s are particularly relevant to the present discussion. The first, titled "Are We Still Jews?", was written by philosopher and educator Ernst Simon.[9] The second, titled "The Nature and Origins of the 'Young Hebrew' (Canaanite) Movement," was written by philosopher and literary critic Baruch Kurzweil.[10] Simon and Kurzweil argue—in my opinion, somewhat justifiably—that it was Zionism that provided the Canaanites with the ideological tools to develop their philosophy.

According to Kurzweil: "The most important and dangerous elements that appear to belong to this movement alone are also shared, albeit in a concealed manner, by other, completely different circles. To be more specific, the Young Hebrews' positions on Judaism, Zionism, the Jewish past, the values of the Jewish religion, and exile actually provide the clearest indicator of the attitude of the vast majority of the younger generation to these issues."

According to Simon, the group, which was "composed of a small minority of the youth in the country, actually expresses the sentiments of many others who are not organized within its framework." Canaanite ideology, which is of course not Zionist ideology, took Zionist ideas to an absurd extreme. Its mood and its anti-Jewish and anti-exile tendencies were also characteristic of much wider circles.[11]

This perspective helps us better trace the evolution of the identity of the native Israeli—the new Israeli persona of the generation of children of the first waves of Zionist immigration. It has changed in character over the years, at first toward the Hebraism which the founding fathers of Zionism aspired to institute,[12] and later, during the 1940s and the early 1950s, toward Canaanism, which as I have said was an ideology that was explicitly espoused by very few. During the period spanning the second half of the 1950s and the first half of the 1970s, Israeliness replaced Hebraism and Canaanism among what by then was the third and fourth generations in the country.

## The Sabra Myth

The concept of "negation of the Diaspora," which at times evolved into negation of the "exilic Jew," has been present to varying degrees in all three phases of the metamorphosis of Israeli identity. During these different periods, attitudes toward Judaism and Jewish values have also been ambiguous at best. The pioneers of the second and third waves of Jewish immigration to Palestine in the early twentieth century cultivated the myth of the "Sabra" with regard to their children, who were completely different from their own ancestors whom they left behind through a painful and tortuous separation. Sabras are sometimes described as people who sprouted out of nowhere. In this way, these pioneers were attempting to erase their exilic past.

From the 1940s onward, and perhaps even earlier, the figure of the Sabra—the "new Jew" who was a native of the Land of Israel—became a common concept, image, and a symbol. This image represented a deep cultural, ideological, and psychological process that, in my view, was the product of the revolutionary nature of Zionist actualization. The Sabra was perceived as an image with vitality and "natural" rootedness that was free of "exilic complexes" and excessive "intellectualism" and "abstraction," and that embodied a new spirit.[13] The native Sabra of the Land of Israel, the "child of the sun," was the "superior Jew" (who to a large extent had freed himself from his Judaism), or the negative of the "exilic," "inferior" Jew.

The Sabra had two specific qualities that were not qualities of exilic Jews: They were farmers, cultivators of land, as well as fighters and soldiers, familiar with war. It is important to remember that in terms of defense and settlement, Zionism's actualizing and revolutionary significance came to be increasingly focused over the course of a number of decades. More than anything else, Zionism in the Land of Israel was in need of and was calling for farmers and fighters. This fact provides a telling indication of the immanent tension in Zionism between continuity on the one hand, and change, revolution, and a yearning for normalcy on the other hand.

The myth of the Sabra—of Israeliness—began to lose currency during the 1970s and has been in continual crisis ever since.[14] During this period, as the Israeli components of our identity weakened, the Jewish components began to gain strength. Thus, we witness the decline of the secular Sabra and the rise of the image of the "religious Sabra"—the member of "Gush Emunim," the political-messianic settler cultivating the new ethos of the Greater Land of Israel. This ethos differs from the religious Zionist and secular Zionist ideal of settlement in that it does not necessarily involve physical labor and social vision. At least initially, the religious Sabra also attracted considerable interest and support as a new type of pioneer in much wider circles.

## Who Is a Jew?—An Attempt to Define Identity

During the 1950s and 1960s, questions concerning the essence of Israeliness and Jewishness remained largely unsolved. The deep divisions within Israeli society were now hidden behind the celebratory words of the Declaration of Independence, and the proclamation of "the establishment of a Jewish state in the Land of Israel to be known as the State of Israel" failed to define the Jewishness of "the Jewish state" (and not "the state of the Jews" to which Herzl referred fifty years earlier).

In 1950, the Israeli government placed the Law of Return before the Knesset to be legislated. The law, which has also been referred to as the "who is a Jew" law, expressly stipulates that "every Jew has the right to come to this country as an *oleh* [Jewish immigrant to Israel]." The underlying premise of the law—that Israel belongs not only to its citizens but to all Jewish people, wherever they may live—is a clear reflection of the Zionist character of the state.[15]

The Declaration of Independence and the Law of Return contain expressions of the uniqueness of Jewish history (the nation's separation from its land, anti-Semitism and the Holocaust, the vision of the ingathering of the exiles, etc.). However, they also reflect the tension between this uniqueness on the one hand, and the aspiration for normalcy and the desire to live "like all other nations" on the other hand. For this reason, Israel has not, and I believe cannot adopt the premise of the modern nation state regarding the equivalence of nationality and citizenship. After all, most Jews in the world choose not live in the Jewish state, and a significant percentage of Israeli citizens (1 out of every 6) are not Jewish.

It is no coincidence that the Law of Return fell short of explicitly defining which Jews were eligible to immigrate to Israel. At that time, like today, Israeli society had no clear-cut answer to this question. Nonetheless, in 1970—after a Supreme Court ruling that inquired about policy in this area and had received no answer—the government and the Knesset were compelled to formulate a clear policy on this issue through Knesset legislation. In 1970, the government of Golda Meir introduced an amendment to the Law of Return, which stated that: "For the purposes of this law, 'Jew' means a person who was born of a Jewish mother or has become converted to Judaism and is not a member of another religion." The different instructions that have been introduced by the various ministers of the interior regarding the registration of Jews for the purposes of the Law of Return have reflected the marked differences between the conceptions of nationality that exist throughout Israeli society and within the Israeli government. Over the years, the difficulties surrounding questions on the nature of Jewish identity, the essence of belonging, the process of joining the Jewish people, and the equating of national identity with religion have only increased.

The history of these debates remains relatively unknown throughout the general public and the Israeli student body. Unfortunately, few people know that Bar-Yehuda is not only the name of the bridge that crosses the Yarkon River but also one of Israel's early interior ministers. In March 1958, Interior Minister Israel Bar-Yehuda issued instructions for registering Jews for the purpose of receiving Israeli identity cards. The instructions read as follows: "A person who declares in good faith that he is a Jew shall be registered as a Jew, and no additional evidence shall be required." However, on 22 June 1958, as a result of the public debate on the issue, the government voted to amend the instructions and resolved that: "A person who declares in good faith that he is a Jew, and is not a member of another religion, shall be registered as a Jew." At the same opportunity, the government resolved that if a mother and father declare that their child is a Jew, the child shall be registered as a Jew.[16]

In response to this resolution, the ministers of the National Religious Party (NRP) resigned from the government, and on 15 July the new instructions were suspended and a three-member committee (consisting of the Prime Minister, the Justice Minister, and the Interior Minister) was appointed to consider the issue. The committee decided to consult with the Jewish sages in Israel and the Diaspora in order to hear their opinions on the matter. Most thought the national component and the religious component could not possibly be separated. Clearly, the disagreement on the matter was one of principle. Without a doubt, closer exploration of the manner in which these disagreements evolved and the nature of the Supreme Court rulings on this and other related issues stands to shed important new light on the question of Jewish-Israeli identity.

The Israeli state leadership, and first and foremost David Ben-Gurion, decided not to decide on these questions out of a desire to prevent a major rupture surrounding fundamental questions during the first years of statehood. Based on his statist approach (*mamlakhtiut*), and apparently due to other factors as well, Ben-Gurion and his colleagues refrained from enforcing their views, which could have led to the emergence of an alternative, secular Jewish nationality. They refrained from a possible political resolution that may have worked against the interests of the religious minority, and this helps explain the "status-quo agreement," the abstention from adopting a constitution, and the dismantling of the workers' sector of the Israeli education system. The subsequent outcome, which they most likely did not expect, was a blurring of the distinction between the national and religious components of Jewish identity and an increased equating of the two. Furthermore, over the years, religious circles have become increasingly extreme in their demands. Some regard this abandonment of the element of change within Zionism as missing a historic opportunity and as something to lament for generations (*bekhiya l'dorot*). In the 1970s and 1980s, a new national ethos that was more religious in nature began to emerge.

Developments in the Israeli education system also reflect a similar trend of statism and amalgamation, which in retrospect appears to imply a degree of concession with regard to the fundamental interests of non-religious Jews. "Jewish consciousness" was introduced into schools in an attempt to chart a more Jewish course for education without actually defining what this course would be.[17] Later, conscious and subconscious attempts would be made to identify Jews with religion. These attempts met with a degree of success.

## After the Six Days War

Individually and together, the Six Days War (1967) and the Yom Kippur War (1973) changed everything from the ground up. Israelis' deep fears concerning their future existence, at least on a subjective level, were replaced with sweeping and sometimes almost messianic enthusiasm that had far-reaching long-term influence on questions of identity. The Six Days War has increasingly come to be regarded as a point of historic rupture in the short history of the state of Israel. In many ways, this war was the most significant event after the Holocaust and the establishment of the state, not only from the perspective of Israeli and Zionist history but in terms of its significance for the Jewish world as a whole.[18] Less than seven years later, Israel suffered the tragedy of the Yom Kippur War, which brought a swift end to the false sense of power that characterized the country during the years following 1967.

Most important for the current discussion is the fact that the combined impact of these two wars resulted in the decline of the mythological Sabra, Israelis' loss of faith in their own power and confidence, and the beginning of a crisis of Israeli identity. The "children of the sun" began to lose their safe horizons, living the war as an existential nightmare and having no idea when the so-called "final war" would be fought. As we will see, Israeli youth perceive wars as decisive events with regard both to their own future and to the destiny of the Jewish people in general.

The combined impact of the Six Days War and the Yom Kippur War, including the effect of the ongoing occupation, accentuated fundamental dilemmas in the Jewish-Israeli experience and the Zionist world-view that had previously been swept under the rug. Disagreements which Israeli society was not strong enough to solve now rose to the surface. Today, forty-three years after the Six Days War, Israeli society is still living out the seventh day of the war and is still standing at a crossroads that demands a clearer definition of its Jewish and Zionist identity.

Below are a number of major dynamics in Jewish-Israeli identity that emerged during the period following the Six Days War:

### *1. First a Jew*

If the period preceding 1967 was characterized by the sentiment "first an Israeli and only then a Jew," the prevalent sentiment following the war was "first a Jew and only then an Israeli." This period witnessed an increasing emphasis on the Jewish components of our identity, a change that was first noticeable in the political realm and among those responsible for shaping the formal education system. As we will see, this emphasis is currently in the process of being internalized by young Israelis, who today express a much weaker level of the sentiment of "first an Israeli." In many ways, the history of the state of Israel has proven the complete reversal described by Yudka in the "Sermon": When Israel could no longer be Zionist—in the original sense of the term—it became Jewish.[19]

However, for most young Israelis, Jewish experience and Jewish life are vague foreign concepts. The members of the generation of their grandparents and great-grandparents who immigrated to the country acquired Jewish roots and knowledge during their childhood, including the ones who rebelled against their religious upbringing. Although they suffered what Schweid has referred to as "the sorrow of severed roots," their roots in Judaism existed, were part of their lives, and were present in their memories. The generation of their parents and grandparents also had alternative means of Jewish expression to take the place of traditional Judaism. However, most young Israelis today share a sense that for them, when it comes to Judaism, something is missing. As we will see, the Holocaust has played a central role in filling this gap and imbuing their Jewish identity with meaning.

## *2. A Nation Dwelling Alone*

Relations between Jews and non-Jews, and Israel's relations with the rest of the world, have been understood in different ways throughout Israel's existence. Without a doubt, the Zionist vision contained elements of openness to the world, integration, and universalism. Zionism was understood as the only possible solution for normalizing Judaism's distorted relations with other nations. In contrast to the state of Judaism during the Diaspora period, Zionism restored Judaism's significance as a responsible, historical force and aspired to return the Jews as a collective to the family of nations.

In one of many similar quotations, Ben Gurion asserted that:

> Since our last national tragedy—the suppression of the Bar Kochba rebellion, we have had "histories" of persecution, of legal discrimination, of the Inquisition and the pogroms, of dedication and martyrdom, of scholars and Jewish personages. But, we did not have Jewish history anymore, because a history of a people is only what the people create as a whole, as a national unit, and not the sum total of what happens to individuals and to groups within the people. For the last eighteen hundred years during which our people has been non-existent as a national unit, we have been excluded from world history, which is made up of the histories of nations.[20]

These words are also reminiscent, indeed almost identical, to the words spoken by Yudka in his "sermon."[21]

Zionism attempted to change this situation at its very foundations. Integration and involvement in the world was now an ideal. The leaders of the new state expressed a distinct desire for normalization, to be a nation like all other nations, and to return to the family of nations. Furthermore, the first years of statehood also witnessed a nurturing of the vision of "a light until the nations"—"a treasured nation," in the sense of Ben-Gurion's secular statism. Since then, and since the Six Days War in particular, a large portion of Israeli society has embraced the approach, the rationale, and often the ideal of "a nation that dwells alone" ("… and shall not be counted among the nations.") in both the religious and non-religious senses. Religious circles, and some other circles as well, advance the idea of "a kingdom of priests and a holy people." In these ways, they highlight differentiation and the chosen aspect of the Jewish existence.

Israel's ongoing conflict with the Arab world, which as we have seen constitutes a meaningful aspect of Jewish identity (the impact of which has yet to be adequately explored) and which some in Israeli society regard as unsolvable, is an important force shaping this approach. Another reason is the emergence of the Holocaust as a key element of collective Jewish-Israeli identity, as well as personal, individual identities. In this way, many Israelis began to consider their country as the heir of the hated and persecuted Jew, in the spirit of "and Esau hates Jacob."

It is of course relatively simple to prove the inaccuracy and unfounded nature of this approach, which was reinforced by government propaganda and the education system even before the political turnover of 1977. Irrationality, fear, and anxiety not only gained legitimacy but began to guide Israeli society and the Israeli leadership. This approach stands in stark contrast to the cold, rational, pragmatic analysis and real-politic approach of Israeli state leadership during the first decades of statehood.

### *3. The Charm of Americanization*

Concurrent with, and ostensibly in contradiction to these processes of withdrawal and seclusion, movement in the opposite direction was also underway. Israeli society had developed a fascination with the charisma of America and Americanization, which emphasizes individualism, consumerism, the quest for a high standard of living, and material status. With this, the primacy of values such as "pioneering," "actualization," and "to build and be rebuilt" declined, and were replaced by the quest for "self-fulfillment" in its spiritual and materialistic sense. Israeli society was thus transformed from a society emphasizing collective values and the needs of the general public into a society based on individualistic values—a society that no longer spoke in first person plural. Instead of the often complete identification of society and state, inclinations toward alienation and division intensified. Many came to regard Zionism and its unique creative expressions as something that had already been completed, concluded, or exhausted. For others, Zionism represented ruin. "Could it be that it's over?" sang Arik Einstein, who for decades was one of the most familiar voices in Israeli pop music:

> They say that there was a wonderful dream here,
> But when I came, I didn't find anything.
> Could it be that it's over?

At the same time, Israeli society had to navigate this challenging terrain and confront questions with profound meaning and great potential impact for the society as a whole and the individual lives and personal futures of all of its citizens. These questions pertained to the essence of Judaism and Zionism; the social and economic fabric of Israel; the relationship between religion and state; Jewish immigration to Israel; and perhaps most important, war and peace. Unfortunately, however, the decline of common myths and visions did not result in the crystallization of new alternative common goals capable of making society's demands worthy of acceptance. During this period, we can clearly identify processes of exhaustion, separation, and polarization, and of people looking out for their own interests at the expense of the unifying aspects of identity. The sense of mutual obligation that was once so strong in Israel began to decline.

The result has been an ongoing identity crisis that has been reflected (among other things) in Jewish emigration from Israel (*yerida*), and perhaps even more cogently in the legitimacy, acceptance, understanding, and at times justification of this phenomenon in the eyes of the Jewish-Israeli public. The change in attitude toward this phenomenon in recent decades offers important insight into the evolution of Jewish-Israeli identity.

Against this background, other processes reflecting different aspects of existing or aspired-to Jewish-Israeli identity began to take place in the different political and ideological groupings and streams that make up Israeli society. The following brief comments relate not to the political dimensions of these processes, but rather to their ideological-theoretical dimensions in Jewish and Zionist context.

### *4. Failing to Meet the Challenge of "the Seventh Day"*

The difficulties and confusion of secular Judaism were perhaps most discernable in its two major sociopolitical constructions: the labor movement—or socialist Zionism—which had constituted the dominant stream within the leadership of the Zionist movement and the state of Israel; and liberal Zionism. Although to a certain degree the problems began prior to the Six Days War, their most significant manifestation emerged in the labor movement's inability to effectively meet the challenge of the seventh day of the Six Days War. In this context, a shift in Zionist and Jewish-Israeli priorities began.

These two streams within moderate secular Jewish-national Judaism and Zionism sought a means of reconciliation with and integration within the family of nations, and this included an effort to achieve co-existence with the Arab world. In addition to emphasizing the unique nature of Judaism, they also demonstrated an openness to universal values. According to their Zionist vision, the Jewish state and the Land of Israel were essential means toward the actualization of Zionism. However, by Ben-Gurion's statist period, the state had already become more important. After the Six Days War, emphasis was now placed on the "homeland." The vision of the "full" (or "greater") land of Israel was increasingly cultivated in some circles within the secular Zionist labor movement and liberal Zionism. As a result of its internal divisions, the labor movement had lost the ability not only to decide but also to take initiative. It had lost its self-confidence and was transformed from a leading force that played an important, proactive role in shaping Israeli and Zionist priorities into a force that simply responded to events and developments. Ten years after the Six Days War and three years after the Yom Kippur War, Israel also experienced a political turnover, which removed the Labor Party from government and replaced it with a government led by Israel's political right wing.

The seventh day of the Six Days War has lasted for forty-three years, and who knows what the future holds. The process that brings an end to the war, whether by annexing the territories or withdrawing from them, will involve some of the most significant decisions made since the establishment of the state.

### *5. The Rise of Radical Nationalism—From National Identification to Chauvinistic Nationalism*

Since 1967, secular and religious Zionist circles alike have experienced an intensification of radical nationalist trends. This has often taken the form of xenophobic nationalism, rejection of the (non-Jewish) other and an unwillingness to recognize the rights of the other party to the conflict. During this period, Israel's political right wing and radical right have grown stronger.

Religious Zionism also underwent a fundamental change in character. Its focus was no longer "Torah and labor" or even "Torah and *derech eretz* [morally upstanding behavior]." Instead, a great deal of significance was now attributed to the wholeness and the sanctity of the land. It was from these circles that *Gush Emunim* (the Bloc of the Faithful) emerged. Moderation and openness toward other ideas, including secular Zionism, were replaced by radicalization in the religious realm (in competition with the increasingly ultra orthodox Judaism, which was also growing stronger) and the nationalist realm (in competition with the increasingly powerful political right wing and the radical right). Now, the national-religious stream of Zionism placed greater emphasis on the religious sanctity of all parts of the Land of Israel.

In addition to the increased significance of the Land of Israel, radical Israeli nationalism is characterized by a number of other elements, such as an emphasis on the importance of the state itself; a more aggressive approach to Jews' relationship with the world in general and the Arab world in particular (based on the belief that "power will solve everything"); a focus on Jews' differences with and separateness from the rest of the world ("a nation that dwells alone"); a growing need to incorporate hatred and anti-Semitism into Zionist ideology (based on the belief that "the whole world is against us" and the lesson of the Holocaust which obligates Jews to be strong).

Radical nationalism attributes greater importance to Jewish tradition and religion than moderate secular nationalism does. It also attempts to reconnect Israeli society and the Israeli state with the Jewish past and the historic destiny of the Jewish people.

## *6. Messianism*

Although manifestations of messianism have been widespread throughout the religious and secular streams of the Zionist movement during its entire existence, until 1967, messianic sentiments had nonetheless never played a dominant role in the Zionist idea or in Zionist policies and actions. After the Six Days War, messianic sentiments grew stronger, and not only in religious circles. One explanation for this development lies in the intensity and power of the abrupt shift from the deep fear of possible annihilation that characterized the period of waiting preceding the Six Days War, to the elation stemming from the sweeping victory in the war itself. Between May and June 1967, our Jewish and Israeli identity underwent a dramatic transformation. Another factor was the degree to which Israeli society was intoxicated with power after the war. Although entirely different, this dynamic can be compared in intensity to the complete helplessness of the Jewish people during the Holocaust, which had come to an end just over two decades earlier. Although the expressions of messianism among secular Zionists gradually declined, religious Zionism continued to relate to the victory in the Six Days War as a divine miracle, and to the occupied territories as "liberated" parts of the Land of Israel.

In this way, messianic tendencies began to play a more important role in Judaism and Zionism, a trend illustrated by the appearance and ongoing influence of movements such as Gush Emunim[22] and by the increasing acceptance of messianic concepts in some circles within ultra-orthodox Judaism (Chabad, to name one). Here, however, lies an internal weakness of at least a portion of today's national-Zionist sector: The fact that it draws on Zionist messianic ideology, which is transcendental and a-historical in nature, means that, sooner or later, it will suffer the fate of all past messianic movements with beliefs and activities not anchored in the practical reality of their time, but rather in transcendental belief.

Although this study does not explore the concept of messianic Zionism, I must nonetheless point out the serious warnings that have been articulated regarding the future of this religious Zionist stream. In 1976, Yeshayahu Leibowitz wrote: "Ultimately, from a Jewish perspective, delusions of *atchalta d'geula* (Aramaic for "the beginning of the redemption") are likely to result in bitter and unfortunate outcomes for those who embrace them. When the messianic bubble bursts ... they will discover 'believers' (*anshei emunim*) that no longer have roots in this Judaism and that no longer find something worthwhile in this Jewish-Israeli reality."[23]

Gershom Scholem, who also directs his comments toward Gush Emunim, asserts clearly and simply that Zionism is not a messianic movement. "...from the moment I grew up and began to think of Zionism in a systematic manner, I concluded that the decisive aspect of Zionism is the fact that it is a process—one of the most legitimate processes—and not a messianic movement. This is its secret, for as a messianic movement it would be predestined for failure ... I think it would be a terrible tragedy if the Zionists or the Zionist movement were to change, to obfuscate the borders between the realms of messianic-religiosity and historical-political reality."[24]

## *7. Ultra-Orthodoxy*

Ultra-orthodox Judaism began to gain strength in the 1970s. During the years immediately following the Holocaust and the establishment of the state of Israel, the ultra-orthodox stream appeared to be growing increasingly marginalized within Jewish society both in Israel and in the Diaspora. Not only had its membership reserve suffered a major blow during the war in Europe, but it also had trouble effectively addressing the religious significance of the Holocaust. How was it possible to explain the murder of 1.5 million innocent children? The ultra-orthodox world also faced the victory of the Zionist movement, its adversary, which had succeeded in establishing a sovereign Jewish state. Indeed, from an ultra-orthodox perspective, the existence of a secular state in the holy land meant either the victory of heresy or an unequivocal confirmation of the failure of religion.[25]

However, as years passed and the original values of Zionism declined, ultra-orthodoxy grew stronger and more self-confident, due among other things to the substantial support of the state of Israel.

Ultra-orthodox Judaism increasingly attempted to present itself as the authentic if not the sole possible Jewish answer. Today, ultra-orthodox Judaism boldly challenges both Jewish secular identity and Jewish national-religious identity. To this end, it stresses the transitory nature of Jewish-Zionist identity and offers a Jewish alternative that negates the impact of the Emancipation, as well as that of the "auto-Emancipation" achieved by Zionism and the state of Israel as a secular state.[26] The 1980s witnessed the emergence of a new ultra-orthodox image and political style that was meant not only to differentiate ultra-orthodox Judaism from the political center, but also to gain greater access to it, influence it, and accrue benefit from it. Some of the ultra-orthodox population—particularly in the Sephardic sector—has become more moderate in its negation of Israeliness, and perhaps in its negation of the state as well.

The Jewish ultra-orthodox worldview consists of a number of basic components, the most important of which are as follows:

1. Rejection of all present or past cultural values that do not originate from Jewish religious sources.
2. Extreme negativity toward, and sectarian seclusion from, all non-ultra-orthodox parts of the Jewish world.
3. Understanding of the Holocaust as a divine punishment for the abandonment of the ultra-orthodox way of life that began with the *Haskala,* or for the sin of Zionism.

4. The repudiation of Zionism and the establishment and existence of the state of Israel as sins aimed at attempting to bring about the messianic era that reject the belief that the ingathering of the exiles will take place at the end of days with the coming of the messiah.

## *8. A Lack of Failure*

Prior to its failure in effectively addressing the challenge of the seventh day of the Six Days War, the troubles facing Israeli society in general and the labor movement and liberal Zionism in particular stemmed largely from the disappointing but natural discrepancy between expectation and reality. The utopian aspirations and vision of Zionism were courageous, all-embracing, and revolutionary, and at times the movement was attributed secular and religious messianic significance. One example of an aspiration which by definition had no chance of complete actualization was the creation of a new model society, a treasured nation and "a light unto the nations."

The same was true of Zionism's failure to create a "new Jew." Zionism not only aspired to return a people to its land, but also sought to give birth to a new type of person—to bring about a revolution within the body and soul of Jews. This aspect of the Zionist worldview resulted in the ideal of the Hebrew and the myth of the Sabra, which portrayed the superior Sabra as the opposite of the inferior exilic Jew. Societies, nations, and revolutionary movements, in particular, set ideals for themselves which they cannot possibly actualize fully. By cultivating a certain myth, such societies may actually inadvertently be sowing the seed of their own failure in the future.

With the wisdom of hindsight, we now know that Zionism, led by the labor movement, went too far in cutting off its roots and cultivating the ethos of rebellion, change, and revolution. It went too far in the intensity of the utopian vision that called for complete destruction of the old world. It goes without saying that Zionism made many mistakes. However, its most serious mistake of all in this context was the division it created between Israelis and Jews—its severing of ties between Jews born in Israel and their brethren abroad. The fulfillment of Zionism, which placed the Jewish people at the top of its agenda, brought the myth of the Sabra—the fruit of its own labor—to a point of rupture.

Consciousness of the homeland cannot come at the expense of consciousness of the nation. The state of Israel exists for the sake of the Jewish people. It has no roots, and its designation for the Jewish people detracts from its importance. From this perspective, Zionism paid a heavy price for its lack of failure in cultivating the myth of the Sabra, which was subsequently shattered.

A rational, critical, sober evaluation of the Zionist enterprise illustrates the fundamental and largely positive change that the Zionist movement and the state of Israel has brought about in the lives of Jews in Israel and the Diaspora. In addition to its far-reaching vision, Zionism was characterized by a pragmatic and realistic style of thinking that facilitated its success, or at least prevented its failure, despite the prevailing circumstances in which success appeared highly unlikely. Critical thinkers have also been hard pressed to ignore Zionism's considerable successes. As Nathan Rotenstreich wrote in the conclusion of his book *On Jewish Existence in the Present:* "Few social movements have achieved what we have achieved. Our utopia was not a complete disappointment."[27] Yaakov Talmon, who typically offers sharp criticism, also acknowledged, "When surveying the history of national liberation movements, we must conclude that of all national movements, only Zionism enjoyed such great success in such a relatively short period of time while facing such enormous difficulties. Even if this remains the only achievement of that generation, its members can stand proud before the generations of the future."[28]

### *9. At a (Second) Crossroads*

Until World War II, the Zionist movement was—in the words of Martin Buber that were initially intended to describe the kibbutz—an "exemplary non-failure." Since then, the Zionist movement and the state of Israel have been at a Jewish and Zionist crossroads. The manner in which it crosses this junction will to a large degree determine not only the future of the state of Israel, but the destiny of Jewish existence in Israel and the Diaspora as a whole.

The Zionist movement offered one approach to the continued existence of Judaism and the Jewish people. Zionists sought the Jewish people's integration as a collective within the family of nations, without sacrificing their differences and uniqueness and without waiting passively on the sidelines of history for the coming of the messiah. Extremely appealing streams and identities within Israeli society aspire to undermine these Zionist premises. One is the secular and religious national Zionist stream, which, with or without its messianic attributes, is represented most clearly by Gush Emunim and its successors. This group attempts to divert the course of Zionism by replacing the redemption of the nation and the individual with redemption of the land and the establishment of a territorial Land of Israel. In parallel, and in partnership with this stream, the secular nationalist stream offers a Jewish-Zionist identity based on a foundation of tribal impulse and political and military power. The non-nationalist ultra-orthodox stream, in contrast, aspires to return Israel to its pre-Zionist past. These approaches may lead Israel and contemporary Judaism to a dead end.

It is a struggle over faith and religion, and a debate between different concepts in Judaism and Zionism. As we have seen, this competition offers three primary options: secular radical messianic nationalism, religious radical messianic nationalism, and ultra-orthodoxy, all of which offer clear, emphatic answers. A fourth option—a return to the original objectives of Zionism—is more vague, ambiguous, and indecisive.

It is doubtful whether these fundamental divisions will be resolved in the foreseeable future. The goal should not be a decision in favor of one of these approaches over the others. Rather, Israeli society has the obligation to learn to live with the divisions, to recognize pluralism and to accept difference. We must accept the legitimacy of different expressions of Jewish identity, even if we do not agree with them. If a new Jewish-Israeli existence is to emerge in Israel, it will undoubtedly be multi-faceted and contain many contradictions. The difficult questions, however, still loom: Will Israeli society succeed in building the consensus necessary to ensure the existence of multiple valid and legitimate conceptions of Judaism? Will it be able to produce the mutual tolerance required to ensure the co-existence of different approaches, based on mutual recognized legitimacy? This is the most important question currently facing Jewish Israeli society.

## The Choice between the "Objective Jew" and "Subjective Jew"

A final major dilemma that has challenged the Zionist movement throughout its entire existence concerns the nature of Jewish individuals' belonging to the Jewish collective, and the correct way of exercising this belonging. The different solutions to this dilemma have practical, personal, theoretical, and educational implications.

A brief review of the debates surrounding this issue from the early years of Zionism is crucial for our understanding of the question today. Zionism emphasized the national component, or the assertion that the Jews are a nation. Herein lies the revolutionary core of the Zionist idea: In the words of the Basel Program adopted by the first Zionist Congress in 1897, "Zionism aims at establishing for the Jewish people a publicly and legally assured home in the Land of Israel." At the time, a wide variety of groups throughout the Jewish world did not accept the presumption of modern Jewish nationhood. Today, some groups play down the revolutionary essence and profound significance of the national concept at the heart of Zionism.[29] Zionist leaders and philosophers have countered Jewish opponents of this idea with the only answer they could: that the Jews constituted a nation in the present, not just in the past. This was because (most) Jews regarded themselves as part of the Jewish nation and wanted to be defined (right to self-determination) as such, and therefore regarded the revival and self-liberation of the Jewish people as their auto-emancipation. The tensions and divisions between religious circles (*Mizrachi*) and other circles within the Zionist movement, which during the early years of Zionism were led by the "Democratic Fraction," have still not been resolved. As I have noted, the ultra-orthodox opposition to Zionism stemmed from the ultra-orthodox world-view itself.

The question of "who is a Jew" was of course not an issue of practical importance during the early days of Zionism. Nonetheless, the essence, substance, and nature of Judaism and its relationship with the non-Jewish world lay at the heart of the movement's theoretical agenda. As the movement was still in its infancy, Herzl worked to prevent a crisis regarding such fundamental questions at any price. Distancing himself from the rabbis who had supported him would most likely have given Zionism the image of an anti-religious movement. Herzl was undoubtedly justified under the circumstances at the time in trying to preserve the appearance of unity within the nascent movement. Although I am unable to discuss this point in detail here, it is important to note that the prevalent attitude among most non-religious groupings within the Zionist movement was markedly different than the approach later adopted by the state of Israel.[30] Below are some examples of this disparity.

In contrast to the religious concept of the "objective Jew"—a person who is Jewish by virtue of Jewish law, heredity, and belonging—new approaches began to stress the "subjective Jew."[31] This emphasis on willful and conscious aspects of Jewish identity—that is, on the decision to be Jewish and Jewish identification and nationality as a sentiment, a bond of belonging, and an internal reality—was not characteristic of the secular socialist labor movement alone. Rather, it was shaped by much larger circles.

At the turn of the twentieth century, when the Zionist movement was busy with everyday business and the major crisis that followed the Uganda affair and the death of Herzl, the Russian Zionists, who were then the most important and deeply rooted group within the Zionist movement, resolved to "work in the present." This meant strengthening the Jews of the Diaspora as a necessary stage in Zionist actualization. The platform of the Russian Zionist movement, approved at its third general convention in 1906 under the influence of Ze'ev Jabotinsky and Itzhak Greenbaum, read as follows: "The Jewish nation encompasses every Jew who has not announced his withdrawal from the nation."[32] The seventh convention of Russian Zionists, which was held in May 1917, passed resolutions that were almost identical to those passed in 1906 in Helsingfors.[33] On the question of who is a Jew, it was decided: "Every Jew who has not announced his withdrawal from Judaism and is not a member of another religion is Jewish."

The willful aspect of Jewish identity is also emphasized by Ehad Ha'am and Martin Buber, two major Jewish and Zionist philosophers closely associated with Jewish tradition, heritage, and, to a certain extent, at least in the case of Buber, religion. In his 1909 article "Judaism and the Jews," Buber asks:

> Why do we call ourselves Jews? And what does it mean that we are Jews? I want to speak to you not about an abstraction, but about your own life, our own lives … Why do we call ourselves Jews? Merely because our forefathers did so? That is to say, out of a habit that we inherited? Juda-

> ism is only meaningful for Jews when it is their internal reality. What is it that makes a person's nation an independent reality in his soul and in his life? What makes a person feel his nation not only around him but within him?[34]

Ahad Ha'am, asks the same question in almost the same words:

> Why are we Jews? How strange the very question! Ask the fire why it burns! Ask the sun why it rises! Ask the tree why it grows! … This is like asking a Jew why he is Jewish. We are incapable of not being what we are. It is within us; it is one of our laws of nature … It emerges from the darkness of our souls, it is part of our heart! It cannot be annulled, overcome or denied, just as the heart itself cannot be annulled, overcome, or denied …[35]

In this context, the Jewish nationalist non-Zionist philosopher Shimon Dubnow reached the following conclusion: "The objective signs of nationality are gradually making way: from the definition of scientific concepts to subjective signs; a spiritual union based on a common cultural inheritance, historical tradition, common spiritual and public ideals, and signs of other characteristic developments."[36] From his perspective, the nation's own self-awareness is the primary criterion of its existence. The guiding principle of the "cultural-national" group was the following formula: "I recognize myself as a nation, therefore I exist."

In an article critiquing the "who is a Jew" law in 1970, philosopher Gershom Scholem, who also had a deep connection to religion, chose a definition that was not based on Jewish law: "A Jew is a person, with at least one Jewish parent, who identifies himself as a Jew and assumes the obligation and right of being a Jew."[37]

Each in their own way, Amos Oz and A. B. Yehoshua, two popular contemporary authors whose literary and journalistic writings deal with these issues, emphasize the elements of choice, freedom, and identification in being a Jew. "A Jew is someone who defines himself as such," writes Yehoshua. "Being a Jew is a matter of choice."[38] Amos Oz also provides a clear answer to the question "who is a Jew?":

> I call Jewish anyone who sees himself as a Jew and anyone who is forced to be a Jew. A Jew is someone who acknowledges his Judaism. A person who acknowledges it in public is usually a Jew by choice. Indeed, a person who acknowledges his or her Judaism to themselves alone is a Jew by fate. Someone who acknowledges no connection to the Jewish people, neither in public nor in secret, in his own torments, is not a Jew, even if Jewish law regards him as a Jew because he was born to a Jewish mother. According to this non-religious definition, a Jew is anyone who chooses or is compelled to share a common fate with other Jews.[39]

Israeli youth, however, are neither exposed to nor familiar with the complexities of the above discussed dilemmas and solutions. It also seems that they do not ponder them. Nonetheless, a mere glance at a daily Israeli newspaper reflects the extent to which we are entangled in and divided about questions regarding the different aspects of our Jewish and Israeli identity. Only rarely do we succeed in creating contexts in which Israeli youth are able to understand the connection between specific newspaper articles, Judaism, and Zionism, as well as the resulting implications for Jewish-Israeli identity. The Israeli education system has not succeeded, and perhaps is not interested in succeeding, in making questions regarding the nature of Judaism, Israeliness, and Zionism relevant for the young people being educated in Israel today. In the context of such issues, the involvement and searching required by all educational processes has rarely been exercised.

Human identity consists of many different elements of a given reality, and only a few components that are actually chosen. In many ways, such elements of choice are the essence of the human struggle and human existence. The fact that someone is Jewish, Israeli, or Zionist is not and should not be obvious or automatic—not even in the state of Israel. Although many would certainly disagree with me, I believe that being Jewish, being Israeli, and being a Zionist are things that should be chosen. Although Judaism and Israeliness constitute part of the objective reality of the life of a Jew born in Israel, they are by no means all-encompassing. Judaism, Israeliness, and Zionism should neither be taken lightly nor taken for granted. They should also not be taken as the precepts of scholars. Young Jewish-Israelis in particular are required to sacrifice many things—at times their lives—for the sake of their Judaism and Israeliness. Their education must provide them with the means to make these choices. Some of us may choose not to be an Israeli, not to be a Zionist, and perhaps not even to be a Jew, and we must recognize the legitimacy of these choices regardless of whether or not we agree with them. The fact of the matter is that a few hundred thousand people who were born as Israelis have already chosen not to be Israeli. This is a phenomenon that must be recognized, even though it may be difficult to accept.

I am aware of the different types of difficulties faced by people trying to change or give up some elements of identity. Still, some people choose to do so, and in some cases are forced to do so. They are also sometimes successful to some degree, albeit at the price of psychological challenges, tensions, and contradictions. I only partially agree with the argument that a Jew cannot cease being a Jew because others will always make him a Jew. The right and obligation to choose is extremely important both from a human perspective and from a Jewish and Zionist perspective. We must recognize people's freedom to choose to belong for themselves. Providing a person with the ability to make such choices is the task of education in the deepest sense of the word. It means enabling a person to understand the issues, to decide among different options, to make a choice based on free will, and to take responsibility for his or her decision. In my view, enabling people to choose their relationship with Judaism and Zionism is the most profound and true meaning of Jewish and Zionist education.

The empirical data presented throughout this study is neither directly nor indirectly related to the decision of someone to be a Jew. However, the study data does appear to demonstrate that the conditions necessary for making such a decision—which are not always entirely sufficient—do not exist within the Israeli education system. Young Israelis possess neither the knowledge nor the awareness required to make such a decision.

## Notes

1. The relationship between religion and nationalism is also not always a given. Consider, for example, the fascinating case of Brother Daniel, who requested to become an Israeli citizen under the Law of Return, and the fundamental questions raised by his subsequent appeal to the Israeli Supreme Court. Ultimately, his request was rejected by a majority opinion. Although there have been few similar cases, Brother Daniel's was certainly not the only one. Another was that of Paris Archbishop Cardinal Jean-Marie Lustiger, who did not regard his position in the Catholic Church as contradicting his sense of belonging to the Jewish people.
2. See Shlomo Avineri, *Varieties of The Zionist Idea* (Tel Aviv, 1980) [Hebrew], particularly the introductory section, titled "Zionist as a Revolution," and the concluding section, titled "Zionism as a Continuous Revolution."
3. Berl Katznelson, "Being Tested (Conversations with Youth Leaders)," in *The Writings of Berl Katznelson,* vol. VI (Tel Aviv, 1950), 388–90 [Hebrew]. Katznelson wrote "Perpetually Enriching Sources" in response to what he referred to as "emotional debates" sparked by his article "Destruction and Uprooting," which discusses the significance of the Ninth of Av for the Land of Israel Labor Movement in general and its young members in particular (365–68).
4. Excerpts from Haim Hazaz, "The Sermon," in *Modern Hebrew Literature,* ed. Robert Alter (New York, 1975), 271–87, 283–85.
5. Hazaz edited this version of the story while he was still alive, in preparation for the publication of all his writings. See Haim Hazaz, *The Sermon and Selected Stories (According to the Curriculum of the Ministry of Education)* (Tel Aviv, 1991) [Hebrew].
6. Although "The Sermon" was written shortly before the extermination of Jews in Europe became public knowledge, its publication at that particular point in time should still be regarded as significant. I believe that "The Sermon" should be understood as a response to the experiences of Jews during that period. It also appears to have been influenced by fear and anxiety stemming from the possibility of an invasion of Rommel's forces into Palestine, and it contains a call for Jewish activism. Regardless, the subject is undoubtedly in need of reassessment. Although "The Sermon" was originally written as one of a number of chapters with a planned continuation, Hazaz never wrote one. Canaanite poet Aharon Amir explains this fact as follows:

   Why?

   Because it made too many waves and toppled too many mountains.

> Because Hazaz had learned of the extent to which his words of rejection and denial took the natural intuition of the masses of Hebrew youth, imprisoned within the confines of Jewish concepts and Zionist education, too far. Because he had learned of the inflamed debates his Sermon had provoked in the meeting places of the different youth movements. Because he had learned of the extent to which the youth understood his words in their simple form, as a sort of "authorization from above" for the sense of uniqueness within them, for their sense of complete detachment from Judaism. Hazaz heard this, and was alarmed. He explained to one of the young Hebrew authors who came to him in those days to discuss his Sermon that he, Hazaz, was allowed to say this and that, as he was completely saturated with Judaism and Jewish values, a Jew down to the very marrow. But those youths who have not read and have not suffered Jewish tribulations—who were they to reject ... For whatever reason, a continuation never appeared. (from *Alef,* June–July 1950)

On the attitude of the Jewish youth movements in Palestine toward the Diaspora during the Holocaust, see Yair Auron, *The Attitude of the Youth Movements of the Land of Israel Labor Movement to the Diaspora during the Holocaust,* Symposium on Youth Movement Research (Efal, 1990) [Hebrew].

7. See Yaakov Shavit, *From Hebrew to Canaanite* (Tel Aviv, 1984), 186–90 [Hebrew], which contains a full reprint of Ratush's "Epistle to the Hebrew Youth."
8. Yosef Gorny, *In Search of National Identity* (Tel Aviv, 1990), 279–92 [Hebrew].
9. Ernst Simon, *Are We Still Jews?* (Tel Aviv, 1982) [Hebrew].
10. Baruch Kurzweil, ["The Nature and Origins of the 'Young Hebrew' (Canaanite) Movement," *Luach Haaretz* 1952/3 [Hebrew]. Excerpts taken from Kurzweil's *Our New Literature—Continuity or Revolt?* (Jerusalem and Tel Aviv, 1965), 270–330 [Hebrew].
11. Although Simon and Kurzweil hold opposing opinions on many issues, both voice harsh criticism of secular Zionism and religious Zionism alike for "being far from engaging the fundamental problem of our entity—the revival of the values of Judaism—in a serious, straightforward, living manner." Ibid., 329. Simon issues a stern warning regarding the false call of redemption and the principle that replaces god with the homeland. He is critical of equating the "kingdom of priests" (of the past) with the "kingdom of soldiers" that had been established in its stead, and expresses great concern regarding the future.
12. In this context, see the chapter titled "The Last Jews or the First Arabs," in Shavit, *From Hebrew to Canaanite,* 16–44 [Hebrew]. Shavit holds that "instead of [Hebraism's] ambiguous attitude toward the Jewish past and Jewish heritage, the 'Canaanites' propose complete, unequivocal separation. Hebraism, therefore, is not 'Canaanism.'" Ibid., 11.
13. Ibid., 160.
14. Only six years elapsed between the publication of Amos Elon's *The Israelis: Founders and Sons* (London, 1971) and Amnon Rubinstein's *To Be a Free Nation in Our Land* (Jerusalem, 1977) [Hebrew], which contains a chapter titled "The Rise and Fall of the Mythological Sabra." Also see Oz Almog, *The Sabra: The Creation of the New Jew* (Berkeley, 2000).
15. Ben-Gurion had the following to say about the Law of Return: "The Law of Return is one of the fundamental laws of the state of Israel. It embodies a central purpose of our state, the purpose of ingathering the exiles. This law stipulates that it is not the state that grants Jews from abroad the right to settle in it, but that this right is inherent in any Jew, wherever he may live, if he desires to join in the settling of the country." Law of Return, 1950, *Knesset Debates,* 1950 (6), 2035–36 [Hebrew].

16. The government resolution amended Bar-Yehuda's instructions in at least two fundamental ways: 1) by adding the stipulation regarding those who declare in good faith that they are "not a member of another religion"; and 2) by striking the clause that said that in the event that a person declares in good faith that he is Jewish, "no additional evidence shall be required."
17. Baruch Kurzweil later added the following important comment to his article "The Nature and Origins of the 'Young Hebrew' (Canaanite) Movement," which as we have seen was published in his 1965 book *Our New Literature:* "For the moment, official circles have responded to the situation by 'inventing' a miracle cure: 'Jewish consciousness.' However, this consciousness, which is most clearly characterized by the fact that no one knows what it is, will do nothing to change the situation, which is marked by emptiness, a loss of values, cynicism, and careerism."
18. On this subject, see Yaakov Talmon, "The Six Days War in Historical Perspective," in *The Era of Violence* (Tel Aviv, 1974) [Hebrew]. The article, which foresaw far-reaching processes, was in fact written prior to the Yom Kippur War.
19. On this subject, see Rubinstein, *To Be a Free Nation in Our Land,* 182.
20. Quoted in Yosef Gorny, "The Attitude of the Poale Zion Party in the Land of Israel toward the Diaspora (During the Second Aliyah)," *Hatzionut* 2 (Tel Aviv, 1970–71), 77 [Hebrew]. Ben-Gurion's article was meant to assess the revolutionary significance of the Balfour Declaration, was originally published in Yiddish, and was titled "Die Geula" (The Redemption).
21. "We have no history at all ... We didn't make our own history, the Goyim made it for us ... What is there in it? Oppression, defamation, persecution, martyrdom. And again, and again, and again without end ... I would simply forbid teaching our children Jewish history. Why the devil teach them about their ancestors' shame? I would just say to them: 'Boys, from the day we were driven out from our land we've been a people without history. Class dismissed. Go out and play football ..." Hazaz, "The Sermon," 274–75.
22. Zvi Raanan, *Gush Emunim* (Tel Aviv, 1980) [Hebrew]; Amnon Rubinstein, *The Zionist Dream Revisited: From Herzl to Gush Emunim and Back* (Tel Aviv, 1980) [Hebrew], particularly the chapter titled "Gush Emunim and its Secular Partners," 111–33; and Danny Rubinstein, *On the Lord's Side: Gush Emunim* (Tel Aviv, 1982) [Hebrew].
23. Yeshayahu Leibowitz, *Faith, History and Values* (Jerusalem, 1983), 219 [Hebrew] (excerpt taken from the article "Faith and the Faithful").
24. Gershom Scholem, *Dvarim be-Go* (Tel Aviv, 1976), 49 [Hebrew].
25. Eliezer Schweid, "The Justification of Religion and the Test of the Holocaust," *Yahadut Zmanenu* 5 (1988–89) [Hebrew]; and Menachem Friedman, "The State of Israel as a Religious Dilemma," *Alapyim* 3 (1990): 24–68 [Hebrew].
26. On ultra-orthodox Jewry in Israel, see (among other sources) Menachem Friedman's books: *Society and Religion: The Non-Zionist Orthodoxy in the Land of Israel, 1918–1936* (Jerusalem, 1978) [Hebrew]; and *The Haredi Ultra-Orthodox Society: Sources Trends and Processes* (Jerusalem, 1991) [Hebrew].
27. Nathan Rotenstreich, *On Jewish Existence in the Present* (Tel Aviv, 1972), 187 [Hebrew].
28. Talmon, "The Six Days War," 378.
29. Instead, they stress the connection between the people of Israel and the Land of Israel, and the religious aspect of the relationship "between Zion and Zionism." In this way, they highlight the continuity of the Jewish presence in the Land of Israel, sometimes through a tendentious presentation of the facts. They also tend to downplay the fundamental dif-

ferences between pre-Zionist Jewish immigration to the Land of Israel and the later waves of Zionist immigration.

30. See Ehud Luz, *Parallels Meet* (Tel Aviv, 1985) [Hebrew]. According to Luz, the place of religion (or tradition) in national life was the most important internal question facing the Eastern European Zionist movement during its early years. Ibid., 10.
31. See Rotenstreich, *On Jewish Existence in the Present,* 107–08.
32. Aryeh Rafaeli, *National Conventions of Russian Zionists: A Source on the Zionist Movement in Russia* (Tel Aviv, 1963–34), 98–99 [Hebrew].
33. The resolutions passed by the convention addressed issues such as the political struggle to ensure national autonomy and the civil and national rights of all minorities in Russia.
34. Martin Buber, *Judaism and the Jews* (Jerusalem, 1959–60) [Hebrew].
35. Ehad Ha'am, "Three Steps," in *Collected Writings of Ahad Ha'am* (Tel Aviv, 1952–53), 151 [Hebrew] (originally published 1899).
36. Shimon Dubnow, "The Doctrine of Israeli Nationalism," in *Letters on Ancient and Modern Judaism* (Tel Aviv, 1936–37), 14–24 [Hebrew] (originally written between 1897 and 1903).
37. Gershom Scholem, "Who Is a Jew?" in *Dvarim be-Go,* 596. Scholem believed that it was the government of Ben-Gurion, not Golda Meir, that bore responsibility for the ancient sin.
38. A. B. Yehoshua, *Toward Normalcy* (Jerusalem, 1980), 110–15 [Hebrew].
39. Amos Oz, "Homeland," in *Under This Blazing Light (Essays)* (Tel Aviv, 1979), 74 [Hebrew] (originally published 1967).

# CHAPTER 1
# ISRAELI IDENTITIES, 2008

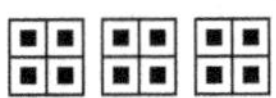

## Introduction

In 1990, I carried out a comprehensive study among college students studying to be teachers in all sectors of Israel's education system. The study served as the basis for a number of articles and a 1993 book titled *Jewish-Israeli Identity*. Although in some ways the current book is a continuation of my earlier study, it also contains a few important differences.

I was inspired to undertake the studies by a sense that young Israelis today are incapable of handling the complex problems of the reality currently presented by the modern Jewish world both in Israel and in the Diaspora. I also believe that young Israelis have not been equipped with the basic tools necessary to attempt to learn about and understand this reality, and to develop their own Jewish-Israeli values or, in the case of young Arab Israelis, their own Arab-Israeli values. Lip service, demagogic pronouncements, preaching, and the emphatic repetition of slogans by educators and leaders cannot replace the ongoing systematic, educational, and pedagogic exploration of these questions.

The past two centuries of Jewish history have been characterized by a number of major processes, including Emancipation; secularization; the emergence of religious streams and national movements among Jews during the nineteenth and twentieth centuries; the emergence of the ideological movement of Zionism; and the Holocaust. Many young Israelis, and many teachers in Israel, know very little about these processes, which must constitute the basis for all study of, and inquiry into the social, political, and material conditions of the Jewish people after the Holocaust and the establishment of the state of Israel.

The Israeli education system teaches preciously little about post-Emancipation Jewish history. Although efforts have been made in recent years to significantly increase the scope and level of instruction about the Holocaust, Israeli students learn almost nothing about the Jewish people in Israel and the Diaspora after the Holocaust and the establishment of the state. Israelis are not teaching, studying, clarifying, or discussing these crucial existential contemporary Jewish issues from a proper perspective of time and space (Israel and the Diaspora). Arab and Palestinians in Israel are taught even less about their history than Israeli Jews are, and students in both sectors are not taught about Jewish-Arab relations or manifestations of racism in Israeli society.

I believe that an effort must be made to bring about a fundamental change in our work in this field. If we are truly interested in such a change, we need to begin with institutions that have a formative influence. This must include institutions involved in the training of teachers and other educators, as it is they who need to initiate the discussion, clarification, and teaching of these issues and to introduce them to different parts of Israeli society, primarily through the education system. Although the attitude and the low level of knowledge of Israeli teens and young adults is repeatedly evident, we too quickly return to our personal and national agenda and the looming, urgent problems that only appear to be unrelated to this broader issue.

Those in contact with young Israelis today quickly reach the conclusion that the population suffers from a high level of ignorance. However, for some reason we refuse to acknowledge the magnitude of this ignorance and the fact that it provides fertile breeding ground for chauvinism; clericalism and, alternatively, intense anti-religious sentiment; anti-Diaspora sentiment; and the belief that "the entire world is against us." Jewish-Arab relations within the green line are deteriorating, and this is even more true in the occupied territories. Our ignorance gives rise to confusion, anguish, and a subjective and objective sense of siege. In the case of some people, for a variety of reasons, it leads to emigration.

Experience in the field of education shows that learning about these issues raises young people's level of knowledge and, equally as important, helps change their attitudes and their level of involvement. Still, according to my assessment, the situation in this realm has not changed in the last eighteen years (since my first study on Jewish-Israeli identity), despite the work of the Shenhar Commission, which was appointed by the Minister of Education to address Jewish education in Israeli schools, and the Kremnitzer Commision, which was appointed by the Minister of Education to address the teaching of democracy in Israeli schools.

I carried out my first study in 1990 among college students studying to be teachers in all three sectors of Israel's education system: the State sector, the State-Religious sector, and the Ultra-Orthodox sector. Its conclusion contained interesting information with comparative potential that I found extremely thought provoking.

A quantitative attitude study cannot provide a comprehensive assessment of Jewish-Israeli identity, and the attitude questionnaire I used to examine the subject left many angles unexplored. Without a doubt, however, such studies certainly have the potential to shed new light on the major issues and to identify trends and directions that can and should be researched by means of other methodologies. As we will see, the depth and detail provided by my study, in conjunction with other work on Jewish-Israeli identity, enhances our knowledge and understanding of the subject.

The 1990 study began with a series of questions which could not all be answered due to the fact that the study was one of the first of its kind. Indeed, some of the issues still require more work or new studies altogether. Such issues include: the national component of personal and group identity (as opposed to the religious component); attitudes toward Diaspora Jewry; the role of anti-Semitism in Jewish identity; the role of the Holocaust in Jewish-Israeli identity; and the impact of the Holocaust on attitudes toward the Arab-Israeli conflict, on the Palestinians in green-line Israel, and on the Palestinians in the occupied territories.

The few studies that have addressed the subject of Jewish identity in recent years have more often than not disregard the influence of the Arab-Israeli conflict. In contrast, I regard the "Palestinian problem" as a force shaping Jewish identity. For this reason, the present study examines the role of this factor as well. I also deemed it necessary to expand the study population and to investigate the identity of Arab students. Initially, I considered designing one questionnaire for Jewish and Arab students, containing uniform questions and a few different questions. Ultimately, however, I reached the conclusion that it was necessary to prepare two separate questionnaires: one for the Arab-Israeli or Palestinian-Israeli population (the term used to classify the identity of this group will be discussed later in the book), and one for the Jewish-Israeli population. Some of the questions pertain to identity, while others are specific questions meant for each sub-population.

In my conclusions of the 1990 study, I presented an analysis of four aspects of Jewish-Israeli identity: attitudes toward the Jewish people; attitudes toward the Jewish religion; attitudes toward the Holocaust; and attitudes toward the state of Israel and Zionism. At the time, I regarded these elements as the main components of an analysis of the Jewish-Israeli identity of young Israelis. However, it was also clear that these components did not encompass all aspects of Jewish-Israeli identity. Examples of issues that were not explored by the study include the role of the Hebrew language in Jewish-Israeli identity and the role of the Arabic language in Palestinian-Arab identity.

I chose the titles "The Jewish People and Me," "The Holocaust and Me," "Zionism and Me," and "Religion and Me" for the chapters of the 1990 study in an effort to draw attention to the personal, subjective dimension and to present things from the perspective of the students themselves. Students' subjective points of view are also of central importance to the 2008 study, which also explores attitudes toward the "other" as a meaningful component of Jewish-Israeli and Palestinian-Israeli identity. In the case of Jewish-Israelis, the "other" refers to non-Jew in general and Arabs and Palestinians in particular. This chapter is titled "The Other and Me."

The 2008 study classifies the identity of the subjects as "Jewish-Israeli" and "Palestinian-Israeli," and the citizens of the state of Israel as "Jewish Israelis" and

"Palestinian Israelis" (nonetheless, throughout the book I use the terms "Palestinian" and "Arab" interchangeably in order to refer to the Palestinian-Arab citizens of Israel, with no intention of unequivocally endorsing one approach or the other, as I believe that it is up to them to define their own identity). This classification reflects my approach to the issue of identity. It differs from approaches that attempt to highlight the Jewish component, and it differs even more markedly from approaches that attempt to highlight the Israeli component (in its different variations) and that speak only of "Israeli identity." Israeliness, however, is not simply one detail on Israeli identity cards; it is a meaningful component of the identity of Jewish Israelis and Palestinian Israelis alike. According to the approach proposed here, identity is not something to be imposed but rather something that must be defined by group members themselves.

This book does not presume to provide symmetrical treatment of Jewish-Israeli identity and Palestinian-Israeli identity. Much more of the book is dedicated to Jewish identity than to Palestinian identity, as my knowledge of the former is richer and more extensive than my knowledge of the latter. Nonetheless, I make a sincere attempt to sensitively present and illuminate the subject of Palestinian-Arab identity in the Israeli context, and it is my hope that this approach will be built upon in the future.

A great deal has been written about the word "identity." The many definitions of this broad and often misleading term cover a wide variety of cultural, social, and socio-psychological dimensions. This book refrains from offering yet another definition and instead draws on the studies of Simon Herman for the theoretical foundation of the research presented, as I explain in more detail below.

Although the following brief text, which was published in the *Haaretz Weekend Magazine* on 1 May 1996, is anarchistic, provocative, and entirely non-academic in nature, it nonetheless provides food for thought for those interested in the different definitions of the term:

> The following letter was sent by the spokesperson of the *Zapatistas* to the editorial offices of *The Advocate,* a homosexual magazine in the United States. The publication sought to ascertain the veracity of the Mexican government's claims that the mysterious Subcomandante Marcos, the leader of the underground, is a homosexual.
>
> *1993: Identities*
>
> Thank you for your inquiry. Marcos is gay in San Francisco, black in South Africa, an Asian in Europe, a Chicano in San Ysidro, an anarchist in Spain, a Palestinian in Israel, a Mayan Indian in the streets of San Cristobal, a Jew in Germany, an ombudsman in the Defense Ministry, a communist in the post-Cold War era, an artist without gallery or portfolio, a pacifist in Bosnia, a housewife alone on Saturday night in any

> neighborhood in any city in Mexico, a reporter writing filler stories for the back pages, a single woman on the metro at 10 PM, a peasant without land, an unemployed worker, a dissident amid free market economics, a writer without books or readers, and, of course, a Zapatista in the mountains of southeast Mexico.
>
> I hope this answers your question.
>
> —The Spokesman

In his book *In the Name of Identity,* Amin Maalouf discusses the multiplicity of factors that make up individual identity:

> What's known as an identity card carries the holder's family name, given name, date and place of birth, photograph, a list of certain physical features, the holder's signature, and sometimes also his fingerprints—a whole array of details designed to prove without a shadow of doubt or confusion that the bearer of the document is so-and-so, and that amongst all the millions of other human beings there isn't one—not even his double or his twin brother—for whom he could be mistaken.

In addition to this type of mundane information, Israeli identity cards, until recently, also contained a section titled "nationality." "My identity," Maalouf continues:

> is what prevents me from being identical to anybody else.
>
> Defined in this way the word identity reflects a fairly precise idea—one which in theory should not give rise to confusion. Do we really need lengthy arguments to prove that there are not and cannot be two identical individuals? ...
>
> Each individual's identity is made up of a number of elements, and these are clearly not restricted to the particulars set down in official records. Of course, for the great majority these factors include allegiance to a religious tradition; to a nationality—sometimes two; to a profession, an institution, or a particular social milieu. But the list is much longer than that; it is virtually unlimited. A person may feel a more or less strong attachment to a province, a village, a neighborhood, a clan, a professional team or one connected with sport, a group of friends, a union, a company, a parish, a community of people with the same passions, the same sexual preferences, the same physical handicaps, or who have to deal with same kind of pollution or other nuisance.
>
> Of course, not all these allegiances are equally strong, at least at any given moment. But none is entirely insignificant, either. All are components of personality—we might almost call them "genes of the soul" so long as we remember that most of them are not innate.[1]

We must also remember that the components of identity and their respective importance are dynamic, and most can be changed. For example, a person can be born with one nationality and die with another.

The title of the findings of the 1990 study—*Jewish-Israeli Identity*—reflects a major point of tension within Israeli society, particularly for the non-religious population: the relationship between the Jewish and Israeli components of Jewish-Israeli national identity. Another point of tension lies in the complex relationship between religion and modern Jewish nationalism. I reject the claim that Judaism is only a religion and that for this reason it is an expression of the religious component of our identity alone, while Israeliness expresses the national component. In my view, Judaism is both a religion and a nationality. Jews in the modern era have chosen to define themselves in relation to one or both of these elements, according to their outlook. Palestinian-Israelis also need to define the components of their national, civil, and religious identity. In the present study, I argue in favor of a balanced, all-inclusive approach that recognizes the complex and intertwined nature of issues of identity for both Arabs and Jews, as well as the inherent tensions between them.

A third point of tension lies in the intricate relationship between the national and civil components of identity. Israel is a democratic state, but it is also a Jewish state. This being the case, what are the rights and obligations of the country's Arab citizens? From this perspective, the tension between the Jewish religion and Jewish nationality has the potential to cause tension between the civil and national poles, and may drift (or may have already drifted) into Jewish and Arab nationalism. Although Israel tends to define itself as a Jewish and democratic state, it sometimes seems that the tension between Jewishness (or Judaism) on the one hand and democracy on the other continues to intensify. The Palestinian-Israeli conflict as manifested outside Israel's borders has also taken on (at least to a certain degree) the characteristics of a national-religious (or even a nationalist-religious) struggle, as reflected in groups such as Hezbollah, Hamas, and Islamic Jihad.

## The Questionnaire and the Study Population—2008

The questionnaire used in the 2008 study was implemented out digitally. It was completed by 934 Jewish students and 258 Arab students of the Open University of Israel during the second half of 2008, and the response ratio was greater among the Jewish student population than it was among the Arabs. The lower response ratio among the Arab students appears to have stemmed from the fact that some had no home Internet access. Some Palestinian-Israeli students might also have been intimidated by the fact that the questionnaire was in Hebrew, despite the fact that most of their university and studies are conducted in Hebrew. Others may have chosen not to take part due to the content of the questionnaire.

The Arab students were primarily from the Triangle and northern Israel (Nazareth and the surrounding area), while the Jewish students were from localities throughout the country, with large groups from Jerusalem, Ashdod, Bat-Yam, Givatayim, Kfar Saba, Herzliya, Haifa, Holon, Rishon Lezion, Ramat Gan, Raanana, and Tel Aviv.

The Open University has an enrolled student population of approximately 45,000 students who study in "study centers" around the country. Open University students are not required to take high school matriculation exams in order to be accepted, and a large portion of Open University students also work. In addition, the average student age is higher than in other universities, although it has dropped somewhat in recent years. The gender breakdown of the Open University student population is similar to that of other universities, with 55 to 56 percent women, and 44 to 45 percent men. I do not believe that these attributes have significant influence on the students' attitudes toward their identity. The comprehensive studies that have been undertaken on identity to date deal primarily with high school students and are referred to below.

Aside from the intentional selection of Arab students for whom the second questionnaire was designed, the students in the 2008 study were selected randomly. In contrast, the students who participated in the 1990 study were selected according to the sector of the Israeli education system with which their teachers' college is affiliated. They were also selected to be representative of the size of that sector in relation to the overall population. The previous questionnaire (1990) underwent two trials. In light of its findings and the conclusions based on analysis of the information gathered in the second trial, additional changes were made and the nationwide questionnaire was finalized. The questionnaires were distributed in April to June 1990.

I regard the studies of Simon Herman as a comprehensive empirical and theoretical endeavor capable of addressing a significant number of the questions that are relevant to my study. For this reason, I adopted Herman's model (Herman, 1980) as a foundation for my study. Herman, who developed the study of Jewish identity in Israel, followed the lead of Kurt Lewin, whose studies in the fields of the social sciences, social psychology, and field theory examined national group identity in general and Jewish national identity in particular. It should be noted that since the publication of Herman's major studies in 1965 and 1974, the more limited studies of Farago in 1985 and 2005, and my study in 1990, Israeli society has experienced major changes.

The concept of identity employed by Simon Herman is based on fundamental components contained in the definitions of Daniel Miller and Erik Erikson. Miller defines identity as "the pattern of observable or inferable attributes 'identifying' a person to himself and others."[2] In his discussion of Freud's articulation of his own "inner identity" with Judaism, Erikson drawn attention to "an essential aspect of a group's inner coherence" that is reflected in the individual.[3] According to Herman:

> Identity reflects both likeness and uniqueness. To quote a popular phrasing of the fact: Every person is in certain respects
> 1. like all other persons (possesses universal human attributes),
> 2. like some other persons (shares certain attributes in common with specific social categories),
> 3. like no other man (has unique personality of his own).[4]

When designing the first trial questionnaire of the 1990 study, I adapted the model that had been designed for high school students for the student population of teachers' colleges instead, in accordance with the events of the 1980s. The second trial questionnaire developed for the 2008 study was also subject to additional modification.

Both studies also made use of elements of other attitude studies on specific issues related to general attitudes toward Zionism and contemporary Judaism, such as Israel-Diaspora relations, Israelis as Jews, and Israelis' identification with state and society. In addition to these issues, I sought to explore various other questions, such as how respondents assess their own level of knowledge in these areas. Re-exploring questions asked by previous studies allowed me to examine continuity and transformation over time with regard to a number of different subjects, and, by comparing the findings from different periods, enabled me to identify changes taking place in Israeli society. In the end, I was forced to remove a number of questions from the research agenda due to limitations resulting from the scope of the study.

The significant number of publications that address the issue of Jewish-Israeli identity are in part theoretical studies. Some of these studies—like works by Baruch Kimmerling, Gershon Shafir and Yoav Peled, Nadim Rouhana, and Sammy Smooha, which are cited in other parts of this book—discuss the question of Arab-Israeli identity from the disciplinary perspectives of sociology, political science, and democracy studies.[5] In contrast, I explore identity-related questions from the perspective of national identity (as well as civil and religious identity) and attempt to apply Herman's model—which was subsequently developed by Farago and then myself—to Israel's Arab (Palestinian) population as well, while adapting it as necessary.

The 2008 study was based on some of the questions of the attitude study undertaken in 1990. This facilitates a comparison between the student population (of teachers' training institutions) of that period with the student population surveyed for the 2008 study. The comparative dimension of similar populations, even if only partial, is extremely significant from a research perspective.

Another important aspect of the 2008 study is its consideration of the Arab student population and Jewish-Arab relations. As I have explained, I constructed a separate questionnaire for Arab students. Both the Arab students and the Jewish students were asked to relate to a wide variety of issues linked to their own individual identity, to the identity of the "other," and to the relationship between them. In this context, I benefited from the attitude studies of Sammy Smooha and, to a lesser extent, from other studies in the field.

The 2008 study was carried out among students of the Open University and is representative of the different religious affiliations within Israeli society (secular, traditional, religious, and ultra-orthodox). It also incorporates representation of Israel's Palestinian population. To this end, I designed a special questionnaire expressly for the Arab population, some of which was similar to the questionnaire intended for Jews and some of which was different. This comparative dimension provides us with new insights and observations regarding our identity.

In this context, the 1990 study differs fundamentally from the 2008 study in that the former completely fails to address the Arab-Israeli conflict. In contrast, the present study regards the ongoing conflict as an important aspect of the dilemmas and problems currently facing young Israelis in the realm of identity. The wars that have been fought throughout the course of modern Israeli history constitute an influential factor in the identity of young Israelis, and the impact of this conflict on our Jewish-Israeli identity has yet to be sufficiently explored. However, it is clear that the Palestinian "other" plays an important negative role in defining our identity by producing (negative) components of identity that are externally unifying, but that do not result in the evolution of positive components of identity. This study also attempts to explicate this aspect of identity in Israel.

Israeli Jews are increasingly coming to regard both Palestinians in general and Palestinian-Israelis as "different," and as the "other." At the same time, Palestinians are also increasingly coming to see Jewish-Israelis as the other, albeit to a lesser extent. In his landmark book *Orientalism* (1978), Edward Said argues that the Orient played an important role in the process by which the Europe and the West defined itself vis-à-vis the East. We need to be asking ourselves which elements of this argument are relevant to Jewish-Palestinian relations in Israel. According to Said, western knowledge defined the imaginary ultimate other as the opposite of western existence. This knowledge was assembled, he holds, to serve the interests of occupation, control, and subjugation. Academics, colonial officials, and others figures succeeded in creating within their own culture the inferior other that was so necessary for producing the enlightened image of the west. European culture acquired additional power and identity by highlighting itself in opposition to the Orient. The East, holds Said, always symbolized threat and danger. This knowledge was presented in the west as objective and ethically neutral.[6]

## Background Traits of the Sample of Respondents' Age

Many of the studies that have addressed aspects of the Jewish identity of young Israelis have focused primarily on high school students (tenth through twelfth graders). These studies were carried out some time ago, and my analysis of the findings must therefore address the influence of changes that have taken place in Israeli society over the past 25 years.

The average age of the 1990 study population (21 to 26) was just a few years older than that of the populations of previous studies on Jewish identity. The sample consisted primarily of young adults who had recently completed their compulsory military service, which is thought to be a period with great influence on Israeli identity. It is therefore reasonable to assume that the identity of the 16- to 17-year-old Israelis examined in previous studies were in the process of being formed, while identity and consciousness among the student population examined in my two studies were at a more advanced stage of development (this issue was not a focus of the study).

The age distribution of the Jewish student population of the present study is as follows: 18–20—2 percent; 20–23—15 percent; 23–26—35 percent; and 26 and older—48 percent. The age distribution among the Arab student population of the present study was: 18–20—6 percent; 20–23—36 percent; 23–26—23 percent; and 26 and older—35 percent. The younger average age of the Arab student population stemmed, among other things, from the military service completed by most Jewish students. Not only do Arabs not undertake this military service, but they also tend not to travel abroad at this age, in contrast to young Jewish Israelis, who typically take long trips abroad following their military service.

## Gender

The 1990 study was overwhelmingly female, with women representing 92 percent of the total number of subjects the study was carried out within teachers' colleges where the majority of the students are female). In the 2008 study, the breakdown is different, with men representing 42 percent of the Jewish subjects, and women representing 58 percent. The female-male ratio is greater in the Arab study population, with 61 percent women and 39 percent men. In my view, the higher percentage of women in the study population has no significant bearing on the issues under discussion.

## Marital Status

Sixty-seven percent of the Jewish study population were unmarried, 15 percent were married without children, and 18 percent were married with children. The breakdown among the Arab students was found to be similar, with 67 percent unmarried, 5 percent married without children, and 28 percent married with children.

## Religion

Researchers who have worked on the issue of Jewish identity have concluded that the religiosity of respondents is "very relevant to the subject," that all studies on the subject have highlighted the great influence of the variable of religion, "that religion influences a wide variety of attitudes,"[7] and that it is the decisive variable in determining the intensity of Jewish identity in Israel, as in all other places."[8] This was also the case in my previous study, which identified religiosity as an independent variable with immense influence. In a separate chapter, I will discuss subjects' attitudes toward religion as a dependent variable. I will employ religiosity as an independent variable to help us understand subjects' attitude toward other subjects.

I asked the study subjects to classify their religious identity, their parents' religious identity, and their level of religiosity in comparison to that of their parents (more religious than their parents, less religious than their parents, or same level of religiosity as their parents). The data is presented in tables 1 to 4.

The religiosity of the Jewish and Arab subjects, as well as their parents, was determined based on the subjects' responses to the following question: "Are you religious, traditional, or non-religious?" I did not think that subjects had a significant reason to intentionally alter their responses regarding their religiosity. Some studies have attempted to define the religiosity of subjects based on seemingly objective criteria, such as the extent to which they perform religious rituals. However, this methodology was too complex to be implemented within the framework of the present study, which aims to explore a broad spectrum of issues related to identity. *For me, it was important to understand the students' own subjective self-definition.*

**TABLE 1.1 Religiosity of Jewish Respondents in Comparison to Religiosity of Their Parents, 2008 (as a percentage):** ***"Are you religious, traditional, or non-religious? Are your parents religious, traditional, or non-religious?"***

| Subject | Parents | |
|---|---|---|
| Religious | Religious | 92 |
| | Traditional | 5 |
| | Non-Religious | 3 |
| Traditional | Religious | 15 |
| | Traditional | 74 |
| | Non-Religious | |
| Non-Religious | Religious | 4 |
| | Traditional | 12 |
| | Non-Religious | 84 |
| $X^2 = 899$ | $df = 4$ | $p < 0.0001$ |

**TABLE 1.2 Religiosity of Jewish Respondents in Comparison to Religiosity of Their Parents, 2008 (as a percentage):** ***"Are you more religious, religious to the same extent, or less religious than your parents?"***

| Subject | Parents | |
|---|---|---|
| Religious | More religious than parents | 29 |
| | Religious to same extent as parents | 52 |
| | Less religious than parents | 19 |
| Traditional | More religious than parents | 15 |
| | Religious to same extent as parents | 38 |
| | Less religious than parents | 47 |
| Non-Religious | More religious than parents | 8 |
| | Religious to same extent as parents | 54 |
| | Less religious than parents | 38 |
| $X^2 = 58.65$ | $df = 4$ | $p < 0.0001$ |

Whereas religious students tended to be more religious than their parents, 42 percent of the traditional students were less religious than their parents, as was a slightly lower percentage of non-religious students (38 percent).

**TABLE 1.3 Religiosity of Arab Respondents in Comparison to Religiosity of Their Parents, 2008 (as a percentage):** ***"Are you religious, traditional, or non-religious? Are your parents religious, traditional, or non-religious?"***

| Subject | Parents | |
|---|---|---|
| Religious | Religious | 88 |
| | Traditional | 10 |
| | Non-Religious | 2 |
| Traditional | Religious | 34 |
| | Traditional | 65 |
| | Non-Religious | 1 |
| Non-Religious | Religious | 18 |
| | Traditional | 36 |
| | Non-Religious | 46 |
| $X^2 = 165.765$ | $df = 4$ | $p < 0.0001$ |

The distribution of the study population reveals interesting findings: Twelve percent of the Jewish students defined themselves as religious; 23 percent defined themselves as traditional; and 55 percent defined themselves as non-religious. The percentage of non-religious students is disproportionately high in comparison to their actual percentage within the general population. This finding may also be related to the differences in cultural behavior among the different groups,

**TABLE 1.4 Religiosity of Arab Respondents in Comparison to Religiosity of Parents, 2008 (as a percentage):** ***"Are you more religious, religious to the same extent, or less religious than your parents?"***

| Subject | Parents | |
|---|---|---|
| Religious | More religious than parents | 15 |
| | Religious to same extent as parents | 42 |
| | Less religious than parents | 43 |
| Traditional | More religious than parents | 4 |
| | Religious to same extent as parents | 44 |
| | Less religious than parents | 52 |
| Non-Religious | More religious than parents | – |
| | Religious to same extent as parents | 37 |
| | Less religious than parents | 63 |
| $X^2 = 17.671$ | $df = 4$ | $p < 0.0001$ |

particularly with regard to ultra-orthodox Jews who seldom study in academic institutions. Sociologist Yeshayahu (Charles) Liebman estimated the breakdown of the Israeli population by religiosity in the early 1990s to be 20 percent religious (including 5 percent ultra-orthodox), 35 percent who classified themselves as traditional, and 45 percent who classified themselves as non-religious. According to Liebman, the two decades that preceded 1990 witnessed a small but consistent decline in the number of traditional Jews, whom he regards as the most difficult to classify. At the same time, this group accounts for the decisive majority of Jews of Sephardic extraction (this data appears in my previous study as well). Liebman also found that, in 1990, approximately 45 percent of Israelis defined themselves as secular, and that this number had increased slightly during the two preceding decades.

Studies of the Guttman Institute and the Avichai Foundation yielded the following breakdown for the year 1999: 5 percent ultra-orthodox, 12 percent religious, 35 percent traditional, 43 percent non-religious, and 5 percent anti-religious. According to theses studies, the percentage of traditional Jews decreased by 7 percent between 1991 and 1999; the percentage of non-religious Jews decreased by 5 percent; and the percentage of the ultra-orthodox increased by 2 percent. During this period, the non-religious replaced the traditional Jews as the largest group. Although my study limits itself to the respondents' classification of their own level of religiosity, Guttman and others have found that some secular Jews perform religious rituals. According to their findings, approximately 29 percent of non-religious Jews perform some rituals.

My two studies provided subjects with the option to classify themselves as "non-religious," which is somewhat more moderate than "secular." Secularism includes an element of universalistic view, and is not simply a definition of identity based on the absence of religion. In the words of Yizhar Smilansky: "It is possible to be non-religious out of ignorance, laziness, or for no particular reason. However, being secular stems from the choice to be secular."[9]

My findings indicate a decrease in the level of religiosity among this group of students in the Jewish population (as well as in the Arab population, as we will see later). The percentage of students who classified themselves as religious (12 percent) is lower than the percentage of students who reported having studied in a religious elementary school or high school. Fifteen percent of the subjects indicated that they attended State-Religious elementary schools, while another 9 percent reported that they attended Ultra-Orthodox schools. It can be assumed that at the time, most or all of these students were religious. For high school, 8 percent attended city religious schools, while 11 percent attended yeshivas or high school *ulpanot* (religious schools for girls).

This decline in religiosity is also discernable in subjects' responses regarding the religiosity of their parents, when comparing the level of religiosity of parents and children. Seventeen percent classified their parents as religious, 25 percent as traditional, and 57 percent as non-religious. When asked to compare their own religiosity with that of their parents, 12 percent of the students said that they were more religious, 50 percent reported maintaining the same level of religiosity, and 38 percent said they were less religious (see tables 1.1 and 1.2).

The percentage of students who are parents was higher among religious students (46 percent) than among the traditional and non-religious groups (14 percent in each group). This most likely stems from the fact that religious Jews tend to marry and have children at a younger age than non-religious Jews.

While the level of religiosity among Arab students was higher than among Jewish students, they too are experiencing a significant decline in religiosity in relation to the religiosity of their parents. Fifty-four percent of the Arab students classified their parents as religious, 34 percent as traditional, and 12 percent as non-religious. At the same time, 44 percent of the Arab students classified themselves as religious, in comparison to 32 percent who classified themselves as traditional, and 24 percent who classified themselves as non-religious. Within the Arab student group, 72 percent classified themselves as Muslims, 11 percent as Christians, and 13 percent as Druze (4 percent classified themselves as "other"). In comparison with their parents, 8 percent classified themselves as more religious, 41 percent said that they had maintained the same level of religiosity, and 51 percent said that they were less religious. These findings contradict the widespread belief that religiosity in Israel is on the rise. In the case of the students participating in the study, the numbers tell a different story (see tables 1.2 and 1.3).

In conclusion, the study findings reflect a generational decline in religiosity among both the Jewish and Arab sub-groups of the study population. I reached similar conclusions during my 1990 study of teaching students. Among the religious students considered in 1990, 25 percent were more religious than their parents, 73 percent had maintained the same level of religiosity as their parents, and 1 percent were less religious than their parents. Among the traditional students, 13 percent were more religious than their parents, 35 percent had maintained the same level of religiosity, and 52 percent were less religious. At the same time, however, it is important to keep in mind that this dynamic is characteristic of the student population and may very well be less discernible in the general population.

## Country of Birth and Extraction

A large majority of the Jewish students (81 percent) were born in Israel. Of those who were born abroad, 85 percent have lived in Israel for more than 10 years, 12 percent have lived in the country for 5 to 10 years, and only a small percentage have been in Israel for less time. This can be compared to my 1990 study, in which 90 percent of the subjects were born in Israel. In the 2008 study, 90 percent of the participating religious students and 91 percent of the traditional students were born in Israel. Five percent of the traditional students were born in the Soviet Union and Eastern Europe, but the figure jumps to 20 percent when I considered this group among the non-religious students. We can therefore expect this significant group of immigrants from the former Soviet Union to have a substantial impact on the overall responses of the non-religious students.

Based on the fact that Israeli society is an immigrant society, it is reasonable to assume that either the parents or grandparents of many of the students immigrated to Israel. Indeed, 73 percent of the fathers of religious students were born in Israel, as were 46 percent of the fathers of the traditional students. Among the traditional fathers, 38 percent were born in Muslim countries and Africa, and 13 percent were born in the Soviet Union and Eastern Europe. Among the non-religious students, 17 percent of fathers were born in Muslim countries, and 47 percent were born in Israel. The figures were similar with regard to the country of birth of students' mothers.

However, when I examined the country of birth of students' paternal grandfathers, the picture changes somewhat, illustrating the fact that Israel is fundamentally a country of immigrants. Only 12 percent of the religious students (their higher percentage may stem from the young age at which they married), 6 percent of the traditional students, and 8 percent of the non-religious students had grandfathers who were born in Israel. The percentage of paternal grandfathers born in Muslim countries was much higher than the percentage of parents, standing at 34 percent among the religious students, 72 percent among the traditional students, and 31 percent among the non-religious students. The percentage of students whose paternal grandfather was born in the Soviet Union was 42 percent among the religious students, 14 percent among the traditional students, and 52 percent among the non-religious students. In the 1990 study, I found ethnic origin to be a relatively insignificant variable with regard to a large number of the questions asked. Statistically, country of birth was not found to influence students' attitudes on different issues. At the same time, correspondence between "traditional" religiosity classification and Middle Eastern extraction is likely to emerge as a factor with influence on attitudes. As in the 1990 study, the variable of extraction was not found to play a significant role, while the variable of religiosity was. Despite these findings, I draw no conclusions regarding Israeli society as a whole.

An overwhelming majority (99 percent) of the Arab students were born in Israel (although a handful reported having been born in Palestine), and this was also true of a decisive majority of the paternal and maternal grandfathers of the Arab study participants. Aside from the approximately 8 percent of grandfathers whose grandchildren (the students in the sample) indicated that they had been born in Palestine, the rest (with the exception of a few) were reported as being born in Israel.

In conclusion, the most important difference between the students appears to be the fact that they belong to two different national groups whose relationship with each other is characterized by a high level of tension and conflict. Within each national group, the variable of religiosity is the most important independent variable, and the variable of extraction has much less influence. Within the Jewish study population, the traditional group had a higher percentage of immigrants from other Middle Eastern countries, while the non-religious students had a higher percentage of immigrants from the former Soviet Union.

## Notes

1. Amin Maalouf, *In the Name of Identity: Violence and the Need to Belong* (New York, 2000), 10–11.
2. D. R. Miller, "The Study of Social Relationships: Situation, Identity, and Social Interaction," in *Psychology: A Study of a Science,* ed. S. Koch (New York, 1963), 673.
3. E. H. Erikson, "The Problem of Ego Identity," in *Identity and Anxiety,* ed. M. R. Stein et al. (Glencoe, IL, 1960), 38.
4. Simon Herman, *Jewish Identity: A Social Psychological Perspective* (New Brunswick, 1989), 28–29.
5. Among other sources, see Ephraim Ya'ar and Ze'ev Shavit, "Processes and Trends in Collective Identity," in *Trends in Israeli Society (Vol. II)* (Tel Aviv, 2003), 1197–1221; Baruch Kimmerling and Joel Migdal, *The Palestinian People: A History* (Cambridge, MA, 1990); Yoav Peled and Gershon Shafir, *Being Israeli: The Dynamics of Multiple Citizenship* (Cambridge, 2002); Nadim Rouhana, *Palestinian Citizens in an Ethnic Jewish State: Identities in Conflict* (New Haven, CT, 1997); Sammy Smooha, *Autonomy for Arabs in Israel?* (Raanana, 1996) [Hebrew]; Sammy Smooha, *Arabs and Jews in Israel* (Boulder, 1989 and 1992).

6. Edward Said, *Orientalism* (New York, 1979).
7. Uri Farago, "The Jewish Identity of Israeli Youth, 1965–1985," *Yahadut Zmaneinu* 5 (1989): 264, 285 [Hebrew].
8. Simon Herman, *Jewish Identity: A Social Psychological Perspective* (Jerusalem, 1977), 173 [Hebrew].
9. Yeshayahu (Charles) Liebman, "Some Thoughts on Relations between Religious and Non-Religious Jews," in *Living Together: Religious-Secular Relations in Israeli Society*, ed. Yeshayahu (Charles) Liebman (Jerusalem, 1990), 10–11, 195. See also Yizhar Smilansky, "The Courage to Be a Secular Jew," *Shdemot* 79 (198—81): 74–80 [Hebrew]. Smilansky distinguishes between the terms "non-religious" and "secular."

# CHAPTER 2
# MY PEOPLE AND ME

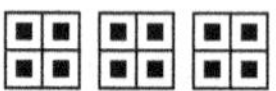

## Jewish Nationality and Me

### *Introduction*

The attitude of young Israelis toward their Jewish-Israeli identity is a subject that is frequently discussed, and when it is, one of the issues focused on is the relationship between "Israeliness" and "Jewishness." While this is a meaningful distinction, I argue that it does not always facilitate a thorough understanding of the concepts in general and of the perspective of young Israelis in particular. Beyond their formal definitions as determined by law, the concepts of Israeli and Jew, and Israeliness and Jewishness, are complex and problematic in many ways.

As we have seen, there is no consensus among Jews regarding the relationship between their Judaism and their Israeliness. In this context, citizenship and national belonging intermingle with one another, as holders of Israeli identity cards belong to a number of different national groups (Jewish, Russian, Ukrainian, Arab, etc.) which until recently were listed in the card's "nationality" section. This being the case, it is clear that Israeli citizenship is not equivalent to nationality. Information regarding the nationality and religion of all Israeli citizens is maintained by the Population Registry of the Ministry of Interior, which is a practice that, to the best of my knowledge, is not typical in other democracies.

Israeli identity can be broken down into two different components: a civil component, and an ethno-national component. This dual identity implies a decisive lack of clarity and a number of contradictions. Evidence of this lack of clarity in the official definitions is reflected in Israeli identity cards—which are supposed to identify and classify us on the formal, official level—dating from the period preceding the elimination of the nationality section. The card bears the following text: "Under Section 3 of the Population Registry Law of 1965, the information on this card—with the exception of nationality, personal status, and name of spouse—constitutes evidence of its accuracy." Moreover, the term Jew is defined differently by the Law of Return and the Population Registry on the one hand, and the (exclusive) rabbinical courts in matters of marriage and divorce on the other hand. In the latter context, Jewish religious law assumes a binding status for all Jewish citizens of Israel listed in the Population Registry, religious and non-religious alike. Young Israelis can often be heard trying in vain to extricate themselves from this confusion with statements such as: "I am Israeli by nationality and Jewish by religion." However, they begin to encounter difficulties when asked whether they and the young Arab (Palestinian) from Umm al-Fahm belong to the same nation.

For these reasons, it was more important for us to assess how subjects see themselves than how they classify themselves, and I did not ask them to define the concepts. The discord surrounding the questions "who is a Jew?" and "who is an Israeli?" will continue to engage us in the future, both in Israel and the Diaspora. After all, Israel's Declaration of Independence defines the country as a "Jewish state," without clarifying its Judaism or Jewishness, and the disagreements surrounding this question are substantive and fundamental.

My research methods were not suitable for assessing who the subjects in particular, and Jews in general, regard as members of their group—that is to say, what they regard as the objective definition of public identity. Rather, I sought to illuminate the criteria that enable Jews to assess their own identities. This chapter focuses on one aspect of young Israelis' Jewish identity: their attitude toward the Jewish people and the Jews of the Diaspora. It is my hope that this discussion will help us better understand the Israeliness and Jewishness of young Israelis.

Zionism's object of reference is the Jewish people, and recognition of the existence of the Jewish people and its aspiration to become a sovereign nation constituted the raison d'être of the state of Israel. Nonetheless, as we have seen, Judaism had and has a variety of definitions. There is no consensus regarding the definition of Jewish identity and Jewish nationalit—that is, of the nature of the Jewish people and who belongs to it—and this is as true in the present as it was in the past.[1] The same is true regarding attitudes toward the exile, or the Diaspora. Did the auto-emancipation of the Jewish people mark the end of exile? What is the relationship between the Diaspora and the national center being created in Israel? What is the status of the Jewish Diaspora in relation to the state of Israel, and how is solidarity between the two entities manifested? Do Jews of Israel and Jews of the Diaspora share a consciousness of mutual responsibility? Are the Jews of Israel and the Jews of the Diaspora really dependent on one another?

Regardless of their particular points of view, all those engaged in the study of the Jewish world following the Holocaust and the establishment of the state of Israel recognize that Israel has become one of the most important forces—if not *the* most important force—in shaping Jewish identification and Jewish identity. At the same time, however, Western (free) Jewry has not exercised its option to immigrate to Israel and does not appear to intend to do so in the future. What, then, is the meaning and significance of "the state of Israel as the state of the Jewish people" and of the "Jewish state," a classification advanced in the summer of

2009 by Israel as a condition for negotiations with the Palestinians? What constitutes the group of belonging or group of reference for Jewish-Israelis: the citizens of the state of Israel, some of whom are not Jewish, or world Jewry, including the Jews in the Diaspora who choose not to make their lives in Israel? How do young Israelis educated in Israel relate to these issues and to other issues not discussed here?

This chapter explores these and other issues, including: the centrality and morality of Israeliness and Jewishness; attitudes toward different periods in Jewish history; attitudes toward Jewish communities in the Diaspora; attitudes toward Diaspora Jews; certain aspects of Israel-Diaspora relations (Israel's contribution to Diaspora Jewry and Diapora Jewry's contribution to Israel); and attitudes toward Jewish immigration to Israel (*Aliyah*) and assimilation. It also explores the relationship among the state of Israel, the "people of Israel" (*Am Israel*, or the Jewish people), and the "religion of Israel" (*Dat Israel*, or Judaism), and, in a parallel section titled "Arab Nationality and Me," it examines Arab students' attitudes toward their own national identity. To a certain extent, this study is a continuation of my previous study on Jewish-Israeli identity. However, it differs from the previous study in a number of significant ways.

### *Israeliness and Jewishness*

My assessment of the intensity of students' Jewish and Israeli identities follows the lead of Herman and Farago (1977, 1978, 1989), whose studies also explored these issues, and who based their assessments on four indicators:

1) The valence of Jewish and Israeli identity
2) The centrality of Jewish and Israeli identity
3) The relative strength of Jewish and Israeli identity
4) Overlap and compatibility between Jewish and Israeli identity

In order to asses these indicators of Jewish and Israeli identity, I made significant modifications to the questions used by Herman and Farago and eliminated questions dealing directly with the third and fourth indicators. At the same time, however, I also added two questions assessing students' positions on the Israeli-Jewish continuum, which was also examined by Herman. I treated Israeliness and Jewishness as separate variables that stand on their own, but I also presented them as one continuum in order to assess the degree of overlap and compatibility between the two.

### *Valence*

Valence is an indicator of emotional sentiment toward, and a desire to be part of a particular group. In my study, valence was assessed by means of a series of questions that presented students with a hypothetical situation in which they had the theoretical ability to choose if they wanted to belong to the Jewish collective. The hypothetical question was worded as follows: "If you could be reborn, would you want to be born Jewish?"

I identified a high valence of Jewish identity and a high valence of Israeli identity among all the students. However, I also found a number of statistically significant differences regarding the intensity of the valence of Jewish and Israeli identity among the three student groups: religious students, traditional students, and non-religious students. The valence of Jewish identity among non-religious students was lower than among the other two groups. The valence of Israeli identity among non-religious students was also lower than among students who classified themselves as religious and traditional.

**TABLE 2.1 Valence of Jewish Identity according to Religiosity, 2008[2] (as a percentage):** ***"If you could be reborn, would you want to be born Jewish?"***

| | Want Strongly | Want | Indifferent | Do Not Want | Total | (N) |
|---|---|---|---|---|---|---|
| Religious | 84 | 13 | 1 | 2 | 100 | 99 |
| Traditional | 75 | 15 | 9 | 1 | 100 | 166 |
| Non-Religious | 42 | 24 | 30 | 4 | 100 | 518 |
| $X^2 = 104.66$ | | $df = 6$ | | $p < 0.0001$ | | |

It should also be noted that the valence of Jewish identity among the subjects of my 1990 study was higher than that identified by Herman and Farago. Among non-religious subjects, the responses "want" and "want strongly" together accounted for 54 percent in 1965, 62 percent in 1974, and 64 percent in 1985. In the 1990 study, these responses accounted for 75 percent, and in the 2008 study they accounted for 66 percent, or less than the 1990 assessment of teaching students. My studies identified the continuation and intensification of the trend of an increasingly positive attitude toward Jewish identity among all the young Israeli subjects, which Herman and Farago found to be particularly prominent among traditional and non-religious Jews.[3]

In Herman's studies, traditional Jews constituted an intermediate group, at times bridging the gap between the religious and non-religious subgroups with regard to intensity of Jewish identity. In the 1990 study and the 2008 study, I also identified a high valence of Jewish identity among the traditional students, which was much higher than that identified among the non-religious students. Moreover, responses provided by traditional students to a number of types of questions were extremely similar to the responses of religious students, while their responses to a number of other types of questions were similar to responses of the non-religious.

The division of the student population into religious, traditional, and non-religious (secular) subgroups provides a better illustration of the real differences between these populations with regard to Jewish-Israeli identity. The role of the traditional group as a statistically significant intermediate group was reflected in all the responses examined in this chapter. Below, I use a number of questions to demonstrate this dynamic.[4]

The valence of Jewish identity was lower when students were asked if they would be willing to be reborn as Jews outside Israel. Among the study population as a whole, the figure dropped from 54 percent ("If you could be reborn, would you want to be born Jewish?") to 43 percent ("If you were going to live your life abroad, would you want to be born Jewish?" [see table 2.2]). The most significant decline was among non-religious students, possibly reflecting the fact that the Jewishness of this group is closely related to its Israeliness. For non-religious students, Israeliness is not an expression of their unique Jewishness (the fact that they are Jewish-Israelis as opposed to American Jews). Rather, in many ways, their Judaism is an expression of their Israeliness. That is to say, non-religious young Israelis are frequently Jewish-Israelis as opposed to non-Jewish Israelis, whether on a religious level (as opposed to Christians and Muslims) or a national level (as opposed to Arabs or the Palestinians).

We can assume that, had they been born outside of Israel, some of the non-religious students would have preferred not to be born Jewish. In contrast, the Jewishness of religious students stands on its own right as a central component of their identity. It is possible that Israeliness is an expression of the Judaism of secular young Israelis who feel no other connection to Judaism aside from the fact that they live in a Jewish state. It is also possible that some of these students may prefer the state of Israel to be an Israeli state.

**TABLE 2.2 Valence of Jewish Identity according to Religiosity, 2008 (as a percentage):** ***"If you were going to live your life abroad, would you want to be born Jewish?"***

| | Want Strongly | Want | Indifferent | Do Not Want |
|---|---|---|---|---|
| Religious | 78 | 16 | 2 | 4 |
| Traditional | 63 | 18 | 9 | 10 |
| Non-Religious | 29 | 22 | 25 | 24 |
| $X^2 = 128.25$ | $df = 6$ | | $p < 0.0001$ | |

Indeed, the valence of Jewish identity decreases significantly with the possibility of the subject being born outside of Israel. Jewishness is dependent on Israeliness in this way particularly among the non-religious students, and to a lesser extent among the traditional students.

In contrast, the valence of Jewish identity among the religious and traditional students turned out to be very high (see table 2.3 below). That is to say, the religious and traditional students tended to select the responses with the highest values in order to describe the valence of both Jewish identity and Israeli identity (although the valence of Israeli identity was lower than that of Jewish identity). In the 1990 study, although the valence of Israeli identity was higher than that of Jewish identity among students of the state teachers colleges, I nonetheless found it to be relatively low.

**TABLE 2.3 Valence of Israeli Identity according to Religiosity (as a percentage):** ***"If you could be reborn, would you want to be born Israeli?"***

| | Want Strongly | Want | Indifferent | Do Not Want |
|---|---|---|---|---|
| Religious | 55 | 23 | 9 | 13 |
| Traditional | 53 | 24 | 15 | 8 |
| Non-Religious | 31 | 28 | 21 | 20 |
| $X^2 = 40.92$ | $df = 6$ | | $p < 0.0001$ | |

In the 2008 study, 66 percent of the non-religious students (table 2.1) indicated that they would like to be born Jewish ("want" and "want strongly" combined), in contrast to 76 percent of the respondents from state teachers colleges in the 1990 study. However, I also identified a decline in their desire to be born Israeli: 59 percent in the present study (table 2.3) in comparison to 80 percent among teaching students of the state system. Another significant development is the fact that a higher percentage of non-religious students want to be born Jewish (66 percent) than want to be born Israeli (59 percent).

In the 1990 study, the valence of Israeli identity among non-religious students was to a large extent lower than among the parallel groups in Herman's study,[5] and it continued to decline until the 2008 study. I believe that the low valence of Israeli identity reflected in the responses may also be an expression of difficulties with Israeli identity among *some members* of the non-religious group. These difficulties may be intensifying in conjunction with developments that have taken place in Israeli society in recent years. This dynamic was expressed in various responses in the 1990 study as well, such as extremely harsh criticism, including being "extremely ashamed" of the events that had taken place in Israel during the preceding decade (this question did not appear in the 2008 study).

### *Centrality*

Centrality is an indicator of the importance of Jewish identity and Israeli identity in the consciousness of individual respondents. It was measured by means of the question: "To what degree does the fact that you are Jewish play an important role in your life?" In contrast to the findings presented above that indicate a higher measure of valence of Jewish identity than Israeli identity, the situation was reversed when I considered the centrality of Jewishness. Seventy-six percent of respondents in the 2008 study answered the question affirmatively ("a large degree" and "a very large degree" combined), indicating that Israeliness played an important role in their lives, in comparison to 62 percent who answered affirmatively regarding Jewishness. Some of the latter group may regard Israeliness as a civil identity.

Jewish identity played a much more minor role in the lives of the non-religious students than for the religious and the traditional students. Indeed, for the non-religious students, Israeli identity was much more central (75 percent) than Jewish identity (47 percent). This finding may stem from the large percentage of immigrants from the former Soviet Union within this group (see tables 2.4 and 2.5). Not surprisingly, the centrality of Jewish identity was much higher among the religious students.

In the 1990 study, the centrality of Israeli identity among students of the State-Religious teaching colleges was comparable to, if not somewhat higher than its centrality among students of the State teaching colleges. According to the 2008 study, the centrality of Israeli identity was 71 percent among the religious students, 79 percent among the traditional students, and 75 percent among the non-religious students (table 2.5).

**TABLE 2.4 Centrality of Jewish Identity according to Religiosity (as a percentage):** ***"To what degree does the fact that you are Jewish play an important role in your life?"***

| | Not at All | A Small Degree | A Large Degree | A Very Large Degree |
|---|---|---|---|---|
| Religious | – | 1 | 8 | 91 |
| Traditional | 1 | 12 | 45 | 42 |
| Non-Religious | 10 | 43 | 37 | 10 |
| $X^2 = 275.22$ | $df = 6$ | | $p < 0.0001$ | |

**TABLE 2.5 Centrality of Israeli Identity according to Religiosity (as a percentage):** ***"To what degree does the fact that you are Israeli play an important role in your life?"***

| | Not at All | A Small Degree | A Large Degree | A Very Large Degree |
|---|---|---|---|---|
| Religious | 1 | 28 | 34 | 37 |
| Traditional | 1 | 19 | 42 | 37 |
| Non-Religious | 5 | 20 | 45 | 30 |
| $X^2 = 11.77$ | $df = 6$ | | $p < 0.0001$ | |

Although the centrality of Jewish identity was low among students of the State teaching colleges in 1990, it was nonetheless higher than in the findings of Herman and Farago. In this way, the trend over the years appears to have been one of increasing centrality of Jewish identity, particularly among traditional students.[6] This trend was also evident in the study of 1990 but appears to have declined by the time of the 2008 study. In contrast, the 1990 study did not identify a "slight but insignificant decline in the centrality of Israeli identity among all the respondents included in previous studies."[7] Rather, Israeli identity remained high among the non-religious and traditional students alike. The 2008 study found Israeliness to be only slightly less central than it had been 18 years earlier, according to the findings of the 1990 study.

For religious students, the fact that they are Jewish plays a more important role in their lives (99 percent, reflecting "a large degree" and "a very large degree" combined) than the fact that they are Israeli (71 percent). Eighty-seven percent of the traditional students indicated that the fact that they are Jewish plays an important role in their lives, in comparison to 80 percent who feel the same way about the fact that they are Israeli. The percentages were lower among the non-religious students: Only 75 percent thought that the fact that they are Israeli played an important role in their lives, while only 47 percent feel this way about their Jewishness.

### *The Israeli-Jewish Continuum*

As I have noted, my study did not include questions regarding the relative intensity, overlap, and compatibility of Jewish and Israeli identity, but rather employed questions (based on the questions posed in Herman's study, with some modification) addressing subjects' Israeli-Jewish continuum, or the relative intensity of the Israeli and Jewish components of subjects' Jewish-Israeli identity. I asked students whether they regarded themselves first and foremost as Jews or as Israelis. Within the overall study population, 60 percent regarded themselves first and foremost as Jews, and 40 percent as Israelis.

Division of the study population into the three religiosity-based sub-groups highlights clear differences on this point (see table 2.6). Non-religious students were more likely to classify themselves as "first and foremost Israelis," while traditional students and religious students classified themselves as "first and foremost Jews" (I have already noted the role of the traditional student as an intermediate group with regard to other questions as well). Response distribution in the context of these questions in the 2008 study was almost identical to the 1990 study, with the exception of an increase in the tendency of non-religious students to favor Jewishness at the expense of Israeliness.

**TABLE 2.6 Jewish or Israeli Identity according to Religiosity, 1990 and 2008 (as a percentage):** ***"Do you regard yourself as more Jewish or more Israeli?"***

| | First and Foremost Israeli | | First and Foremost Jewish | |
|---|---|---|---|---|
| | **2008** | **1990** | **2008** | **1990** |
| Religious | 2 | 1 | 98 | 99 |
| Traditional | 19 | 20 | 81 | 80 |
| Non-Religious | 55 | 66 | 45 | 34 |
| 1990 | $X^2 = 160.831$ | $df = 6$ | | $p < 0.0001$ |
| 2008 | $X^2 = 110.57$ | $df = 2$ | | $p < 0.0001$ |

In a different question, I asked respondents to indicate their location on a multi-level scale (six levels in 1990, and seven levels in 2008) ranging between an extreme identification with Israeliness and an extreme identification with Jewishness:[8] "Indicate on the scale provided whether you feel more *Israeli* or more *Jewish*. The word "Jewish" appears on one end of the scale and the word "Israeli" appears on the other end of the scale. Circle the number that is most applicable to you" (table 2.6). In students' responses to this question, I found clear religiosity-based differences, with the religious students classifying themselves characteristically as Jewish, and two-thirds of the non-religious students classifying themselves as Israeli. Although the traditional students constituted an intermediate group, 80 percent nonetheless classified themselves as "first and foremost Jewish." The 2008 study identified an increase in Jewishness among the non-religious, with 45 percent classifying themselves as "first and foremost Jewish," in comparison to 34 percent in 1990.

**TABLE 2.7 Israeli-Jewish Continuum, 2008 (as a percentage):** ***"To what extent do you regard yourself as more Jewish or more Israeli?"***

| | Jewish Israeli | | | | | | |
|---|---|---|---|---|---|---|---|
| | 7 | 6 | 5 | 4 | 3 | 2 | 1 |
| All Jewish Subjects | 8 | 11 | 16 | 19 | 18 | 12 | 16 |
| Religious | 52 | 30 | 10 | 7 | 1 | – | – |
| Traditional | 26 | 16 | 21 | 25 | 9 | 2 | 1 |
| Non-Religious | 6 | 7 | 19 | 20 | 21 | 15 | 12 |
| F = 115.29 | | $df = 2$ | | | $p < 0.0001$ | | |

Higher Score = More Jewish; the numbers have no value-oriented significance.
As I have noted, findings reported for all the subjects are not significant (see the note for table 2.1 above).

The mean position for the entire study population was 4.3 (4 marks the midpoint of the scale), and the mean position for the religious students was 6.2. Among non-religious respondents, there was a slight tendency toward Israeliness over Jewishness, with both variables on one continuum. In contrast, the traditional and religious students exhibited a clear tendency toward Jewishness. This is consistent with Herman, who also identified an increasing tendency toward Jewishness. The mean position in his 1965 sample tended toward the Israeli side of the scale (3.5). However, by 1974 it had moved to 4.2, crossing over the midpoint of the seven-level scale (4) from the Israeli side to the Jewish side. The non-religious students, whose position in 1965 was on the Israeli side of the scale (2.6), remained on the Israeli side but moved slightly closer to the midpoint (3.1). This ongoing trend was also reflected in my 1990 study and my 2008 study.

The non-religious students who participated in this study frequently selected positions on the Israeli side of the continuum. Whereas the mean position of the non-religious students was 3.66 (another 20 percent selected 4, the scale's midpoint), the religious students clearly positioned themselves on the Jewish side of the continuum, with a mean position of 6.23.

This difference was further illustrated by the distinction between traditional students and non-religious students. Non-religious (secular) students exhibited a clear tendency toward Israeliness (in addition to the 48 percent of non-religious students who selected Israeli values, another 20 percent chose 4—the midpoint of the scale), while traditional students tended toward Jewishness. Sixty-three percent selected positions on the Jewish side of the scale, and 25 percent selected 4, the midpoint. To a moderate extent, non-religious students regarded themselves as more Israeli than Jewish. In contrast, the traditional students and, to a greater extent, the religious students saw themselves as much more Jewish than Israeli. The religious students were not only extremely Jewish but extremely Israeli as well, as I saw in their responses to other questions. Nonetheless, it is clear that as far as they are concerned, Judaism preceded Israeliness and was what guided their worldview.

Indeed, non-religious students today tend to see themselves as first and foremost Israeli, although less than in the past. However, they also see themselves as both Israeli (more than in the past) and Jewish in a manner that is more balanced (although still clearly unbalanced) than in the past. As we have seen, their responses to questions regarding centrality reflected Israeliness much more than Jewishness, whereas their responses to questions assessing valence reflected Jewishness much more than Israeliness. That being the case, we cannot be certain that the intensification of Jewishness is necessarily related to a fundamental change in position on their part. The change may also be more declarative in nature—an expression of external changes that the education system successfully instilled in them. It is also possible that the intensified Jewishness among the traditional, and particularly the non-religious students, has to do with the weakening of Israeliness, and does not exist on its own. I examined the depth and significance of these changes through a series of questions exploring additional aspects of the Jewish and Israeli identity of the subjects.

### *Attitudes toward the State of Israel, the People of Israel, and the Religion of Israel (Comparative Data)*

Here, I wish to examine the claim that young Israelis regard their attitude toward the Jewish people and their belonging to the Jewish people as less important, and perhaps even much less important than other aspects of their identity, such as their attitude toward the state of Israel and the Land of Israel (due to the already large number of questions included in the questionnaire, I did not explore these questionsin the study). For young religious Israelis, it may also be less important than their attitude toward religion.

I argue that the Israeliness of young Israelis is expressed *primarily* in their attitude toward the state of Israel and the Land of Israel, whereas their attitude toward their Jewishness is expressed *primarily* with regard to the "religion of Israel" (Judaism) and "the people of Israel." If in fact some young non-religious Israelis lack a meaningful attitude (and at times display a negative attitude) toward religion as well as toward their belonging to the Jewish people, I am of the opinion that their Jewishness may be lacking in some way.

Below, I explore this assumption by means of a series of questions that examine different aspects of the subject. During the study, I presented respondents with questions directly addressing the degree of connection they felt toward the state of Israel, the Jewish people, and the Jewish religion. My findings suggest that it is the non-religious students who feel the strongest bond to the state of Israel. In response to the statement "I feel a strong bond to the state of Israel," 53 percent chose the answer "strongly agree," and 32 percent indicated that they "agree." This was the only one of the three statements (attitude to people, state, and religion) in which the bond felt by the non-religious students was stronger than the bond felt by the two other groups.[9] The religious students indicated a weaker bond with the state of Israel than the traditional and non-religious students, with 77 percent selecting either "agree" or "strongly agree," in comparison to 91 percent among the traditional students and 84 percent among the non-religious students.

The religiosity variable became significant in response to questions regarding attitude toward the two other components: the Jewish religion and the Jewish people. In response to the statement "I feel a strong bond to the Jewish religion," the vast majority of religious students chose "strongly agree" (87 percent), and another 10 percent chose "agree." In response to the statement "I feel a strong bond to the Jewish people," 88 percent selected "strongly agree," and another 11 percent selected "agree." In my 1990 study, I found that all respondents who felt a strong bond to the Jewish religion also felt a strong bond to the Jewish people. Of those who described their bond to religion with the response "yes, definitely" (4 on a scale of 1 to 4), 98 percent also chose answer 4 to characterize their attitude toward the Jewish people. The remaining 2 percent chose answer 3. The responses of the non-religious students in the 1990 study were much more moderate. Although their responses indicated a relatively strong bond to the Jewish people, it was nonetheless significantly weaker than that indicated by the students in the other groups. The responses of the non-religious students also indicated a bond to the Jewish people that was weaker than their bond to the state of Israel.

**TABLE 2.8 Attitudes toward the State of Israel, the People of Israel, and the Religion of Israel, Comparative Data, 2008 (as a percentage): *"I feel a strong bond to the state of Israel/the People of Israel/the Religion of Israel"***

| | State of Israel | | People of Israel | | Religion of Israel | |
|---|---|---|---|---|---|---|
| | Agree | Disagree | Agree | Disagree | Agree | Disagree |
| Religious | 77 | 23 | 88 | 12 | 96 | 4 |
| Traditional | 91 | 9 | 94 | 6 | 86 | 14 |
| Non-Religious | 84 | 26 | 78 | 22 | 36 | 64 |
| Jewish People | $X^2 = 97.6$ | $df = 6$ | $p < 0.0001$ | Significant | | |
| State of Israel | $X^2 = 12.47051$ | $df = 6$ | $p < 0.0001$ | Marginally Significant | | |
| Jewish Religion | $X^2 = 279.06$ | $df = 6$ | $p < 0.0001$ | Significant | | |

The bond that the 1990 students of the State teaching colleges expressed toward the Jewish religion was significantly weaker, with 25 percent indicating a strong bond to the Jewish religion; 46 percent indicating a medium bond; 23 percent indicating a weak bond; and 6 percent indicating no bond whatsoever.[10]

Again, it must be emphasized that the sense of connection to the Jewish people and the Jewish religion expressed by the non-religious students was obviously weaker than that expressed by the traditional students. Only 12 percent of the non-religious (secular) students from the 1990 study expressed an extremely strong bond to religion, while 49 percent indicated a medium bond. The 2008 study identified another trend: an increasingly weaker bond with religion among the non-religious students. In response to the statement "I feel a strong bond to the religion of Israel," 9 percent strongly agreed; 27 percent agreed (total: 36 percent; see table 2.8); 44 percent expressed minimal agreement; and 20 percent did not agree (total: 64 percent).

**TABLE 2.9 Sense of Connection with the Jewish People, 2008 (as a percentage): *"I feel a strong bond to the Jewish People"***

| | 4<br>Strongly Agree | 3<br>Agree Moderately | 2<br>Agree Minimally | 1<br>Strongly Disagree |
|---|---|---|---|---|
| Religious | 88 | 11 | – | 1 |
| Traditional | 73 | 21 | 5 | 1 |
| Non-Religious | 39 | 38 | 19 | 4 |
| $X^2 = 97.6$ | $df = 6$ | | $p = 0.0001$ | |

I also regard it as extremely important that the bond between young Israelis and the Jewish people is diminishing: 39 percent of the non-religious students indicated a strong bond (see table 2.9) with the Jewish people, down from 59 percent in 1990; among traditional students and religious students, the figure dropped from 91 percent to 73 percent and from 98.5 percent to 88 percent respectively.

I presented students with two additional statements relating to the Jewish people: 1) "It is important for me that the Jewish people always exist"; and 2) "It is important for me that Jews outside Israel continue to maintain their Judaism." The vast majority of the subjects in the 1990 study (teaching students) and the 2008 study (university students) said that it was very important for them that the Jewish people always exist. This was the response of 100 percent of the subjects from the State-Religious and the Ultra-Orthodox sectors (4 on a scale of 1 to 4) surveyed in the 1990 study, as well as 92 percent of the religious students in the 2008 study. Responses from students in the state system were also high, but lower in comparison to the other groups: Eighty-three percent said that it was "very important" for them that the Jewish people always exist, and 14 percent said that it was "important" (3 on a scale of 1 to 3). Of the non-religious students examined in the 2008 study, 72 percent said that it was very important.

A significant difference could be detected in subjects' responses (according to religiosity) to the other statement: "It is important for me that Jews outside Israel continue to maintain their Judaism." Eighty-six percent of the religious students indicated that this was very important for them, and almost all those remaining indicated that they regard it as important (3 on a scale of 1 to 4). Among the traditional students, responses were more varied: Sixty-nine percent indicated that it was very important; 25 percent said that it was important; 14.5 percent said that it was of minor importance; and 6 percent said that it was of no importance at all. Response distribution increased even more among the non-religious students, with 36 percent indicating that it was of great importance to them; 33 percent indicating that it was important; 21 percent indicating that it was of minor importance; and 10 percent disagreeing altogether.

The differences of opinion among study participants regarding the importance of the state of Israel and the Jewish religion were also reflected in their responses to two other statements: "the Jewish people cannot survive without the Jewish religion," and "the Jewish people cannot survive without the state of Israel." The vast majority of religious students (96 percent) agreed that the Jewish people cannot survive without the Jewish religion (86 percent strongly agreed and 10 percent agreed). Agreement within the traditional group was more moderate, with 61 percent agreeing strongly and 27 percent agreeing, 9 percent expressing minimal agreement, and 3 percent not agreeing at all. Among the non-religious students, response distribution was even wider, with 27 percent agreeing strongly, and 33 percent agreeing, 26 percent expressing minimal agreement, and 14 percent not agreeing at all. I consider the responses to this statement in greater detail below.[11]

The picture changes somewhat when I considered the students' responses to the statement regarding their bond to the state of Israel: "the Jewish people cannot survive without the state of Israel." The non-religious students strongly agreed more than the religious students, but to a significantly lesser extent than the degree to which the religious students strongly agreed with the statement regarding the role of the Jewish religion in safeguarding the existence of the Jewish people. Again, the traditional students functioned as an intermediate group between the religious and the non-religious students, with responses that were usually more similar to those of the religious than those of the non-religious. Of all the groups, their responses to this statement expressed the greatest level of support.

**Table 2.10 Agreement with the Statement, *"The Jewish people cannot survive without the state of Israel,"* 2008 (as a percentage)**

| | 4<br>Agree Strongly | 3<br>Agree | 2<br>Agree Minimally | 1<br>Disagree |
|---|---|---|---|---|
| Religious | 24 | 20 | 16 | 40 |
| Traditional | 59 | 25 | 12 | 4 |
| Non-Religious | 47 | 25 | 17 | 11 |
| $X^2 = 73.46$ | $df = 6$ | | $p < 0.0001$ | |

In this context as well, the traditional students expressed the most "Zionist" or "nationalist" approach (as we have seen, they also articulated the strongest bond with the state of Israel). Eighty-four percent agreed that the Jewish people cannot survive without the state of Israel ("strongly agree" and "agree" combined), in comparison to 72 percent of the non-religious students. In the 1990 study, a higher percentage of respondents agreed with the statement; for example, 58 percent of the students from the State teaching colleges strongly agreed and 25 percent agreed, for a total of 83 percent in agreement.

Attitudes toward the state of Israel, Zionism, and religion will be discussed in subsequent chapters. However, it is nonetheless interesting to note here that the different points of view regarding the future of the Jewish people are reflected in this context as well. The religious students held that the Jewish religion is what maintained, maintains, and will continue to maintain the Jewish people. From their perspective, the state of Israel plays a much more minor role in ensuring the existence of the Jewish people. Indeed, according to the ultra-orthodox perspective, as reflected in the 1990 study of teaching students, the state's role in this context is marginal.

## *The Perspective of Time: Attitudes toward Jewish History*

"Just think ... What is there in it? ... Oppression, defamation, persecution, martyrdom. And again, and again, and again without end. . . . That's what's in it, and nothing more. After all, it's ... it's ... it bores you to death, it's just plain dull!"

—Yudka in "The Sermon," by Haim Hazaz

The students' attitudes toward the Jewish people were also reflected in their attitudes toward Jewish history and their perspective of time regarding their Jewishness. Some thinkers have been critical of young Israelis' approach to Jewish history and have posited that their roots are short or displaced. Another approach prevalent in some circles in Israeli society has called for disengaging from the exilic past of the Jewish people.

In an open-ended question that appeared as the first question in the survey, the subjects were asked to:

1) List three historical events that in your opinion influenced the destiny of the Jewish people; and
2) list three historical events that you feel are especially relevant to you or your destiny

**TABLE 2.11 Important Events in Jewish History,[12] 1990 (as a percentage)**

| The Ultra-Orthodox Education System | | | | | | | | |
|---|---|---|---|---|---|---|---|---|
| | Historical Events that Influenced the Destiny of the Jewish People | | | | Historical Events that are Especially Relevant to You or Your Destiny | | | |
| Event | 1 | 2 | 3 | Total | 1 | 2 | 3 | Total |
| Holocaust | 18.0 | 14.5 | 32.7 | 66.0 | 44.7 | 7.7 | 20.0 | 72.4 |
| Establishment of Israel | 0.0 | 3.2 | 9.1 | 12.3 | 4.3 | 10.3 | 6.7 | 21.3 |
| Exile | 7.8 | 6.5 | 9.1 | 23.4 | 4.3 | 10.3 | 3.3 | 17.9 |
| Giving of the Torah | 28.1 | 16.1 | 5.5 | 49.7 | 21.3 | 10.3 | 16.7 | 48.3 |
| Exodus from Egypt | 15.6 | 8.1 | 7.3 | 31.0 | – | 5.1 | 6.7 | 12.8 |
| Destruction of the Temple | 6.2 | 29.0 | 7.3 | 42.5 | 4.3 | 7.2 | – | 12.0 |
| Expulsion from Spain | 6.2 | 9.7 | 7.3 | 23.2 | – | 5.1 | 3.3 | 8.4 |

| The State Education System | | | | | | | | |
|---|---|---|---|---|---|---|---|---|
| | Historical Events that Influenced the Destiny of the Jewish People | | | | Historical Events that are Especially Relevant to You or Your Destiny | | | |
| Event | 1 | 2 | 3 | Total | 1 | 2 | 3 | Total |
| Holocaust | 54.4 | 27.6 | 8.7 | 90.7 | 41.6 | 13.8 | 8.2 | 63.6 |
| Establishment of Israel | 5.1 | 33.3 | 30.4 | 68.8 | 22.2 | 23.6 | 9.6 | 55.4 |
| Giving of the Torah | 2.3 | 0.6 | 1.6 | 4.5 | 0.3 | – | 0.5 | 0.8 |
| Exile | 4.8 | 1.4 | 1.6 | 7.8 | 0.6 | – | – | 0.6 |
| Destruction of the Temple | 7.9 | 2.9 | 3.8 | 14.6 | – | – | – | – |
| Zionist Events[13] | 5.6 | 5.8 | 8.2 | 19.6 | 4.2 | 6.6 | 9.9 | 20.7 |
| World War II | 6.2 | 3.7 | 1.3 | 6.0 | 1.6 | 3.6 | 0.5 | 5.3 |
| War of Independence | 1.4 | 8.9 | 4.8 | 15.1 | 2.6 | 4.7 | 1.9 | 9.2 |
| Six Days War | 0.3 | 2.3 | 12.8 | 15.4 | 3.9 | 8.4 | 9.1 | 21.4 |
| Yom Kippur War | – | 0.6 | 3.2 | 4.8 | 2.9 | 6.9 | 7.7 | 17.5 |
| First Lebanon War | – | 0.6 | 4.2 | 4.8 | 6.1 | 14.5 | 13.0 | 33.6 |
| Wars of Israel[14] | 0.3 | 1.7 | 3.2 | 5.2 | 0.6 | 6.5 | 5.8 | 12.9 |
| First Intifada | – | 0.3 | 1.9 | 2.2 | 2.3 | 4.0 | 12.5 | 18.8 |
| Peace Treaties with Egypt and Jordan | 0.6 | 0.6 | 4.8 | 6.0 | 1.6 | 3.6 | 12.0 | 17.2 |
| | | | | | | | | |
| The State-Religious Education System | | | | | | | | |
| | Historical Events that Influenced the Destiny of the Jewish People | | | | Historical Events that are Especially Relevant to You or Your Destiny | | | |
| Event | 1 | 2 | 3 | Total | 1 | 2 | 3 | Total |
| Holocaust | 19.5 | 34.4 | 28.2 | 76.7 | 17.7 | 27.4 | 6.0 | 51.1 |
| Establishment of Israel | 1.6 | 16.8 | 44.7 | 63.1 | 19.5 | 21.7 | 34.5 | 75.7 |
| Giving of the Torah | 23.4 | 12.0 | 0.8 | 36.2 | 25.7 | 6.6 | 7.1 | 39.4 |
| Exodus from Egypt | 31.3 | 2.4 | 4.4 | 38.1 | 4.4 | – | – | 4.4 |
| Destruction of the Temple | 14.1 | 6.5 | 3.5 | 24.1 | 3.5 | 3.8 | 3.6 | 10.9 |
| Zionist Events | 2.3 | 1.6 | 4.1 | 8.0 | 7.1 | 9.4 | 8.3 | 24.8 |
| Six Days War | – | 3.2 | 2.4 | 5.6 | 1.8 | 9.4 | 7.1 | 18.3 |

**TABLE 2.12 Important Events in Jewish History,[15] 2008 (as a percentage)**

| Religious | | | | | | | | |
|---|---|---|---|---|---|---|---|---|
| | Historical Events that Influenced the Destiny of the Jewish People | | | | Historical Events that are Especially Relevant to You or Your Destiny | | | |
| Event | 1 | 2 | 3 | Total | 1 | 2 | 3 | Total |
| Biblical Events | 55 | 22 | 11 | 83 | 25 | 6 | 5 | 31 |
| Holocaust | 12 | 26 | 16 | 50 | 33 | 12 | 3 | 41 |
| Establishment of Israel | 7 | 6 | 35 | 43 | 6 | 22 | 23 | 40 |
| Destruction of the Temple | 14 | 22 | 9 | 43 | 8 | 6 | 3 | 14 |
| Exile | 6 | 9 | 0.5 | 15 | – | 8 | 8 | 12 |
| Withdrawal, Evacuation, Transfer of Territory | | | | | 8 | 6 | 5 | 16 |
| | | | | | | | | |
| Traditional | | | | | | | | |
| | Historical Events that Influenced the Destiny of the Jewish People | | | | Historical Events that are Especially Relevant to You or Your Destiny | | | |
| Event | 1 | 2 | 3 | Total | 1 | 2 | 3 | Total |
| Holocaust | 52 | 25 | 8 | 77 | 34 | 14 | 7 | 45 |
| Establishment of Israel | 11 | 28 | 21 | 51 | 18 | 28 | 4 | 40 |
| Biblical Events | 18 | 5 | 3 | 24 | – | – | – | – |
| Zionist Events | 2 | 7 | 13 | 17 | 7 | 11 | 2 | 15 |
| Exile | 2 | 10 | 5 | 14 | – | – | – | – |
| Destruction of the Temple | 8 | 4 | 5 | 14 | – | – | – | – |
| | | | | | | | | |
| Second Lebanon War | | | | | 4 | 2 | 15 | 13 |
| Events in Israeli Society | | | | | 7 | 6 | 13 | 18 |
| Withdrawal, Evacuation, Transfer of Territory | | | | | – | 6 | 13 | 12 |

| Non-Religious | | | | | | | | |
|---|---|---|---|---|---|---|---|---|
| | Historical Events that Influenced the Destiny of the Jewish People | | | | Historical Events that are Especially Relevant to You or Your Destiny | | | |
| Event | 1 | 2 | 3 | Total | 1 | 2 | 3 | Total |
| Holocaust | 48 | 27 | 12 | 80 | 42 | 11 | 4 | 44 |
| Establishment of Israel | 8 | 34 | 25 | 59 | 13 | 24 | 11 | 36 |
| The Exile, Exiles | 10 | 7 | 5 | 20 | – | – | – | – |
| Zionist Events | 5 | 6 | 8 | 16.5 | 7 | 9 | 10 | 10 |
| Biblical Events | 10 | 4 | 3 | 16 | | | | |
| Destruction of the Temple | 7 | 4 | 2 | 12 | | | | |
| Events in Israeli Society | 2 | 4 | 9 | 13 | 3 | 3 | 5 | 11 |
| Second Lebanon War | – | – | – | – | 3 | 7 | 14 | 17 |

Here, I presented the events that accounted for more than 10 percent of the total number of responses. Less frequently (and in descending order), the religious students listed other events that influenced the destiny of the Jewish people, such as withdrawal, evacuation, and transfer of territory; Zionist events; the Yom Kippur War, the War of Independence; the rise of secularism; events in Jewish history; the Intifadas; anti-Semitism; the Six Days War; the rise of the Nazis; peace treaties; the liberation and conquest of territory; and the rise of Islam and Christianity. Although not always in the same order, these events were also listed by religious students relatively infrequently (alongside terrorist attacks in Israel and abroad, which were also listed very infrequently) as events that influenced their personal destiny.

The events listed relatively infrequently by the traditional students (in less than 10 percent of responses) as events that influenced the destiny of the Jewish people included events in Israeli society, wars (the Six Days War, the War of Independence, the Yom Kippur War together listed at a rate of 26 percent), and the first and second Lebanon wars (together listed at a rate of 5 percent). They also listed peace treaties, the Intifadas, and the liberation and conquest of territory. As events that influenced their personal destinies, traditional students also listed terrorist attacks, events in the history of humanity, peace treaties, the Six Days War, the Yom Kippur War, the First Lebanon War, and the War of Independence.

As events that influenced the destiny of the Jewish people, the non-religious students listed the wars fought by Israel (Six Days War, the Yom Kippur War, and the War of Independence) in a total of 25 percent of the responses, and made less frequent mention of the first and second Lebanon wars. Events such as anti-Semitism, the rise of Islam and Christianity, and events in human history were also listed relatively infrequently. As events related to their personal destiny, they mentioned events related to the military history of the state, wars fought by Israel (the Six Days War, the Yom Kippur War, the War of Independence, and the First Lebanon War), military withdrawal and the transfer of territory to the enemy, peace treaties, the fall of the Soviet Union, the exile of the Jewish people, and terrorist attacks in Israel and abroad.

In my 1990 study, I found that young non-religious Israelis tended to regard only events from the later period of Jewish history (primarily events that took place during the twentieth century) as events with importance for the Jewish people. Of these, three events appear with great frequency: the Holocaust, the establishment of the state of Israel, and the wars fought by Israel. These three events were the most frequently listed as historical events that influenced the Jewish people and as historical events "that you feel are especially relevant to you or your destiny."[16]

Of these three events, the Holocaust was the most frequently cited both as an event with general, objective significance for the Jewish people and as an event with special subjective relevance for the respondents themselves. Indeed, the Holocaust was cited in both the 1990 and 2008 studies more than any other event, although this has not been the case in the past.[17] It was cited with a similar level of frequency within all subgroups as an event influencing respondents' personal destinies: It was cited in this manner by 45 percent of the traditional students, 44 percent of the non-religious students, and 41 percent of the religious students. Differences between the subgroups were greater with regard to events that influenced the destiny of the Jewish people. As I have said, as in the previous study, all the sub-groups in the 2008 study continued to list the Holocaust and the establishment of the state much more frequently than any other event, but less than they did in the past.

The students participating in the 1990 study cited the wars fought by Israel as important events on both a general Jewish and a personal level with relatively high frequency within the state system, and low frequency (the Six Days War) within the State-Religious system. These events, however, were not even mentioned by the students of the ultra-orthodox system. Despite the time that has passed, the Six Days War, the Yom Kippur War, and the War of Independence also emerged as frequently mentioned events to a much greater degree than the first and second Lebanon wars.

Students pointed to the War of Independence (which was inextricably linked to the establishment of the state) and the Six Days War (which many students regard as a decisive event in the history of the state of Israel) as events with general importance. As an event with personal significance, the Six Days War of 1967 is still regarded as more significant than the Yom Kippur War, which was fought six years later, in 1973. It is important to remember that a large portion of the respondents were either very young or were not yet born when the Six Days War broke out. They tend to regard the first Lebanon War (1982), which they experienced as adolescents and in some cases as adults, as a more significant event on a personal level. The peace treaties with Jordan and Egypt and the Intifada are also regarded as significant events on a personal level.

These events, it should be remembered, are related to Jewish national history, Zionist history, and Israeli history, and from this perspective the non-religious students have "short roots." Although the Holocaust is clearly a different type of event in this context, it appears that many young Israelis tend to regard it more (and perhaps primarily) from a Zionist and Israeli perspective than from either a Jewish or a universal perspective.

In contrast, the perspective of time of young religious Israelis prominently highlights ancient historical events, such as the exodus from Egypt, the giving of the Torah, the destruction of the temple, and the exile. These events were hardly mentioned by students in the State education system. Aside from the fact that this is a longer-term perspective of time with "long roots," it should also be noted that these are events related to the national-religious history of the Jews and to a national-religious identification with the Jewish entity. They are the events that shaped the Jewish existence in the past and—according to a religious Jewish conception—in the present. They are also the events that shaped a Jewish-Israeli national-religious existence with religion as its center.

In contrast, the three most frequently cited events—the Holocaust, the establishment of the state of Israel, and the wars fought by Israel—were also cited in the 2008 study, but less frequently. For example, in 1990, the Holocaust was cited by students from the state system as an event that influenced the destiny of the Jewish people at a level of 91 percent, and as a historical event with special personal relevance at a level of 64 percent. In the present study, 80 percent of the non-religious students chose the Holocaust as a historical event that influenced the destiny of the Jewish people, which was much more than any other event, while only 44 percent chose the Holocaust as an event with personal relevance. Percentages were similar for the traditional group, which also selected the Holocaust the most frequently. In contrast, when selecting events that influenced the Jewish people, religious students chose the Holocaust less frequently (50 percent) than biblical events (83 percent). The Holocaust was also cited frequently (41 percent) as a personally relevant event, slightly more than the establishment of the state of Israel (40 percent). In the 1990 study, religious students cited the establishment of the state as a personally relevant event more than any other event, with 76 percent. Wars were also cited less frequently in the 2008 study, perhaps due to the fact that, aside from the Second Lebanon War, there have not been any "major" wars in recent years. Instead, non-religious students chose events such as the Jewish exile and the destruction of the temple, and biblical events such as the exodus from Egypt more frequently than in the previous study. This may be an expression of the move from Israeliness to Jewishness reflected in the responses to other questions.

Unfortunately, we must also consider the significance of the fact that the Holocaust and wars—which are difficult, painful, and negative events—play such a large role in shaping the identity of non-religious young Israelis, who regard their life experience as having little to do with the long history of the Jewish people.

### *Attitudes toward Different Periods in Jewish History*

I asked additional direct, closed-ended questions relating to students' attitudes toward different periods in Jewish history. Based on these questions, I present the attitudes toward two periods: the period of the Shtetl in Eastern Europe, and the period of the Holocaust (attitudes on the behavior of the Jews during the Holocaust). The responses of the students revealed significant differences stemming from education-sector belonging. They also generated extremely interesting findings pertaining to the entire study population as a whole.

In the past, some have claimed that Israeli youth—or at least secular Israeli youth—are ashamed of Jewish history, particularly history from the period of exile. However, my findings show that attitudes toward Jewish history have changed in recent years, as students expressed virtually no sense of shame with regard to these historical periods. Their responses to the two statements relating to the period of Jewish exile with which they were presented ranged from pride to complete indifference ("I have no particular feeling about it") and lack of knowledge ("I do not know enough about the period"). Below, I present student responses according to education system belonging.

Whereas 50 percent of the religious students expressed pride with regard to the period of the Shtetl in Eastern Europe, the percentage dropped to 21 percent among the traditional students and 10 percent among the non-religious students. Indeed, the most prevalent responses among the non-religious students were that they had no particular feeling about the period (60 percent) (which can be interpreted as indifference or a sense of irrelevance) and that they did not know enough about the period (28 percent). Two percent said that they were ashamed of it. Overall, these responses were somewhat similar to the responses of the students in the 1990 study. Among the traditional students (which included a large contingent of Jews from Middle Eastern countries), the most frequent responses were also that they had no particular feeling or that they had insufficient knowledge.[18]

A completely different picture emerged when I examined the students' attitude toward the period of the Holocaust. In the past, many young Israelis understood the Holocaust as a clear and extreme expression of exile and frequently placed blame on the Jews themselves for going "like lambs to the slaughter." Over the years, attitudes toward this subject have changed a great deal. My findings show that a large majority of the students were proud of the behavior of the Jews during the Holocaust, albeit to a significantly lesser degree than the teaching students surveyed in the 1990 study.

**TABLE 2.13 Attitudes toward the Behavior of the Jews during the Holocaust, 1990 and 2008 (as a percentage):** ***"What are your feelings regarding the behavior of the Jews during the Holocaust?"***

| | 1990 | | | 2008 | | |
|---|---|---|---|---|---|---|
| | Ultra-Orthodox | State | State-Religious | Religious | Traditional | Non-Religious |
| (1) I am proud of the behavior of the Jews during the Holocaust. | 97.1 | 77.4 | 88.7 | 76 | 70 | 65 |
| (2) I have no particular feeling toward the behavior of the Jews during this period. | 2.9 | 10.1 | 0.8 | 20 | 21 | 25 |
| (3) I am ashamed of the behavior of the Jews during this period. | – | 4.9 | 3.2 | 2 | 4 | 7 |
| (4) I do not know enough about the behavior of the Jews during this period. | – | 6.4 | 5.6 | 2 | 5 | 3 |
| (5) Provided responses on their own initiative. | – | 1.2 | 1.6 | – | – | – |

The difference found among the education sectors in the 1990 study was statistically significant ($X^2 = 26.69$ $df = 8$ $p < 0.001$). Nonetheless, they appear to have been more moderate than differences regarding other subjects. In the 2008 study, it was not possible to determine whether a significant difference existed between the different sectors due to the insufficient number of responses provided by some of the sub-groups.

It should be noted that this question was intentionally placed within a series of questions on attitudes toward different periods in Jewish history and not within the group of questions focusing specifically on the Holocaust, which I will discuss in a different section.

I found consistency in the responses of the students from the Ultra-Orthodox education sector, the religious students, and, to a certain degree, the traditional students. In contrast, I found inconsistency in the attitudes of the non-religious students, which raises some questions. Specifically, the non-religious students are not interested in the lives of the Jews in the Shtetl, which covers a period of centuries preceding the Holocaust, and if they know nothing about the period itself, this makes it somewhat harder to understand the source of their pride regarding the behavior of the Jews during the Holocaust. After all, the Holocaust marks the conclusion of Jewish life and the period of the Shtetl in Eastern Europe, and for this reason, the students' sense of historical continuity appears to be lacking to a certain degree. The Holocaust has been removed from its Jewish historical context and its general-universal context, and, as a result of Israeli education and the role of the Holocaust in Israeli society, it is currently understood as a free-standing historical period, unrelated to what went on before it and what went on after it.

It is interesting to note that the subjects of the 2008 study expressed less pride than the future teachers surveyed in the 1990 study, who expressed more pride than the Israeli high school students surveyed in 1965, 1974, and 1985.[19] This response is consistent with other responses in the 2008 study and additional data, which allow me to conclude that the Holocaust is becoming an even more important component of the Jewish identity of Israelis (this will be discussed further below) than it has been in the past.[20] The greater sense of pride might also be explained by the fact that the subjects in the 1990 study constituted a defined group within the larger young Israeli population.

As I have noted, greater pride in the behavior of the Jews during the Holocaust was not an indicator of greater pride, interest, or knowledge regarding the lives of the Jews prior to the Holocaust or the history of the Jews of Mediterranean countries (a question posed during the 1990 study).

Another important finding has to do with the differences in responses according to country of origin. As we have seen, the vast majority of respondents in the 1990 study (90 percent) were born in Israel. Most, however, had at least one parent who was born abroad: In the case of 24.5 percent of the subjects, one parent was born abroad, while in the case of 56.5 percent of the subjects, both parents were born abroad.

I found only small differences in the responses of subjects regarding these periods (in the 1990 study, which also explored students' attitudes toward the life of Jews in Mediterranean countries) according to country of origin (parents' country of birth). Respondents with both parents born in Israel and respondents with one parent born in a western country (Europe or the United States) tended to express the absence of a particular feeling or the lack of knowledge regarding the period to a slightly lesser degree regarding the Shtetl period. They also tended to express slightly more pride in the period. Both of these differences, were not found to be statistically insignificant.[21]

At the same time, and to a much larger degree, students of Israeli extraction and western extraction expressed an absence of any particular feeling (more than 30 percent) and the lack of sufficient knowledge (almost 50 percent) regarding the history of Jews in Mediterranean countries. The combined total of these two responses accounted for more than 80 percent of all responses of this group. In fact, lack of sufficient knowledge was the most common response among all the respondents (40 percent) with regard to the history of Jews in Mediterranean countries, while 30 percent indicated the absence of a particular feeling.

With regard to the Holocaust, however, even these small extraction-based differences disappeared. The great majority of respondents (83 percent) expressed pride in the behavior of the Jews during the period of the Holocaust, and I found no significant difference stemming from country of origin. In fact, Jews from Middle Eastern origins tended to express slightly more pride than the other groups (86 percent). Thus, the different attitudes regarding the behavior of the Jews during the Holocaust that apparently once existed among Jews of different extractions could not be detected in the responses of the subjects of the studies of 1990 and 2008. I believe that this is a reflection of the role of the Holocaust as a central component of the Zionist-nationalist ethos and of the so-called "civil religion" of Israeli society.

This approach was reflected in students' responses when asked to indicate the degree to which they identified with the Jews who suffered during the Holocaust (this question, too, was not asked in the context of other questions regarding the Holocaust, which will be discussed below).

**Table 2.14 Identification with the Jews Who Suffered during the Holocaust, 2008 (as a percentage):** ***"Do you identify with the Jews who suffered during the Holocaust?"***

| | 4<br>None | 3<br>Weak | 2<br>Strong | 1<br>Very Strong |
|---|---|---|---|---|
| Religious | 1 | 5 | 24 | 70 |
| Traditional | 2 | 10 | 36 | 52 |
| Non-Religious | 1 | 9 | 41 | 49 |

The correspondence between religiosity and level of identification was not found to be significant.

## *Attitudes toward Jews in the Diaspora*

In order to assess future teachers' attitudes toward Jews abroad, my 1990 study asked a number of questions pertaining to Jewish communities and Jews living outside of Israel. Of course, these questions did not facilitate a complete exploration of students' attitudes toward Diaspora Jewry or Israel-Diaspora relations.

Due to space constraints, the 2008 study did not include questions regarding Jewish communities in the Diaspora and retained only the questions on Jews in the Diaspora. Students' responses to these questions indicate a much closer relationship than that reflected in their responses to the general, somewhat abstract question on perceived connection to the Jewish people.

In response to the statement "I feel a strong bond with the Jewish people," in my 1990 study of Israeli teaching students, the vast majority of subjects selected "strongly agree," indicating the strongest possible bond (4 on a scale of 1 to 4). This was the response of 100 percent of the Ultra-Orthodox sector and 92.5 percent of the State-Religious sector. Approximately two-thirds (68 percent) of the non-religious students also chose this option, while 29 percent selected option 3, "agree moderately." Only a small number of respondents chose option 2 ("agree minimally") and option 1 ("strongly disagree"). The 2008 study revealed a weaker bond than the one identified in 1990, both throughout the study population as a whole and among the non-religious student sub-group in particular.

In contrast to this strong (in the non-religious sector) and extremely strong (in the religious sectors) sense of connection, students indicated a much weaker bond when asked about Jews and Jewish communities outside of Israel. I consolidated the four possible responses into two sub-categories, classifying "very close" and "close" as "close," and "minimally close" and "distant" as "distant." The results are presented in the tables below.

The present study did not inquire into student attitudes toward Jewish communities in the Diaspora but rather focused on Jews with different qualities. Based on students' responses to the other questions, we can assume that their sense of connection with foreign Jewish communities would be even weaker than that identified in the 1990 study.

**TABLE 2.15 Sense of Closeness toward Jewish Communities in the Diaspora, 1990** (as a percentage): *"What is your attitude toward the Jewish communities in the following countries?"*

| Jewish Community | Close | | | Distant | | |
|---|---|---|---|---|---|---|
| | State | State-Religious | Ultra-Orthodox | State | State-Religious | Ultra-Orthodox |
| United States | 36 | 47 | 65 | 64 | 53 | 35 |
| Soviet Union | 34 | 58 | 58 | 66 | 42 | 42 |
| Western Europe | 27 | 33 | 60 | 73 | 67 | 40 |
| Arab Countries | 25 | 43 | 44 | 75 | 57 | 56 |
| Ethiopia | 26 | 38 | 27 | 74 | 62 | 73 |

Students expressed the greatest sense of closeness toward the Jewish community in the United States, followed by the Soviet Union (except for students of the State-Religious teaching colleges, who expressed a greater sense of closeness toward the Jews of the Soviet Union), Western Europe, the Arab countries, and Ethiopia. When the 1990 study was being carried out, the number of Israeli students from the former Soviet Union was still small.

Whereas the sense of distance students expressed toward the Jewish community in the United States was moderate, they expressed an increasingly accentuated sense of distance toward other Jewish communities, particularly the Jewish community in Ethiopia. I believe that this phenomenon contradicts the frequently repeated slogans of "one people" and *Klal Israel* ("All of Israel"). Some young Israelis may also interpret these slogans as referring either primarily or exclusively to Israeli Jews. At least to a certain degree, the students appear to regard the "people of Israel" as being limited to the "people of Israel" living in Israel.

The negative attitude toward Ethiopian Jewry emanating from within the State-Religious and Ultra-Orthodox sectors of the Israeli education system stem from these sector's doubts regarding the Judaism of Ethiopian Jews. However, a sense of distance was not only expressed toward Ethiopian Jewry, but rather, to some extent, toward Diaspora Jewry as a whole. In this context, the sense of distance varied from sub-group to sub-group, increasing from the Ultra-Orthodox sector, to the State-Religious sector, to the State sector. This held true except in the case of the distance expressed by the students of the Ultra-Orthodox sector toward Ethiopian Jewry, which was more accentuated than the attitude of students from the State-Religious sector and similar to the attitude of the non-religious students.

The sense of distance is even greater among the non-religious students from the State sector. The study of ninth grade Jewish Israeli students cited above reported strikingly similar findings, which also reflected an increasing sense of distance from Jewish youth from the United States, the Soviet Union, France, Ethiopia, and Arab countries. The sense of closeness expressed by the subjects of both of my studies was substantially lower than the sense of distance identified by Herman.[22] A similar trend emerged in a study carried out by Mina Zemach in 1987.[23]

Responses of the future teachers of the 1990 study to statements concerning different groups of Diaspora Jews, and responses to similar questions in the 2008 study, also painted an interesting picture. These statements were intended to assess young Israelis' personal attitudes toward Jews living outside of Israel. The two major factors among young Israelis that appear to produce a sense of closeness toward Jews of the Diaspora are as follows:

1) A willingness on the part of the Diaspora Jew to immigrate to Israel
2) The religiosity or non-religiosity of the Diaspora Jew

Students of the teaching colleges of the state and State-Religious sectors expressed a strong sense of closeness toward Jews who were willing to immigrate to Israel.

In contrast, students of the State teaching colleges expressed a greater sense of distance from religious and non-religious Jews from abroad, regardless of the latter's position on immigration to Israel. Although the religiosity of Jews abroad did influence the students' sense of closeness toward them (the students expressed less distance from non-religious Jews outside of Israel than from religious Jews outside of Israel), the influence of this factor appears to have been relatively moderate.

**TABLE 2.16 Sense of Closeness to Diaspora Jews of Students from State Teaching Colleges (1990) and Non-Religious Students (2008):** ***"How close do you feel to each of the following groups?"*** **(as a percentage)**

| | 4 Distance | | 3 Minimal Closeness | | 2 Significant Closeness | | 1 Great Closeness | |
|---|---|---|---|---|---|---|---|---|
| | 1990 | 2008 | 1990 | 2008 | 1990 | 2008 | 1990 | 2008 |
| Religious Jews Abroad | 49 | 42 | 33 | 45 | 11 | 11 | 7 | 2 |
| Non-Religious Jews Abroad | 23 | 20 | 51 | 50 | 20 | 24 | 6 | 6 |
| Jews Willing to Immigrate to Israel | 7 | 14 | 28 | 40 | 36 | 32 | 29 | 14 |
| Jews Unwilling to Immigrate to Israel | 45 | 33 | 37 | 53 | 13 | 12 | 7 | 2 |

Both of my studies identified significant correlation between student religiosity and student attitudes toward religious Jews abroad. Understanding student attitudes in the context of student religiosity also provided important insight into their feelings toward each of the following groups: 1) Jews willing to immigrate to Israel; 2) Jews unwilling to immigrate to Israel; 3) assimilating Jews; 4) non-Jews abroad; and 5) Arab citizens of Israel, a subject that was explored by the 2008 study alone, and which will be discussed in greater detail later in this book. Responses regarding non-religious Jews abroad according to student religiosity were not found to be statistically significant.

The vast majority of Jews in the western world have neither the intention, the desire, nor the willingness to immigrate to Israel in the foreseeable future. In this context, it is important to consider the nature of the relationship between young Israelis living in Israel and young Jews who live abroad and do not intend to move to Israel and how this relationship will look in the future.

Students expressed interesting attitudes toward non-Israeli Jews classified as assimilating Jews. Although it is most likely that many of the respondents did not fully understand the concept of assimilation, they nonetheless made frequent use of the term with regard to the Jews of the Diaspora. The prevalent attitude toward assimilating Jews, which is prominent throughout all three sectors, was a sense of distance. The degree of distance is strikingly similar to the degree of distance that students expressed toward non-Jews (state sector students from the 1990 study actually expressed a slightly greater sense of distance from assimilating Jews than from non-Jews).

**Table 2.17 Responses to the Question, *"What is your attitude toward assimilating Jews?"* (as a percentage)**

| 1990 | | | | |
|---|---|---|---|---|
| | 4 Distance | 3 Minimal Closeness | 2 Significant Closeness | 1 Great Closeness |
| State | 48.7 | 32.9 | 11.0 | 7.1 |
| State-Religious | 22.7 | 50.7 | 20.4 | 5.9 |
| Ultra-Orthodox | 6.8 | 27.9 | 36.3 | 29.0 |
| $X^2 = 30.045$ | $df = 6$ | | $p < 0.0001$ | |
| | | | | |
| **2008** | | | | |
| | 4 Distance | 3 Minimal Closeness | 2 Significant Closeness | 1 Great Closeness |
| Religious | 42 | 45 | 11 | 2 |
| Traditional | 20 | 50 | 24 | 6 |
| Non-Religious | 14 | 40 | 32 | 14 |
| $X^2 = 16.75$ | $df = 6$ | | $p < 0.0103$ | |

In the past, members of the non-religious Zionist movements believed that it was their responsibility and obligation to maintain a connection with assimilating Jews and to bring them closer to Zionism. However, it appears that the second and third generations of these movements received only the rejectionist component of this attitude toward assimilating Jews, and not the important aspect of knowing and understanding assimilating Jews, which was emphasized by the founding generation.

In response to a different statement, a large portion of the students answered that large-scale assimilation is a possibility within the Jewish population of the United States. In fact, in this instance there was no significant difference between the responses of the different sectors. Eighty-five percent of the students of State teaching colleges surveyed in the 1990 study indicated that they believe that large-scale assimilation in the American Jewish community is a real danger ("significant degree" and "great degree" combined), as did 90 percent of the students from the Ultra-Orthodox sector and 97 percent of the students from the State-Religious sector.

Many young Israelis undoubtedly regard the danger of assimilation as an extremely serious threat to the future of Diaspora Jewry. To a large extent, they see Jews living in the Diaspora as assimilating Jews or potential assimilating Jews. In many cases, Israeli students believe that only immigration to Israel can save Diaspora Jews from this eventuality. My findings based on these two groups of questions (on attitudes toward Jewish communities and Jews abroad) reveal that young Israelis feel only a minimal sense of closeness to Jews of the Diaspora. In contrast to Liebman's contention that "Israel is no longer detached from the Diaspora as it once was,"[24] I found that, although it is true that Israel is not detached from the Holocaust, young Israelis are indeed detached from the Diaspora of the past, and from the Jews of the Diaspora in the present.

For students of the Ultra-Orthodox and State-Religious colleges surveyed in the 1990 study, and for the religious students surveyed in the 2008 study, the religiosity of the Diaspora Jews in question was another decisive factor influencing attitudes. The sense of closeness to Jews in the Diaspora they expressed was greater than that of the non-religious students, and was significantly stronger when the Diaspora Jews in question were religious.[25] As reflected in the following table, the education sector-based differences regarding non-religious Jews abroad were not found to be statistically significant. However, they were found to be significant when the Diaspora Jews in question were religious.

**TABLE 2.18 Responses to the Question, *"What is your attitude toward religious Jews and non-religious Jews in the Diaspora?"* (as a percentage)**

| Attitudes Toward Non-Religious Jews Abroad | | | | |
|---|---|---|---|---|
| **1990** | | | | |
| | 4<br>Distance | 3<br>Minimal<br>Closeness | 2<br>Significant<br>Closeness | 1<br>Great<br>Closeness |
| State-Religious | 17.6 | 43.5 | 29.0 | 9.9 |
| Ultra-Orthodox | 22.4 | 50.7 | 16.4 | 10.4 |
| State | 22.7 | 50.7 | 20.4 | 5.9 |
| | | | | |
| **2008** | | | | |
| | 4<br>Distance | 3<br>Minimal<br>Closeness | 2<br>Significant<br>Closeness | 1<br>Great<br>Closeness |
| Religious | 14 | 39 | 36 | 11 |
| Traditional | 16 | 44 | 31 | 9 |
| Non-Religious | 20 | 50 | 24 | 6 |
| $X^2 = 11.39$ | $df = 6$ | $p < 0.072$ | Marginal Significance | |

| Attitudes Toward Religious Jews Abroad | | | | |
|---|---|---|---|---|
| **1990** | | | | |
| | 4<br>Distance | 3<br>Minimal<br>Closeness | 2<br>Significant<br>Closeness | 1<br>Great<br>Closeness |
| State-Religious | 10.8 | 26 | 34.6 | 28.5 |
| Ultra-Orthodox | 6 | 9 | 17 | 68 |
| State | 49 | 32 | 11 | 8 |
| $X^2 = 222.138$ | $df = 6$ | | $p = 0.0001$ | |
| | | | | |
| **2008** | | | | |
| | 4<br>Distance | 3<br>Minimal<br>Closeness | 2<br>Significant<br>Closeness | 1<br>Great<br>Closeness |
| Religious | – | 27 | 37 | 36 |
| Traditional | 16 | 40 | 34 | 10 |
| Non-Religious | 42 | 45 | 11 | 2 |
| $X^2 = 195.11$ | $df = 6$ | | $p = 0.0001$ | |

Religious students' sense of closeness was influenced by the religiosity of the Diaspora Jews in question and by their willingness to immigrate to Israel.

The 2008 questionnaire also contained two statements meant to assess student attitudes toward elements of the broader, non-Jewish world. One of these questions concerned students' sense of closeness to non-Jews abroad, and another had to do with students' sense of closeness to Arab citizens of the state of Israel (a subject that will be discussed in more detail below). Student attitudes toward both of these groups were characterized by a great sense of distance. Ninety percent of all Jewish respondents indicated either distance or only a minimal sense of closeness toward non-Jews living outside of Israel (to whom they sometimes referred as "the *goyim*") while the figure with regard to Arab citizens of Israel was only slightly higher: 91 percent (see table 2.20).

**TABLE 2.19 Responses to the Question, *"What is your attitude toward non-Jews abroad?"* (as a percentage)**

| | Distance | Minimal<br>Closeness | Significant<br>Closeness | Great<br>Closeness |
|---|---|---|---|---|
| Religious | 70 | 27 | 1 | 2 |
| Traditional | 59 | 36 | 4 | 1 |
| Non-Religious | 44 | 44 | 10 | 2 |
| $X^2 = 26.97$ | $df = 6$ | | $p < 0.00016$ | |

The profound sense of distance from Arab citizens of Israel reflected in table 2.20 is striking and thought provoking.

**TABLE 2.20 Responses to the Question, *"What is your attitude toward Arab citizens of the state of Israel?"* 2008 (as a percentage)**

| | Distance | Minimal Closeness | Significant Closeness | Great Closeness |
|---|---|---|---|---|
| Religious | 70 | 25 | 5 | – |
| Traditional | 55 | 37 | 7 | 1 |
| Non-Religious | 48 | 42 | 8 | 2 |
| $X^2 = 15.62$ | $df = 6$ | | $p < 0.159$ | |

Although the percentage of non-religious students who reported such a sense of distance was slightly lower than among the traditional and religious students, it was nonetheless extremely high. I did not ask the Arab students the same question. However, as we will see, my analysis of student responses to similar questions strongly suggests that Arab Israelis are more interested in a sense of closeness with the Jews than vice-versa.

## Jewish Immigration to Israel, Assimilation, and Anti-Semitism as Aspects of Attitudes toward Diaspora Jewry

### *Attitudes toward Jewish Immigration to Israel*

In some ways, many young Israelis regard Jewish immigration to Israel as the major, often primary, and in some cases sole factor relevant to Israel-Diaspora relations. This perspective is reflected in student responses to a number of immigration-related questions contained in the questionnaire. Again, however, it is important to keep in mind that these statements do not facilitate a complete exploration of student attitudes toward Jewish immigration to Israel.

The future teachers of the State-Religious sector surveyed in 1990 regarded the statement "every Jew must immigrate to the state of Israel" as one of the most important lessons to be learned from the Holocaust (for a detailed discussion of this point, see chapter 3). Future teachers from the State sector expressed the same sentiment, albeit to a lesser extent. In the 2008 study, this lesson emerged as less important (58 percent of the non-religious students disagreed with it, as did 37 percent of the traditional students and 41 percent of the religious students). Above, I noted that students had different attitudes toward Jews abroad who are interested in immigrating to Israel and Jews abroad who are not interested in immigrating to Israel.

During the 1990 study, I presented teaching students with a series of questions dealing with the importance of Israel's potential contribution to the Jewish communities in the Diaspora on the one hand, and the importance of American Jewry's potential contribution to Israel on the other hand. In their responses to both series of questions, students viewed immigration to Israel as the most important factor. In this way, they viewed Israel's willingness and ability to absorb those Jews who are interested in immigrating to Israel as a significant contribution made by the state of Israel to the Jewish communities in the Diaspora. When I asked the same question in the opposite direction—what contribution can American Jewry make to Israel?—students again cited immigration as a contribution of extreme importance (students from the State sector regarded Jewish immigration to Israel as equally important as political support, and students from the Ultra-Orthodox sector attributed greater importance to maintaining Jewish education within Jewish community institutions in the United States).

Again, it is important to note that the students of the State teaching colleges surveyed in 1990 were much less supportive of large-scale immigration to Israel than students of the State-Religious colleges and students of the Ultra-Orthodox education sector. When asked explicitly if they supported large-scale Jewish immigration from the United States and the Soviet Union (the 1990 study was undertaken at the beginning of the great Soviet immigration of the 1990s), the students' answers were somewhat more moderate, but nonetheless reflected support of Jewish immigration to Israel.[26]

The question posed as part of the 2008 study was worded slightly differently: "To what extent do you agree with large-scale Jewish immigration to Israel, if it may result in a decline in the standard of living of those already living ?"Students' responses were different as well.

**Table 2.21 Attitudes toward Large-Scale Jewish Immigration to Israel, 2008 (as a percentage):** ***"Do you agree with Jewish immigration to Israel if it may result in a decline in standard of living for those already living there?"***

| | Strongly Agree | Agree | Disagree | Strongly Disagree |
|---|---|---|---|---|
| Religious | 2 | 10 | 33 | 55 |
| Traditional | 1 | 28 | 49 | 22 |
| Non-Religious | 5 | 31 | 46 | 18 |
| $X^2 = 58.301$ | $df = 6$ | | $p < 0.0001$ | |

The student population of the 2008 study expressed a much lower level of support for large-scale immigration than the student population of the 1990 study, and the response-distribution by sub-group was different as well. In the

1990 study, support for large-scale Jewish immigration to Israel was very high, particularly among students from the State-Religious and Ultra-Orthodox sectors. In the 2008 study, the highest percentage of support for large-scale immigration was expressed by the non-religious students, followed by the traditional students and then by the religious students. This may be the result of concern that immigrants include large numbers of people who are not considered to be Jewish according to Jewish law, as well as concerns regarding the influence of immigrants from the former Soviet Union on the increasing presence of non-kosher food in the country and on the issue of civil marriage.

**TABLE 2.22 Attitudes toward Jewish Immigration from the United States and the Soviet Union, 1990 (as a percentage): *"To what extent are you interested in mass Jewish immigration to Israel from the U.S. and the U.S.S.R.?"***

| | State | | State-Religious | | Ultra-Orthodox | |
|---|---|---|---|---|---|---|
| | From USSR | From US | From USSR | From US | From USSR | From US |
| Very Interested | 39.2 | 42.2 | 87.7 | 88.3 | 75.5 | 58.5 |
| Interested | 49.0 | 48.6 | 11.5 | 10.9 | 20.8 | 35.8 |
| Indifferent | 8.9 | 8.1 | 0.8 | 0.8 | 3.8 | 5.7 |
| Opposed | 2.9 | 1.2 | – | – | – | – |
| Test for the statistical significance of attitudes regarding Jewish immigration from the Soviet Union: $X^2 = 102.102$ $df = 6$ $p < 0.0001$<br>Test for Jewish immigration from the United States: $X^2 = 81.878$ $df = 6$ $p < 0.0001$ | | | | | | |

The students expressed different levels of support for large-scale immigration from the U.S.S.R. and from the United States, with students from the Ultra-Orthodox sector expressing greater support for immigration from the Soviet Union than from the United States, and the other sectors tending to favor immigration from the United States. This difference, however, was not found to be statistically significant.

Although the immigration-related questions posed to students in 1990 and 2008 were not identical, it is nonetheless clear that the percentage of students surveyed in the 2008 study that were interested in large-scale immigration to Israel was lower than the percentage of like-minded students in the 1990 study. At the same time, however, 2008 responses to the statement "all Jews should immigrate to Israel" as a lesson from the Holocaust were much more supportive, with 59 percent among the religious, 63 percent among the traditional, and 28 percent among the non-religious. In this way, although Israelis appear to want immigration, it seems that they want immigrants much less. Studies show that young Israelis have related to, and often continue to relate to new immigrants with indifference, alienation, and at times hostility. In my opinion, this is especially visible in attitudes toward the most recent waves of immigration from Ethiopia and the Soviet Union, which are similar to attitudes toward the mass immigration of Jewish Holocaust survivors and Jews from Arab countries that occurred in the late 1940s and the 1950s.

Although the issue certainly requires additional research, I posit that young Israelis do not regard Jews of the Diaspora as part of their collective "we"—that is, the "Jewish people." For them, the Diaspora Jew is to some degree the "other," someone who is different and foreign—the "exilic Jew." During their first years in the country, new immigrants who either choose or are forced to immigrate to Israel experience and often suffer from their unique otherness. Until they become "Israeli," they are French, Russian, Ethiopian, and American. In the past, this transformation was dependent on their relinquishing of what makes them different and unique, and, to a certain extent, this continues to be true today.

A change in attitude toward Jewish immigration to Israel on the part of Israeli Jews will only occur after a change in their attitude toward the Jewish people living outside of Israel. Such a change also requires a better understanding of the Jewish and Zionist significance of immigration, not only from the perspective of Israeli society but from the perspective of the immigrants themselves. The sense of distance I found in student attitudes toward Jewish communities in the Diaspora are also reflected in the absence of personal and social interaction with immigrants. Immigrants' severed roots, or the discontinuation of their pre-immigration lives, make their absorption into the country difficult. Israelis know very little about these severed roots, and are largely uninterested in them.

### *Assimilation and Anti-Semitism*

Israelis tend to relate to Diaspora Jews as a collective entity facing two dangers: assimilation and intermarriage on the one hand, and anti-Semitism on the other hand. Eighteen percent of the 2008 study population held that non-Jews are not anti-Semitic, and 39 percent held that only a small portion are anti-Semitic. In contrast, 40 percent held that some non-Jews are anti-Semitic and 3 percent held that almost all are. In this context, response differentiation by student religiosity is significant: Fifty-eight percent of the religious students believed that non-Jews are anti-Semitic, in contrast to 48 percent of the traditional students, and 38 percent of the non-religious students.

Above, I briefly mentioned that young Israelis regard assimilation and anti-Semitism as serious threats to Diaspora Jewry.[27] Later in this book, I discuss attitudes toward anti-Semitism in greater detail. Here, however, I limit myself to pointing out that, from the perspective of young Israeli Jews, anti-Semitism and assimilation constitute the two most important aspects of Jewish life in the Diaspora. These phenomena are also the chief aspects cited by students who regard Jewish life in the Diaspora as inferior to life in Israel. In contrast, young Jews in the Diaspora tend to take the dangers of anti-Semitism and assimilation less seriously. This view of Jewish life in the Diaspora is instilled in young Israelis by the Israeli education system. This system teaches very little about Diaspora Jewry, and, unfortunately, the little it does teach on the subject is superficial and, to a certain degree, tendentious.[28]

### *Knowledge Assessment*

The study questionnaire was designed based on the premise that it should not incorporate questions assessing knowledge. I did, however, ask questions about what they had learned about various subjects related to the study. Although the information I received may certainly not be regarded as objectively accurate, it nonetheless provided me with an indication of the degree to which high schools and institutions of higher education (colleges and universities) have been addressing the subject, as well as the way the students assess their own knowledge.

The answers to these questions will be discussed in detail elsewhere. Here, I simply note that the subjects related to the topic of this study are taught much more frequently on the high school level than in colleges and universities. In fact, they are hardly ever taught in institutions of higher education, except for when students themselves select courses on these subjects. The most commonly studied subjects are Zionism and the Holocaust. Subjects taught less frequently at the high school and college or university levels include nineteenth century Diaspora Jewry and the Arab-Israeli conflict.

Students offer relatively similar assessments of their own knowledge: in their own opinion, they know more about the Holocaust than about any other subject about which they were asked, followed by Zionism, Israeli society, and the Arab-Israeli conflict. The subject about which they know the least, according to their own assessment, is nineteenth and twentieth century Jewish history (prior to the Holocaust) and the history of Diaspora Jewry after the Holocaust. Students of the State teaching colleges ranked their level of knowledge lower than students of the State-Religious and Ultra-Orthodox sectors.

Here, I present my findings regarding two areas of knowledge: the Holocaust, the subject about which students believe they know the most; and Diaspora Jewry, the subject about which they believe they know the least (a knowledge level similar to that of nineteenth and twentieth century Jewish history prior to the Holocaust) (see tables 2.23 and 2.24).

**Table 2.23** Knowledge about the Holocaust according to Respondents' Assessment of their Level of Knowledge, 1990 and 2008 (as a percentage)

| 1990 | | | | |
|---|---|---|---|---|
| | 4<br>Extremely<br>Knowledgeable | 3<br>Knowledgeable | 2<br>Minimally<br>Knowledgeable | 1<br>Not<br>Knowledgeable |
| State | 34.5 | 59.1 | 5.8 | 0.6 |
| State-Religious | 38.9 | 45.2 | 6.9 | – |
| Ultra-Orthodox | 72.1 | 23.2 | 4.7 | – |
| | | | | |
| **2008** | | | | |
| | 4<br>Extremely<br>Knowledgeable | 3<br>Knowledgeable | 2<br>Minimally<br>Knowledgeable | 1<br>Not<br>Knowledgeable |
| Religious | 36 | 47 | 17 | – |
| Traditional | 28 | 56 | 15 | 1 |
| Non-Religious | 28 | 54 | 18 | – |

Due to an insufficient number of answers in some of the cells, I was unable to determine whether there was a statistically significant difference.

**Table 2.24** Knowledge about Diaspora Jewry according to Respondents' Assessment of their Level of Knowledge, 1990 and 2008 (as a percentage)

| | | 1990 | | |
|---|---|---|---|---|
| | 4<br>Extremely<br>Knowledgeable | 3<br>Knowledgeable | 2<br>Minimally<br>Knowledgeable | 1<br>Not<br>Knowledgeable |
| State | 1.4 | 25.0 | 63.7 | 7.3 |
| State-Religious | 25.0 | 40.0 | 30.0 | 5.0 |
| Ultra-Religious | 8.5 | 46.9 | 37.7 | 6.9 |
| | | | | |
| | | **2008** | | |
| | 4<br>Extremely<br>Knowledgeable | 3<br>Knowledgeable | 2<br>Minimally<br>Knowledgeable | 1<br>Not<br>Knowledgeable |
| Religious | 19 | 28 | 49 | 4 |
| Traditional | 15 | 32 | 47 | 6 |
| Non-Religious | 9 | 25 | 58 | 8 |
| $X^2 = 13.65$ | $df = 6$ | | $p < 0.05$ | |

As I already noted, subjects' assessment regarding their own knowledge must not be regarded as an objective criterion. Actually, I believe that they possess less (and in some cases significantly less) knowledge than they thought.

I believe that it is also necessary to examine the relationship between knowledge (or lack of knowledge) and opinions and attitudes (which I was unable to do in the present framework). Specifically, it is necessary to assess whether lack of knowledge is a significant cause of generalizations (in some ways, lack of knowledge may be the result of generalizations), stereotypical attitudes, and the perceived distance of young Israelis from Diaspora Jews.

I conclude this section by commenting on two claims regarding the Jewish-Israeli connection: one that is research-oriented, and another that emerges from the field of literature. Herman argues that throughout the Israeli public there is a large degree of overlap and compatibility between Israeliness and Jewishness. His studies show "that a large majority of Israelis indicate that when they feel more Israeli, they feel more Jewish, and that when they feel more Jewish, they feel more Israeli."[29] According to Herman, "the increasingly strong relationship between Judaism and Israeliness and an almost complete absence of a sense of their incompatibility constitute a consistent distinction between Jewish identity in the Jewish state and Jewish identity in the Diaspora."[30] In Israel, he argues, reinforcing one component of identity (sub-identity) reinforces the second component (sub-identity) as well. In the Diaspora, however, things work in the opposite direction. For example, strengthening the Jewish component of the identity of an American Jew either has no bearing on his sense of being American or weakens it.

I am only in partial agreement with these points. Jewish identity in Israel has the potential to develop in the direction delineated by Herman. Nonetheless, I hold that in significant parts of secular Israeli society, strong Israeli feelings are accompanied by weak and sometimes negative feelings toward Jewish identity. The trend underway today, which I identified in my studies of 1990 and 2008, is not the reinforcement of both components of Israeli identity, but rather the weakening of Israeliness and the strengthening of Jewishness. In the Ultra-Orthodox sector, which was examined as a separate group in the study of 1990, extremely strong Jewish feelings are accompanied by weak, and at times negative Israeli feelings. Only in the traditional and religious study populations do strong Jewish and Israeli components of Jewish-Israeli identity exist simultaneously.

On this point, I also disagree with A. B. Yehoshua, who is troubled by the idea that "Israeliness is not understood as the most complete and perfect expression of being Jewish."[31] According to Yehoshua, "[B]eing Israeli means being a total Jew," while "the concept Jewish is one of partial existence that can only appear to be total." Defining the concept Israeli, he holds, reveals "the total Jewish dimension of the concept Israeli" and highlights "the clear difference between Israeli and Jewish, relating to the whole and a part of the whole."[32] Although Israeliness on a theoretical level can perhaps be understood as Yehoshua describes it, this is not how things are in reality. Israelis are not total Jews. Unfortunately, and I would like it if the situation were different, Israelis are Jews that are lacking, partial, imperfect, and limited.

## Arab Nationality and Me

The identity of Arab Israelis or Palestinian Israelis (I will return to the self-definition of this group later) is even more complex and difficult to analyze than that of Jewish Israelis, which, as I've shown, is sufficiently complicated as it is. As we have seen and as we will see later, the two primary sites of tension within Jewish-Israeli identity are between Israeliness and Jewishness, and between religious identity and belonging and national identity and belonging.

Israeli Arabs—who refer to themselves as Israeli Palestinians, Palestinian citizens of Israel, Arab citizens of Israel, or just plain Palestinians—are citizens of a self-defined Jewish state. The Declaration of Independence, which is a formative document of Israeli society and government, reads as follows: "We … hereby declare the establishment of a Jewish State in the land of Israel, to be known as the State of Israel." Today, like then, Israel is still in a state of war with some of its neighboring Arab states. For this reason, aside from Israel's Druze citizens and some of its Bedouin citizens, Arab Israelis do not serve in the I.D.F., and this excludes them from many frameworks of belonging and identification. To compound the situation, Israel's relationship with the Palestinian citizens of the Gaza Strip and the West Bank are extremely complicated and at times violent. Although Israel promised its Arab citizens equal rights, the equal rights with which they have been provided (if it is at all possible to describe the situation in this manner) are de jure, and certainly not de facto.

The national identity of Arab Israelis is Arab and/or Palestinian. I can perhaps simplify the situation by saying that Palestinianess indicates a connection and belonging to the Palestinian people, while Arabness refers to their belonging to a nation, a larger entity that incorporates a number of nationalities or peoples. In addition, Arab society in Israel incorporates a number of different religious groupings, including a majority of Muslims, a minority of Christians and Druze, and two villages of Circassians. This diversity is another source of periodic discord and tension within Israeli-Arab society. The identity of Israeli Arabs is made even more complex by the fact that they constitute a minority in a Jewish majority society and a Jewish state that is rejected by a significant portion of Jewish Israelis (which I discuss in more detail below), who see them as a "dangerous minority," a "demographic problem," a "time-bomb," etc.

Until 2003, when the practice was eliminated, the "nationality" of every Israeli citizen was indicated in a special section of his or her identity card. This nationality section, which until its elimination was the focus of extended debate, was the cause of considerable unpleasantness (to put it mildly) for Arab citizens, as influential daily-life figures such as bank employees and police officers could easily identify them as minorities. The elimination of the nationality section from Israeli identity cards (the information itself is still maintained by the Interior Ministry) did not stem from concern for the feelings of Israel's Arab citizens, but rather from a 2002 Israeli High Court of Justice ruling that ordered the registration of converts to Judaism who underwent a Reform conversion process. In order to prevent a person's Jewish identity as determined by the High Court of Justice from being included in an official document, Eli Ishai of the Shas party, who was serving as Israel's interior minister at the time, ordered the elimination of the nationality section.

I am unable to undertake a detailed analysis of the identity of Arab Israelis in the limited framework of this book. At this juncture, I wish only to draw the reader's attention to two important processes currently underway in Israeli Arab identity: Palestinization and Israelization. We will return to these two processes, which do not negate but rather complement one another, in my analysis of the responses.

As I have noted, the percentage of Arab students who completed the questionnaire was lower than the relatively high percentage of Jewish students who did so. One possible explanation for this difference (the importance of which I cannot be certain) may be the Arabness of the students and all this implies. This includes the fear or hesitation of exposing themselves, even when assured that the questionnaires were anonymous, as I wanted to enable them to express their feelings and opinions anonymously and with dignity. Because there were only 258 Arab student respondents, some of their responses are presented below without dividing them into religiosity-based subgroups (religious, traditional, non-religious), as I did in the case of the Jewish population.

Nonetheless, I attempt here as much as possible to examine the issue of Arab-Israeli identity in the same way I examined the Jewish-Israeli responses, while at the same time making the necessary adjustments. This section will discuss the valence and centrality of Israeliness, Arabness, and Palestinianess, and Arab students' attitudes toward selected periods in Arab and Palestinian history.

## *The Valence of Palestinianess, Arabness, and Israeliness*

I asked Arab respondents three questions pertaining to valence, which is a measure of emotional sentiment toward, and a desire to be part of a particular group. The three questions pertained to Palestinianess, Arabness, and Israeliness, and the students' responses were clear. If they could be born again, 75 percent of the Arab students would want to be born Arabs (desire and strongly desire combined) and 51 percent would want to be born Palestinians. A much lower percent—34 percent—would want to be born Israeli.

**TABLE 2.25** Valence of Palestinian, Arab, and Israeli Identity among the Entire Arab Study Population (as a percentage): *"If you were going to be re-born, would you want to be born Palestinian, Arab, or Israeli?"*

| | 4 Would Not Want | 3 Indifferent | 2 Would Want | 1 Would Want Strongly |
|---|---|---|---|---|
| To Be Born Palestinian | 28 | 21 | 18 | 33 |
| To Be Born Arab | 14 | 11 | 17 | 58 |
| To Be Born Israeli | 35 | 31 | 21 | 13 |

**TABLE 2.26** Valence of Palestinian, Arab, and Israeli Identity Among Arab Students by Sector (as a percentage)

| *"If you were going to be re-born, would you want to be born Palestinian?"* | | | | |
|---|---|---|---|---|
| | 4 Would Not Want | 3 Indifferent | 2 Would Want | 1 Would Want Strongly |
| Religious | 21 | 16 | 22 | 41 |
| Traditional | 25 | 24 | 19 | 32 |
| Non-Religious | 48 | 26 | 10 | 16 |
| $X^2 = 13.273$ | $df = 6$ | | $p < 0.005$ | |
| | | | | |
| *"If you were going to be re-born, would you want to be born Arab?"* | | | | |
| | 4 Would Not Want | 3 Indifferent | 2 Would Want | 1 Would Want Strongly |
| Religious | 9 | 3 | 20 | 68 |
| Traditional | 8 | 19 | 18 | 55 |
| Non-Religious | 37 | 13 | 7 | 43 |
| $X^2 = 27.13$ | $df = 6$ | | $p < 0.0001$ | |
| | | | | |
| *"If you could be re-born, would you want to be born Israeli?"* | | | | |
| | 4 Would Not Want | 3 Indifferent | 2 Would Want | 1 Would Want Strongly |
| Religious | 38 | 29 | 26 | 7 |
| Traditional | 35 | 33 | 17 | 15 |
| Non-Religious | 29 | 32 | 20 | 19 |
| $X^2 = 4.667$ | $df = 6$ | | $p < 0.05$ | |

I assumed that the percentage of respondents in the present study who would indicate a desire to be born Israeli would be much higher in all categories of the Jewish-Israeli students (religious, traditional, non-religious) than among the Arab students. The teaching students surveyed in the 1990 study were unequivocal in their responses regarding their desire to be born Israeli.

Although Israeliness is a question of citizenship, many Israelis, particularly among the non-religious, see it also, and perhaps primarily, as the national identity of the Jewish population. This may explain the low valence of Israeliness among the Arab students. The valence of Arabness, which had the highest valence of all the options presented to the Arab students, was lower than the valence of Jewishness among the Jewish students, except in the case of the non-religious group. The valence of Palestinianess among the Arab students was also lower than the valence of Israeliness among the Jewish students in all three of the sub-groups.

The responses to questions aimed at assessing valence provided by both the Jewish Israelis and the Arab Israelis appear to indicate that Arab Israelis' desire to belong to either the Israeli, the Palestinian, or even the Arab group is less than the desire among Jewish Israelis to belong to the Jewish group (75 percent of the entire study population and 66 percent of the non-religious Jewish students) and the Israeli group. Sixty-three percent of the Jewish-Israeli students indicated that if they were going to live their life abroad, they would want to be born Jewish. From this perspective, the Arab students are facing a more complex question of identity.

When I examined the valence of Palestinianess, Arabness, and Israeliness according to the variable of religiosity, I found that religiosity also played an influential role among the Arab students. The religious students wanted very much to be born Arab (88.5 percent, representing want and want very much combined) and wanted to be born Palestinian (63 percent), but did not want to be born Israeli (33 percent). The other groups also did not want to be born Israeli, accounting for 61 percent of the non-religious students (indifferent and do not want combined), 68 percent of the traditional student, and 67 percent of the religious students. I will return to the role of the traditional students as the intermediary group between the secular and the religious students later in the book.

### *The Centrality of Palestinianess, Arabness, and Israeliness*

Centrality is an indicator of the importance of sub-identities in the consciousness of the individual. In the case at hand, the sub-identities in question are the Palestinian, Israeli, and Arab, as well as the religious sub-identities of Muslim, Christian, and Druze. Centrality was assessed by means of four separate questions: 1) "How important a role does the fact that you are a Palestinian play in your life?"; 2) "How important a role does the fact that you are an Israeli play in your life?"; 3) "How important a role does the fact that you are an Arab play in your life?"; and 4) "How important a role does the fact that you are a Muslim/Christian/Druze play in your life?"

Of the Arab student population, 44 percent classified themselves as religious, 32 percent as traditional, and 24 percent as non-religious, reflecting a much higher percentage of Arab religious students than Jewish religious students. In the Jewish sector, 17 percent classified themselves as religious, 23 percent as traditional, and 65 percent as non-religious (both the Jewish and Arab sample groups were constituted at random with regard to religiosity). Of those Arab students who defined themselves as religious or traditional, 72 percent classified themselves as Muslims, 11 percent as Christians, 13 percent as Druze, and 5 percent as "others." This had clear implications for their answers to the questions.

**TABLE 2.27 Centrality of Palestinian, Israeli, Arab, and Religious Identity (as a percentage):** ***"To what extent is it important in your life that you are Palestinian, Arab, Israeli, or religious?"***

| | 4<br>Not at All | 3<br>A Small<br>Degree | 2<br>A Large<br>Degree | 1<br>A Very Large<br>Degree |
|---|---|---|---|---|
| Palestinian | 13 | 30 | 40 | 17 |
| Israeli | 12 | 33 | 41 | 14 |
| Arab | 7 | 18 | 23 | 52 |
| Muslim/ Christian/ Druze | 9 | 15 | 24 | 52 |

The students were asked to answer each question separately.

**TABLE 2.28 Centrality of Different Identities (Palestinian, Israeli, Arab, and Religious) by Sector (as a percentage)**

| Centrality of Palestinian Identity by Sector (as a percentage) | | | | | |
|---|---|---|---|---|---|
| | Not<br>Relevant | 4<br>Would Not<br>Want | 3<br>Indifferent | 2<br>Yes | 1<br>Definitely<br>Yes |
| Religious | 12 | 12 | 29 | 32 | 15 |
| Traditional | 14 | 14 | 30 | 26 | 16 |
| Non-Religious | 39 | 17 | 17 | 22 | 6 |
| It could not be determined whether there was a statistically significant difference due to the insufficient number of responses in some of the cells. | | | | | |
| | | | | | |
| **Centrality of Israeli Identity by Sector (as a percentage)** | | | | | |
| | Not<br>Relevant | 4<br>Would Not<br>Want | 3<br>Indifferent | 2<br>Yes | 1<br>Definitely<br>Yes |
| Religious | 9 | 3 | 32 | 41 | 15 |
| Traditional | 10 | 16 | 21 | 37 | 16 |
| Non-Religious | 11 | – | 28 | 39 | 22 |
| It could not be determined whether there was a statistically significant difference due to the insufficient number of responses in some of the cells. | | | | | |

| Centrality of Arab Identity by Sector (as a percentage) | | | | | |
|---|---|---|---|---|---|
| | Not Relevant | 4 Would Not Want | 3 Indifferent | 2 Yes | 1 Definitely Yes |
| Religious | 3 | 3 | 21 | 26 | 47 |
| Traditional | 3 | 3 | 21 | 26 | 47 |
| Non-Religious | 11 | – | 22 | 28 | 39 |
| It could not be determined whether there was a statistically significant difference due to the insufficient number of responses in some of the cells. | | | | | |

| Centrality of Religious Identity by Sector (as a percentage) | | | | | |
|---|---|---|---|---|---|
| | Not Relevant | 4 Would Not Want | 3 Indifferent | 2 Yes | 1 Definitely Yes |
| Religious | 3 | 3 | 9 | 32 | 53 |
| Traditional | 5 | 9 | 21 | 12 | 53 |
| Non-Religious | 11 | 6 | 28 | 12 | 33 |
| It could not be determined whether there was a statistically significant difference due to the insufficient number of responses in some of the cells. | | | | | |

In response to a different question, 49 percent of the religious students defined their identity "first and foremost as religious identity" (Muslim, Christian, Druze) and 43 percent as "first and foremost Arab." Far fewer—only 9 percent—defined themselves as "first and foremost Palestinian." Of the traditional students, 52 percent defined themselves first and foremost according to their religious identity, 39 percent according to their Arab identity, and 9 percent according to their Palestinian identity. The difference according to the variable of religiosity was found to be statistically significant ($X^2 = 21.98$ $df = 9$ $p = 0.001$).

As we can see, Arabness and religiosity (primarily Islam) play an important role in the lives of the Arab students. This was confirmed by the subjects themselves, 72 percent of whom indicated that Arabness plays an important role in their lives and 74 percent of whom indicated that religion plays an important part in their lives. In contrast, Israeliness and Palestinianess play less important roles in the lives of the students, with approximately 50 percent noting the importance of Palestinianess and 62 percent noting the importance of Israeliness. When I break down these responses according to respondent religiosity, considerable differences appear. Arabness plays a central role in the lives of 73 percent of the religious students, 67 percent of the non-religious students, and 63 percent of the traditional students. The centrality of Palestinianess was relatively high among the religious students (47 percent), somewhat lower for traditional students (42 percent), and much lower for the non-religious (28 percent). The fact that they are Israeli is also of great importance to them (62 percent of the religious, 53 percent of the traditional, and 61 percent of the non-religious).

### *Israeli-Palestinian Continuum*

Israeli students were asked to mark their location on an Israeli-Jewish continuum, and in this way to indicate whether they saw themselves as more Israeli or more Jewish. In a parallel question, Arab students were asked to indicate whether they were more Israeli or more Palestinian. Their responses can be summarized as follows: A large percentage selected the scale's midpoint (4) on a scale of 1 to 7. This was the highest percentage of respondents indicating one particular point on the scale, and this phenomenon is well-known in attitude questionnaires. The remaining responses were divided relatively equally between those who located themselves at various points on the Palestinian side of the scale (indicating that they are more Palestinian) and those who located themselves at various points on Israeli side of the scale (indicating that they are more Israeli). When broken down by religiosity, the statistical significance was found to be marginal.

As we have seen, the Arab students ranked the sub-identities of Israeliness and Palestinianess low in terms of centrality, much lower than Arabness and the religious sub-identities.

The importance of religious sub-identities among the Arab students was elicited by another question they were asked about how they see themselves: Are you first and foremost an Arab, a Palestinian, or a Muslim/Christian/Druze? In response to this question, 51 percent chose their religious sub-identity, 40 percent chose the Arab sub-identity, and 9 percent chose the Palestinian sub-identity. Arab students' responses are consistent on this point. They assign greater importance to their religious and Arab identity than to their Palestinian and Israeli identity.

Religious respondents expressed a high level of identification with regard to the other Arab and Palestinian sub-identities (like the religious and traditional Jewish students, who ascribed great importance to their Jewishness and Israeliness). They attributed great importance to the fact that they were Palestinians (47 percent, representing great importance and extremely great importance combined), while the traditional students attributed less importance (42 percent) and the non-religious even less importance (27 percent). The religious students ascribe great importance to their religiosity (90 percent), in contrast to lower levels among the traditional students (68 percent) and the non-religious (28 percent). Fifty-six percent of religious students also ascribed great importance to their Israeliness, in comparison with 53 percent of the traditional students, and 61 percent of the non-religious. Comparison between the Jewish Israeli and Arab Israeli students on this issue does not have to do with questions of identity but rather with similar questions in the same area. As we have seen, 76 percent of the overall Jewish Israeli study population ascribed importance to the fact that they were Israeli, as opposed to 62 percent who indicated that the fact that they were Jewish played an important role in their life.

Arab students ranked the Palestinian sub-identity lower than any other Arab Israeli or Palestinian Israeli sub-identity.

I asked Arab students a number of questions related to Palestinianess that were parallel, though not identical, to the questions I asked the Jewish Israelis. The vast majority of respondents (90 percent) indicated that it was very important for them that the Palestinian people always exist, while 18 percent indicated that it was important for them. Among the Jewish Israeli students, a slightly lower percentage indicated that it was important for them that the Jewish people always exist (78 percent answered very important, and 16 percent answered important). It was more important for the Arab students (89 percent) than for the Jewish students (78 percent) that their brethren outside of Israel and Palestine continue to preserve their identity. In responses to this question, significant differences emerged among the various sub-identities (religious, traditional, non-religious). The non-religious Jewish students were much less concerned that Jews outside Israel continue to preserve their identity, and non-religious Arab students found it much less important that Palestinians living outside Israel and Palestine continue to preserve their identity.

I also asked two additional questions: one dealing with religion and the other dealing with the state (I will return to these subjects in more detail later in the book). In response to the statement that the Palestinian people cannot survive without religious belief (I did not indicate a specific religion, as not all Palestinians are Muslim), 59 percent Arab students agreed, compared to the 70 percent (or approximately 10 percent more) of Jewish students who agreed with the parallel statement: "The Jewish people cannot survive without the Jewish religion."

With regard to the state, 76 percent of the Arab students indicated that the Palestinian people could not survive without an independent state (which it still has not achieved), in comparison with 71 percent of the Jewish students who said they believed that the Jewish people cannot survive without the state of Israel.

## *The Perspective of Time*

As with the Jewish students, I also asked Arab students questions about historical events related to their personal destiny, the destiny of the Palestinian people, and the destiny of the Arab nation. As we have seen, the Holocaust was the event most commonly listed by Jewish students, although it was listed by a lower percentage of students in the 2008 study than it was in the 1990 study. For the Arab students, the *Nakba* (the Arabic term, which literally means "tragedy" or "catastrophe" and is commonly used to refer to the events of 1948) was the event most commonly listed as influencing their personal destiny (42 percent), the destiny of the Palestinian people (53 percent), and the destiny of the Arab nation (25 percent).

In this context, two points are extremely relevant. The first is the fact that the Palestinian Israeli students were third- and sometimes fourth-generation with regard to the events of the Nakba and the feeling that the Nakba was a formative, decisive event. The second is the fact that they were students in an Israeli university which, like all Israeli universities, is Jewish, Israeli, and Zionist in character, even though they are open to students from different ethnic backgrounds. They therefore had come into contact (theoretically, that is—I did not check this point) with Jewish students more than other groups within the Arab-Israeli population. I do not know the meaning of the fact that the Nakba was cited much more than any other historical event (a thorough inquiry into this question would have required additional questions, which I could not introduce due to the large number of questions already included in the questionnaire). Nonetheless, I think that at the very least, the Jewish public should be aware of the Nakba's authentic place in Palestinian identity, and of all this implies. In any event, commemoration of the Nakba is not something to be struggled against through legal prohibition, like the bill which, at the time this book was being written in 2009, was about to be legislated by the Knesset.

The Jewish and Arab students' selection of the Holocaust and the Nakba respectively as the formative, most important historical events for them and their peoples illustrates that both Jews and Palestinians suffer from a great sense of victimization and regard themselves not only as victims, but perhaps as *the* victims. In addition, the fact that the Jews were the ones who carried out the Nakba (by this, I do not mean to say that they were responsible or bear guilt for it) complicates matters further. After all, the instigators are not far away. They are here. They are the majority society and this is their country, and they are the ones who usually determine how things are handled, including the state's position on the Nakba and whether it will be commemorated or taught in schools (indeed, it is not taught at all in Jewish schools and is taught only minimally in Arab schools).

Upon examining the religiosity-based breakdown of responses regarding the Nakba as an event influencing the destiny of the Palestinian people, I found clear differences: only 35 percent of the religious students cited the Nakba, as opposed to 56 percent of the traditional students and 67 percent of the non-religious students. I also found religiosity-based differences when I asked the Arab students, in an open-ended question, to list historical events which they thought influenced their personal destiny: Thirty-one percent of the religious students listed the Nakba, in contrast to 62 percent of the traditional students, and 73 percent of the non-religious students.

Although I am not sufficiently familiar with Arab society in Israel, it may be possible to argue cautiously that the Nakba constitutes a more significant factor of identity among non-religious Arab Israelis (I return to these subjects in the subsequent chapter on the Holocaust and the Nakba), just as the Holocaust constitutes a significant factor of identity for the non-religious Jews. This is because the religious have other meaningful factors of identity related to their religious faith, and perhaps to their Arabness as well.

The other events listed, which were cited much less frequently, included the Intifadas, Land Day, the wars fought by Israel with the Arab states, events in modern Arab history, events in Muslim history, and the death of Arab leaders.

In both the Jewish and Arab sub-groups, I observed ongoing processes that may still serve to exacerbate the relationship between them.

To conclude this chapter, I reflect upon the processes taking place in Jewish and Arab Israeli society. Among Jewish Israelis, the major process underway is the continuation of the gradual movement from Israeliness to Jewishness. Although Israeliness may have been capable of including the Israeli Arabs, Jewishness as expressed in Israel is much less capable of doing so. As expressed in Israel, Jewishness or Jewish Israeliness rejects the Palestinian Israeli other. In recent years, the trend among Arab Israelis is said to be the development of an increasing sense of Israeliness on the one hand, and an increasing sense of Palestinianess on the other hand. However, this process does not appear to be affecting the Arab study population. For them, the valence and centrality of Palestinianess is low in comparison to that of Arabness and religiosity, and Israeliness is also not strong.

It is also important to note the development and intensification within both groups of major elements of the identity of victimization—the Holocaust and the Nakba, which I discuss in detail in the next chapter. The central role of this sense of victimization in the identity of Jewish and Arab Israelis has far-reaching implications in different realms of life for the Jews and the Arabs and the relationship between them.

## Notes

1. In employing this concept, I draw on the work of Horowitz and Lissak. See Dan Horowitz and Moshe Lissak, *Trouble in Utopia* (Tel Aviv, 1990) [Hebrew].
2. Note for Table No. 2.1: The figures indicating total number of responses are insignificant due to the great differences among the three sub-groups, which are based on the independent variable of religiosity (religious, traditional, and non-religious), as well as the fact that they are influenced by the relative representation of each group in the overall sample. For this reason, responses are typically presented according to the variable of religiosity, and in some cases according to other variables that I also found to be relevant.

   For readers who are unfamiliar with the fine points of research methodology, it should be noted that statistical data will be listed at the bottom of the tables only when found to be significant. Tables with statistically insignificant results will not appear in the body of the text. In some cases, it was not possible to determine whether a statistically significant difference existed due to an insufficient number of responses in some of the sub-groups, and in such cases this will be indicated.

3. Farago, "The Jewish Identity of Israeli Youth," 266.
4. For example, see table 2.9.
5. See Herman, *Jewish Identity,* 161 [Hebrew]. Herman identifies three different responses to the question: "yes" (accounting for 83 percent of the responses in 1965, and 81 percent in 1974); "it makes no difference to me" (accounting for 16 percent in 1965, and 17 percent in 1975); and "no" (accounting for none of the responses in 1965, and 3 percent in 1974).
6. Farago, "The Jewish Identity of Israeli Youth," 266.
7. Ibid.
8. A six-level scale has no midpoint. The midpoint of a seven-level scale is four.
9. The classification of teaching students as "traditional" and "non-religious" in the 1990 study changed the picture somewhat. Ninety-six percent of the traditional students and 87 percent of the non-religious students indicated an extremely strong connection to the state of Israel.
10. I discuss this subject in more detail in chapter 6 of this book ("Religion and Me").
11. See chapter 6.
12. Note for Table 2.11: Respondents were asked to list three events for each question. The order in which they listed the events was also significant. For this reason, the events listed are presented as percentages in the order listed from left to right (first event listed, second event listed, etc.).
13. Note 2 for Table 2.11: This category included events such as the first Zionist Congress, the Balfour Declaration, Israel's acceptance as a member of the UN, and different waves of Jewish immigration, including the immigration of Ethiopian Jews and the Jews of the former Soviet Union.
14. Note 3 for Table 2.11: This category refers to wars in general, without indication of any war in particular.
15. Note 1 for Table No. 2.12: Respondents were asked to list three events of their choice for each question. The order in which they listed the events was also significant. For this reason, the events listed are presented as percentages in the order listed from left to right (first event listed, second event listed, etc.). The column titled "total" reflects the percentage of times an event was listed out of the total number of responses to the question, whereas the percentages in columns 1, 2, and 3 reflect how often an event appeared in a particular column.
16. Responses to the question about the historical events that influenced the Jewish people differed from responses to the question about the historical events that influenced "your destiny."
17. With the exception of students of the State-Religious sector, who listed the establishment of the state of Israel as related to their destiny more often than they listed the Holocaust.
18. The remaining students either did not have sufficient knowledge about the period (6 percent) or were indifferent about it (3 percent). None of the respondents indicated being ashamed of it.
19. See Herman, *Jewish Identity,* 218 [Hebrew].
20. In a study of 200 ninth grade students in an integrative State school in the Tel Aviv area (unpublished), I found similar responses indicating a trend of increasing pride in the behavior of Jews during the period of the Holocaust: 72.5 percent expressed pride in the behavior of the Jews during the Holocaust; 8.4 percent said they were ashamed of their

behavior; 15.7 percent were indifferent; and 3.4 percent did not know enough about the behavior of the Jews during the Holocaust to form an opinion.

21. In my 1990 study, 44 percent of the teaching students surveyed who had two parents who were born in Israel indicated that they were proud of the period of the Shtetl, in contrast to 39 percent of those with one parent of western origin. 30 percent of the entire study population expressed pride with regard to the Shtetl period.
22. See Herman, *Jewish Identity,* 219 [Hebrew]. In this study, Herman gave subjects the option of five different responses. The 1990 study provided subjects with four options, which means that that they were unable to select a median response.
23. In the representative study of the adult Israeli population published by Mina Zemach in 1987, 6 percent of the study population felt an extremely great closeness to the Jews of the United States, and 37 percent felt great closeness. In contrast, 44 percent felt no closeness and 13 percent were "not sure." Zemach also notes a tendency in Israeli Jews over the years toward increasing distance from the Jews of the United States but notes that this may be coincidental. Mina Zemach, *Through Israeli Eyes: Attitudes Toward Judaism, American Jewry, Zionism and the Arab-Israeli Conflict* (New York, 1987), 15–16.
24. See Yeshayahu (Charles) Liebman, "The Holocaust Myth in Israeli Society," *Tefutsot Israel* 19, nos. 5 and 6 (Winter 1981) [Hebrew].
25. The sector-based difference regarding attitudes toward religious Jews living outside Israel in the 1990 study was found to be statistically significant. In contrast, the sector-based difference in attitude regarding non-religious Jews was found not to be statistically significant ($X^2 = 222.93$ $df = 8$ $p < 0.0001$). State teaching college students' sense of distance from non-religious Jews abroad was much less than their sense of distance from religious Jews abroad, and their sense of closeness to all Jews living outside of Israel is therefore low.
26. The questionnaire used in the 1990 study was distributed in April, May, and early June 1990 during the wave of immigration from the Soviet Union to Israel, but before it had reached its peak. The differences between the sectors were found to be statistically significant.
27. See table 2.17.
28. This question was not considered in the 2008 study, and to the best of my knowledge, the issue has hardly been explored at all. Ruth Firer has examined the way this subject is addressed in school text books. See Ruth Firer, *Agents of Zionist Education* (Tel Aviv, 1985) [Hebrew], and *Agents of the Holocaust Lesson* (Tel Aviv, 1989) [Hebrew].
29. Herman, *Jewish Identity,* 50–51 [Hebrew].
30. Ibid., 53.
31. A. B. Yehoshua, *Toward Normalcy* (Jerusalem, 1980), 129 [Hebrew].
32. Ibid., 133, 135, 137.

# CHAPTER 3

# The Holocaust and Me, the *Nakba* and Me

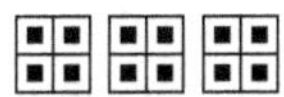

## The Holocaust and Me

Salem Jubran, who for years has been active in efforts to develop methods for teaching the Holocaust to Jews and Arabs together, wrote the following in *Bishvil Hazikaron,* the journal of the Education Department of Yad Vashem:

> The historical process of Israeli-Palestinian peace-making obligates us to eliminate historical stereotypes and distortions, and requires us to discover the person facing us and to understand the human aspirations of the other side. This framework also requires the development of a new approach, on the part of both Arabs and Jews, to the subject of the Holocaust.[1]

### *Introduction: The Holocaust and Me*

This chapter examines the attitudes of Jewish and Arab Israeli students toward the Holocaust and the *Nakba* and the consequences of each. The questions posed to the students did not facilitate a complete exploration of the different issues related to the Holocaust and the Nakba, which are two subjects of incomparable scope and complexity. It is impossible to understand Jewish history after the Holocaust without being aware of the profound ongoing impact of this event. Attitudes toward the Holocaust and its consequences constitute a central component of contemporary Jewish identity, despite the more than sixty years that have passed since the atrocities actually took place. Moreover, from many perspectives, the Holocaust is more present, more prominent, and more externalized throughout the Jewish public both in Israel and the Diaspora today than it has been in the past. I stress that I am not attempting to draw a parallel between the Holocaust and the Nakba, which was a trauma for the Palestinian public but which was nonetheless neither a holocaust nor a genocide. Nevertheless, and although I am less knowledgeable on the subject, it appears clear that the Nakba too has become more present, more prominent, and more externalized with the time that has passed, and that today it represents a major trauma in Palestinian identity, not only for those directly affected by it but by the third and fourth generations as well.

Attitudes toward the Holocaust in Israeli society have undergone significant changes over the past six decades. During the years immediately following World War II, the role of the Holocaust in public life remained relatively shrouded. In the late 1940s, Jewish society in Palestine, and subsequently Israel, was immersed in an existential struggle for a state that was born during war. At that point and during the years that followed, large numbers of displaced Jewish refugees from Europe and Jewish immigrants from Muslim countries arrived in Israel. During the 1950s, the Holocaust was pushed into the collective subconscious, at least to a certain extent. Memories of the terrors of the Holocaust burst into public consciousness with the trial of Adolf Eichmann in Jerusalem in the early 1960s. Indeed, an important goal of the trial was to expose the Holocaust, its consequences, and its lessons to Israeli society as a whole and to the younger generation in particular.

Israel's recurring wars also awakened the memory of the Holocaust and public discussion of the subject. It was the weeks of waiting that led up to the Six Days War and the fear of annihilation then threatening Israel that caused the memory of the Holocaust to emerge forcefully in Israel and the Diaspora. The period during and following the Yom Kippur War, including the UN resolution that equated Zionism with racism, also served to rejuvenate the memory of the Holocaust. Since then, we have witnessed a process—which gained speed in the 1970s, the 1980s, and the 1990s—by which the Holocaust has been transformed into a major component of Jewish-Israeli identity on the collective, national level, and often on the individual level as well. As we will see, the Holocaust is present and relevant for young Israelis today, regardless of their family history. It functions as a major force shaping the attitudes of Jewish Israelis toward themselves as Jews, Israelis, and Zionists and its influences find expression in many realms of life.[2]

Some accuse the state and its institutions of making manipulative use of the Holocaust in the context of the Jewish-Palestinian conflict. Two figures who have voiced harsh criticism in this spirit are Yehuda Elkana, in an article titled "The Need to Forget" (*Haaretz,* 2 March 1988), and Avraham Burg, in a book titled *Defeating Hitler* (Yediot Aharonot, 2007). Both publications elicited heated reactions. According to Elkana: "Symbolically speaking, two people left Auschwitz: a minority, insisting that 'it would never happen again,' and a frightened majority insisting that 'it would never happen to us again.' Israeli society and public debate wanders between these two versions, through the tension between the universal and the particular." Understanding this tension is crucial for this discussion.

Israel's education system also relates to the Holocaust as a primary element of Jewish-Zionist education. For this reason, I regard clarification of certain aspects of young Israelis' attitude toward the Holocaust as crucial for an overall understanding of Jewish identity. The Holocaust's increasingly central role in collective Israeli identity and the country's formal curricula serves to highlight the connection between the Holocaust—the existential and institutional justification for Zionism—and the state of Israel.

In the late 1980s, a number of schools began sending groups of students on study trips to Poland on their own initiative. In 1989, the Education Ministry also began efforts to organize such trips, and since then the number of participants has continued to grow each year. Although the trips aroused debates regarding their character, their aims, their agenda, and the manner in which they were carried out almost from the outset, student delegations to Poland have become an important method for teaching the Holocaust in Israel, and an important force in shaping its memory. The fundamental intention underlying the Poland trips is to make the Holocaust a major, if not primary, aspect of the Jewish-Israeli identity of young Israelis. It is estimated that in the early years, approximately 10,000 eleventh and twelfth graders participated in such trips to Poland on an annual basis. These trips were primarily to Poland, but in some cases to Hungary and the Czech Republic as well. In recent years, numbers have increased to 18,000 to 20,000 students per year and even reached 21,000 in 2002. For five years, between 2003 and 2007, almost 1,500 groups made trips to Poland, including more than 100,000 Israeli high school students (this included 25,367 in 2006 and 27,305 in 2007). Since then participation has dropped slightly. About one-third of the students have participated in trips organized by the Israeli Ministry of Education, while the rest have participated in private delegations organized by their schools themselves. In addition, the March of the Living (a program officially recognized by the Israeli government) takes place in Poland every two years, with Jewish youth from Israel and the Diaspora participating. In recent years, military delegations of more than 1,000 soldiers and officers have taken part in tours of the extermination camps.

The student trips to Poland undoubtedly elicit strong emotional reactions from young Israelis. The combination of the preparations for the trip, the actual visit itself, and the students' processing of their impressions after returning to Israel provide a unique educational-study framework based on emotional experience. The question I must ask, however, is whether such trips can and should become one of the *main, formative* educational forces in the life of young Israelis. Do these trips provide the answers to the difficulties faced by the Israeli education system in the realms of Jewish history and tradition, the transmission of Zionist values, or the complex question of Jewish identity? Or, alternatively, might they actually be helping to repress the problems currently facing Jewish and Zionist education by providing national or even nationalistic answers?[3]

Uriel Simon explains the move from identification with the Bible to identification with the Holocaust as an expression of pragmatic Zionism, which aims at preventing another Holocaust, as opposed to ideological Zionism, which is now passé ("the magic of the Bible has expired"). He also suggests that the Holocaust might reflect the longing for an undisputed national mythos with a uniqueness and exclusiveness that must be fiercely defended.[4] I am of the opinion that by placing such emphasis on the Holocaust, the Israeli education system has been attempting to base Zionist ideology on ideas that differ from its initial foundation. This study neither assessed the impact of the trips to Poland nor examined which study participants had participated in such a trip. However, as we will see below, a decisive majority (81 percent) of Jewish respondents believe that as many teens as possible should visit the death camps.

From time to time, a small number of Arabs (including Arab youth) have participated in trips to Poland, whether as part of the joint educational frameworks in which they study or frameworks aimed at Jewish-Arab reconciliation. In late 2002, Father Emile Shufani, a Greek Catholic priest from Nazareth, undertook an innovative initiative aimed at imparting knowledge of the Holocaust and its role in shaping Jewish consciousness. This project was part of an effort to break the cycle of fear and violence and to create a foundation for a better shared Arab-Jewish future by understanding the pain of the other. The initiative culminated in late May 2005 with a joint visit of 250 Arabs and Jews from Israel, and a group of Arabs and Jews from France, to the Auschwitz-Birkenau death camp. The visit was a profound experience for the Arabs and Jews who participated. At the same time, despite efforts to limit discussion to the Holocaust itself and to isolate it from the political debates regarding the status of the Palestinians, tensions nonetheless emerged, and some participants called for the Jews to recognize the Palestinian Nakba. Other participants—Jews and Arabs alike—rejected this call, and held that the Arabs' participation in the joint visit was unconditional. After the trip, the group disintegrated, primarily due to disagreements regarding the nature of its activities.[5]

Another such trip took place in 2006, when thirty students (fifteen Jews and fifteen Arabs) participated in a visit to the death camps as part of a course titled "Holocaust and Existence—Human and Multicultural Aspects of the Holocaust."[6] Another thought-provoking effort was the decision of residents of the village of Na'alin, which by that point had become a prominent symbol in the Palestinian struggle against the Israeli separation barrier in the West Bank, to display a photo exhibit on the Holocaust, which the residents acquired from Yad Vashem, in the village.[7] The exhibit was held in honor of International Holocaust Remembrance Day on 27 January 2009.

This chapter will discuss the lessons of the Holocaust as understood by Israeli students, the perspective that holds that all Jews today are Holocaust survivors, and the place of the Holocaust in the historical consciousness of young Israelis.

It also explores the teaching of the Holocaust and students' own assessments of their own knowledge on the subject. Certain aspects of students' attitudes toward the Holocaust are also discussed in a previous chapter (chapter 2).

The population of the 1990 study consisted for the most part of students born in the 1960s, and often the late 1960s. In contrast, most subjects of the 2008 study were born in the 1970s and 1980s. Thus, if the students who participated in these two studies had any personal connection with the Holocaust, it was only through their parents or, more likely, their grandparents. In other words, they are what are referred to as the "third generation." Furthermore, the students in both samples were socialized after the Holocaust had become a major component of Jewish and Zionist education.

## *The Lessons of the Holocaust*

Ideological streams and movements attempt to derive lessons from historical events, and particularly from major ones. Without a doubt, the Holocaust is regarded as a decisive historical event that has helped shape the destiny of the Jewish people in the recent past and in the present, and that has important implications for the future. This is how the Zionist movement and its leadership understood the Holocaust as it was taking place, and it is certainly how they have understood it in the years that have passed since then. The Holocaust also had a crucial influence on the spectrum of Zionist and non-Zionist Jewish religious worldviews.

The Holocaust was a tragic, exceedingly complex event in the modern history of the Jewish people, and it raises many questions. One way of dealing with it is by trying to learn lessons from it. Commemorating the Holocaust and learning its lessons have been of great importance in the Israeli education and socialization system, even during periods when the subject was rarely pursued as a subject of study. In his classic work *Imagined Communities,* Benedict Anderson argues that as a rule, the biographies of nations tend to appropriate acts of suicide that have become examples to emulate, holy victims, murders, executions, wars, and holocausts. In order to serve these narratives, the establishment representing the nation makes sure that these violent deaths are remembered—or forgotten—as if they happened to "us ourselves." In this spirit, Anderson asserts that "the ancestor of the Warsaw uprising is the state of Israel."[8] Of course, the uprising did occur as an historical event with importance in its own right. Nonetheless, posits Anderson, it was the state of Israel that created the pivotal importance it has attained in historical memory. Indeed, it is clear that the Israeli political and educational systems attempted to influence young Israelis' effective and cognitive attitudes toward the Holocaust and to direct them on a course that was consistent with the Zionist point of view. Some have gone further and have accused the Israeli education system of intentionally using the Holocaust to further the aims and interests of the state of Israel.

The Martyrs' and Heroes' Remembrance (*Yad Vashem*) Law of 1953 (19 August 1953), which defines the role of Yad Vashem as a national remembrance authority, was one of the most important laws passed by the Knesset on this subject. According to the law, Yad Vashem is authorized "to gather, research and publish all testimony on the Holocaust and the heroism and to impart its lesson to the people" (section 12). It is perhaps for good reason that the law did not indicate precisely what this lesson was.

"A lesson is a conclusion based on past experience that is meant to provide benefit in the future,"[9] and as I have said, the law does not specify the "lesson" (singular, not plural) of the Holocaust. We tend to speak about lessons of the Holocaust, and not about messages and significance. Ruth Firer, who examined the lessons of the Holocaust as reflected in various textbooks, and the changes they underwent between 1948 and 1988, concludes her book on the subject with the following words: "I believe that text books can and should be transformed from 'agents of the lesson' to 'agents of significance.'"[10]

But does the Holocaust have a lesson? Clearly, the Holocaust has no one single lesson. Rather, it can generate different lessons, significances, meanings, and interpretations. Indeed, opinions in Israeli society, the Jewish world, and human society in general are divided about how to understand the lessons and significance of the Holocaust. Here, I am not particularly interested in which issues and difficulties arising from the Holocaust are raised, discussed, taught, and emphasized within the Israeli education system. Rather, I am interested in how Israeli students understand the lessons of the Holocaust and the relative importance they attribute to them (in the future, it will also be important to assess the extent to which the education system actually influences the attitudes of young Israelis). In any case, it is reasonable to assume that the Israeli education system, and the teachers working within it, exercise some degree of influence in this context.

The State Education Law of 1953, which set the goals for the Israeli education system, has been amended only once, in 1980, when the Knesset added the following sentence: "The goal of state education is to base education in the country on the consciousness of the memory of the Holocaust and the heroism." The spirit of this amendment is clear—to establish and nurture a consciousness of the Holocaust and its memory from a Jewish-Zionist perspective, as reflected in the Yad Vashem Law of 1953.

A survey on the importance of the Holocaust in Jewish Israeli society undertaken by Yad Vashem in November 1999 reflected the approach prevalent in Israeli society in a number of different ways.[11] In this survey, virtually the entire Jewish-Israeli population (98 percent) expressed belief that the education system should teach about the Holocaust, while the vast majority of respondents (91 percent) believed that all students in Israel should visit Yad Vashem at least once during their time in school. Fifty-eight percent of Jewish Israelis held that the youth trips to Poland should continue, while 28 percent thought they should continue but only after students have undergone thorough preparation. Nine percent opposed the trips altogether, and 5 percent had no opinion in the matter. Another finding was that 44 percent of Jewish Israelis thought that the time dedicated to the Holocaust in the curriculum was insufficient, 38 percent thought that enough time was being spent on the subject and 2 percent thought that too much time was being spent on the Holocaust.

Participants in the survey were asked why they think the Holocaust should be studied, and the results were as follows (percentages are greater than 100 because participants could select more than one answer):

**TABLE 3.1 Reasons Why the Holocaust Should Be Studied**

| | |
|---|---|
| To learn about Jewish history/roots/heritage | 67 percent |
| To learn/remember/avoid forgetting | 35 percent |
| To ensure it does not happen again to the Jewish people | 17 percent |
| Because it is a very important subject | 10 percent |
| To enhance students' obligation to the future of the Jewish people | 8 percent |
| To increase our sensitivity when dealing with minorities and manifestations of racism | 3 percent |
| To ensure that something similar does not happen to any other people in the future | 0.8 percent |
| To ensure that we do not do to others what was done to us | 0.2 percent |

The few people who said that the Holocaust should not be taught explained their position as follows: We need to be optimistic, not to frighten our children, and to teach more modern subjects. At the same time, a very small number of respondents cited "humanistic reasons" or universal lessons as reasons for teaching about the Holocaust. Seventeen percent thought that the Holocaust should be taught "to ensure it does not happen again to the Jewish people," while only 0.8 percent (twenty-one times fewer!) held that the Holocaust should be studied "to ensure that something similar does not happen to any other people in the future." This is reminiscent of Yehuda Elkana's assessment (discussed above) that on a symbolic level, two people left Auschwitz: a frightened majority insisting that it would never happen to us again, and a minority, insisting that it would never happen again.

I presented respondents with ten possible lessons to be learned from the Holocaust, and I asked them to indicate the extent to which they agreed with each one.[12] The lessons can be divided into three categories:

**Zionist Lessons:** Respondents were asked to indicate the extent to which they agreed with lessons of the Holocaust that are understood as Zionist lessons. These include:

1) All Jews in the Diaspora must move to Israel.
2) It is not safe in the Diaspora.
3) Israel is the safest place for Jews to live.
4) The existence of a strong, sovereign, well established Jewish state is a crucial necessity.

The first two Zionist lessons are much more extreme and far-reaching than the third and the fourth. In fact, many Jews living in the Diaspora would most likely agree with lesson four, including those who do not see themselves as Zionist or even as pro-Zionist. The first two lessons express the concept of negation of the Diaspora and call for its elimination: "it is unsafe," and "all Jews should move to Israel." The lesson "Israel is the safest place for Jews to live" is a different, somewhat more moderate version of the lesson that "it is not safe in the Diaspora."

**Jewish Lessons:** Some lessons of the Holocaust relate not only to Israel but to Jewish existence in general. These lessons hold that "there is a necessity for Jewish unity, self-defense, and reliance on ourselves alone," and that "we need to be aware of all manifestations of anti-Semitism and to fight them as soon as they appear."

**Universal Lessons:** The lessons in this category, such as "it is necessary to defend the rights of minorities everywhere in the world" and "it is necessary to fight against anti-Democratic phenomena" do not relate to a particular Israeli-Zionist or Jewish context, but rather to a universal context. In addition to these two lessons, I presented respondents with another two statements with general ethical content. The first, "the world will not allow another Holocaust to happen," appears to have not been phrased with sufficient clarity and was open to multiple interpretations. The second was somewhat philosophical in nature: "human beings are primarily negative in nature."

### *Zionist Lessons*

Students of the state and State-Religious teaching colleges who participated in the 1990 study expressed a high level of agreement with the Zionist lessons. The lesson that received the highest level of agreement was the one holding that "the existence of a strong, sovereign, well established Jewish state is a crucial necessity." Eighty-four percent of the students from the State stream and 88 percent of the students from the State-Religious stream were in strong agreement with the statement (response 4). Aside from a small handful of respondents, the rest agreed with the statement. Students of the Ultra-Orthodox teaching colleges expressed a different approach, one that reflects much greater dissent against the Zionist lessons of the Holocaust. Only 41 percent strongly agreed with the statement, while another 21 percent agreed. In contrast, 13 percent expressed minimal agreement and 21 percent disagreed.

The different approaches between the State teaching students and the State-Religious teaching students were reflected in their positions on the more extreme Zionist lessons of the Holocaust. The level of agreement among State-Religious students was much higher than that of State students with regard to the following statements: "All Jews in the Diaspora must move to Israel," and "It is not safe in the Diaspora." The level of agreement among the State students was somewhat higher than among the Ultra-Orthodox students.

The State teaching students expressed less agreement with the lesson "Israel is the safest place for Jews to live" than the State-Religious students did, and much more than the students of the Ultra-Orthodox teaching colleges.

In all the sub-groups of the 2008 study as well, the lesson "The existence of a strong, sovereign, well established Jewish state is a crucial necessity" received the highest level of agreement, with 98 percent among the non-religious and 84 percent among the religious. The vast majority of those who agreed chose the response "strongly agree" (response 4). The level of agreement with the statement was even higher than the already extremely high level of agreement expressed in the 1990 study.

The 2008 study also reflected differences in the attitudes of religious, traditional, and non-religious students toward the more extreme Zionist lessons of the Holocaust. With regard to the statement "All Jews in the Diaspora must move to Israel," the level of agreement among the religious (59 percent) and traditional students (63 percent) was higher than among the non-religious students (28 percent). In the case of the statement "It is not safe in the Diaspora," 54 percent of the religious students and 58 percent of the traditional students agreed, in comparison to 40 percent of the non-religious students (see table 3.2).

A statistically significant difference was found to exist between the groups with regard to the statement "All Jews in the Diaspora must move to Israel."

In all the groups, there was great support for the statement "The existence of a strong, sovereign, well established Jewish state is a crucial necessity."

The findings according to education sector and religiosity appearing in the tables dealing with lessons of the Holocaust were found to be statistically significant.

In the 1990 study, the lessons of the Holocaust, and particularly the Zionist lessons, elicited written comments from the respondents from the Ultra-Orthodox education sector. One student noted: "I object. These lessons are possible even without the Holocaust." Another student commented that the Zionist lessons "are not correct. This is not the lesson that should be learned from the Holocaust."

The lesson that "the existence of a strong, sovereign, well established Jewish state is a crucial necessity" provoked comments from a number of respondents, who either expressed complete agreement with the lesson of "a religious Jewish state," or stipulated agreement only "on the condition that it [the state] is based on the true values of the people of Israel, the values of the Torah and Judaism. Such a state will be established with the coming of the Messiah." Other students,

Table 3.2 Level of Agreement with Zionist Lessons of the Holocaust (as a percentage)

| 1990 | | | | | | | | | | | | | |
|---|---|---|---|---|---|---|---|---|---|---|---|---|---|
| | State | | | | State-Religious | | | | Ultra-Orthodox | | | | |
| | 4 | 3 | 2 | 1 | 4 | 3 | 2 | 1 | 4 | 3 | 2 | 1 | $X^2$* |
| 1. All Jews in the Diaspora must move to Israel. | 32 | 44 | 17 | 7 | 75 | 18 | 7 | – | 39 | 24 | 26 | 11 | 82.416 |
| 2. The existence of a strong, sovereign, well established Jewish state is a crucial necessity. | 84 | 13 | 2 | 1 | 87.8 | 10.7 | 0.8 | 0.8 | 41 | 21 | 13 | 25 | 125.546 |
| 3. It is not safe in the Diaspora. | 29 | 47 | 21 | 3 | 59.5 | 32.1 | 6.9 | 1.5 | 29 | 40 | 10 | 21 | 84.970 |
| 4. Israel is the safest place for Jews to live. | 50 | 33 | 13 | 4 | 66 | 23 | 10 | 1 | 12.9 | 11.4 | 32.9 | 42.9 | 174.292 |
| 1–Do Not Agree; 2–Agree Minimally; 3–Agree; 4–Strongly Agree | | | | | | | | | | | | | |
| * For all the lessons: $p$ <0.0001 $df$ = 6 | | | | | | | | | | | | | |

| 2008 ** | | | | | | | | | | | | | |
|---|---|---|---|---|---|---|---|---|---|---|---|---|---|
| | Non-Religious | | | | Traditional | | | | Religious | | | | |
| | 4 | 3 | 2 | 1 | 4 | 3 | 2 | 1 | 4 | 3 | 2 | 1 | $X^2$* |
| 1. All Jews in the Diaspora must move to Israel. | 7 | 21 | 37 | 35 | 24 | 39 | 22 | 15 | 38 | 21 | 26 | 15 | 95.082 |
| 2. The existence of a strong, sovereign, well established Jewish state is a crucial necessity. | 71 | 21 | 6 | 3 | 82 | 16 | 2 | – | 73 | 11 | 9 | 7 | – |
| 3. It is not safe in the Diaspora. | 9 | 31 | 38 | 22 | 21 | 37 | 33 | 9 | 32 | 22 | 27 | 19 | 44.428 |
| * For lessons 1–3: $p < 0.0001$ $df$ = 6. For lesson 2: It could not be determined whether there was a statistically significant difference due to the insufficient number of responses in some of the cells. | | | | | | | | | | | | | |
| ** The lesson "Israel is the safest place for Jews to live" did not appear on the 2008 questionnaire. | | | | | | | | | | | | | |

who did not agree with the statement, responded with statements such as "I do not agree at all—only if it is a Torah state."

Many respondents who expressed opposition to the lesson "it is not safe in the Diaspora" added comments such as: "the holy one, blessed be he protects us in the Diaspora," "the holy one, blessed be he is everywhere, in the Diaspora as well," and "god protects us and can rescue us from anywhere," etc.

The lesson "All Jews in the Diaspora must move to Israel" elicited the following stipulating comment from a student who expressed agreement: "…under a regime that will enable Jews to practice Torah and to elevate themselves with works of god, and not to immigrate to Israel in order to throw off the burden and rebel against Torah and rituals, as was the case in the 'Magic Carpet' immigration, and many other immigration waves."

The non-religious students in the 2008 study expressed less, and in many cases much less support for the Zionist lessons than the students of the State teaching colleges surveyed in 1990: Twenty-eight percent of the non-religious students in the 2008 study agreed with the lesson that all Diaspora Jews must move to Israel, as opposed to 76 percent of the State teaching students of 1990. In the 2008 study, 91 percent agreed with the lesson that the existence of a strong, sovereign, well established Jewish state of Israel is a crucial necessity, in comparison to 97 percent in the 1990 study. Moreover, 40 percent of the non-religious students in the 2008 study agreed that it is not safe in the Diaspora, as opposed to 75 percent of the State teaching students in 1990.

### *Jewish Lessons*

The level of agreement among students of the State-Religious teaching colleges in the 1990 study was also extremely high with regard to the statements with Jewish significance. As we have seen, they also expressed the highest level of agreement with statements expressing Zionist lessons.

In contrast, the level of agreement of all students of the Ultra-Orthodox sector with all the statements was markedly low. This is because the lessons relating to religion and faith which the Ultra-Orthodox students tend to regard as important were not among the options I offered. From their perspective, the religious lessons were the lessons that were most important, and it appears that I did not pay sufficient attention to the unique perspective of this population from the outset.

Many respondents from the Ultra-Orthodox sector added written comments regarding the lessons that should be learned from the Holocaust. For example, the lesson pertaining to "Jewish unity, self-defense, and reliance on ourselves alone" elicited many responses from students who did not agree with the final part of the lesson: "reliance on ourselves alone." Here and in other places, they tried to emphasize divine supervision with comments such as: "We will not achieve anything based on our own help, only on the help of god"; "good things happen because we rely on god"; "we do not rely on ourselves, rather on the holy one blessed be he"; "can a creature like me rely only on himself, on the strength and power of his own hand? Nonsense!!" A significant number of those who expressed agreement with the lesson crossed out the part about "reliance on ourselves alone." One student, who chose not to select an answer, added: "it is important to distinguish between the Jewish unity to which I aspire and agree and reliance on ourselves alone, with which I certainly do not agree." When asked to chose the lesson which they regarded as most important, a significant number of respondents added lessons such as: "we must take it upon ourselves to increase the study of the Torah and strengthen it," "there is no particular lesson but to repent," etc.

In the 2008 study, as in the 1990 study, respondents expressed a high level of agreement with the two Jewish statements. The level of agreement with the statement pertaining to Jewish unity, self-defense, and reliance on ourselves alone was 74 percent among the religious students, 81 percent among the traditional students, and 70 percent among the non-religious students. The level of agreement with the statement dealing with the struggle against anti-Semitism was 80 percent among the religious, 95 percent among the traditional, and 92 percent among the non-religious. The level of agreement with the Jewish lessons expressed by the non-religious students in the 2008 study was also lower than that expressed by the State teaching students in the 1990 study.

### *Universal Lessons*

When we examine the responses to the universal lessons, the order of agreement among the groups changes, with the non-religious students expressing a significantly higher level of agreement.

At the same time, I found that the percentage of State teaching students in the 1990 study that agreed (agree and strongly agree [answers 3 and 4] combined) with the universal statement "it is necessary to fight against anti-democratic phenomena" (95 percent) was higher than the percentage of non-religious students that agreed with the statement in the 2008 study (89 percent). And while 93 percent of the state students in the 1990 study agreed with the statement "it is necessary to defend the rights of minorities everywhere in the world," agreement was considerably less (84 percent) among the non-religious students surveyed in 2008.

In previous studies, the questions pertaining to the Holocaust were not posed as separate questions for which agreement levels were assessed. Rather, in earlier studies, respondents were asked to select one lesson, from a list of possible lessons, that they regarded as the most important. At the end of the list of lessons in the 1990 study, I added an additional question, in which subjects were asked to indicate which of all the possible lessons of the Holocaust they regarded as most important.

**TABLE 3.3 Level of Agreement with the Jewish Lessons of the Holocaust (as a percentage)**

| 1990 | | | | | | | | | | | | | |
|---|---|---|---|---|---|---|---|---|---|---|---|---|---|
| | State | | | | State-Religious | | | | Ultra-Orthodox | | | | |
| | 4 | 3 | 2 | 1 | 4 | 3 | 2 | 1 | 4 | 3 | 2 | 1 | $X^2$* |
| 1) There is a necessity for Jewish unity, self-defense, and reliance on ourselves alone. | 46 | 40 | 10 | 4 | 78 | 16 | 2 | 4 | 27 | 12 | 7 | 54 | 212.145 |
| 2) We need to be aware of all manifestations of anti-Semitism and to fight them as soon as they appear. | 64 | 30 | 6 | – | 73 | 19 | 6 | 2 | 41 | 24 | 13 | 22 | 108.286 |
| * For all the lessons: $p < 0.0001$ $df = 6$ | | | | | | | | | | | | | |
| 2008 | | | | | | | | | | | | | |
| | Non-Religious | | | | Traditional | | | | Religious | | | | |
| | 4 | 3 | 2 | 1 | 4 | 3 | 2 | 1 | 4 | 3 | 2 | 1 | $X^2$* |
| 1) There is a necessity for Jewish unity, self-defense, and reliance on ourselves alone. | 35 | 35 | 21 | 9 | 47 | 34 | 18 | 1 | 39 | 35 | 11 | 15 | 20.56 |
| 2) We need to be aware of all expressions of anti-Semitism and to fight them as soon as they appear. | 65 | 27 | 7 | 1 | 73 | 22 | 5 | – | 55 | 25 | 15 | 5 | 19.06 |
| Lesson 1: $df = 6$, $p < 0.001$<br>Lesson 2: $df = 6$, $p < 0.01$ | | | | | | | | | | | | | |

**TABLE 3.4 Level of Agreement with the Universal Lessons of the Holocaust (as a percentage)**

| 1990 | State | | | | State-Religious | | | | Ultra-Orthodox | | | | |
|---|---|---|---|---|---|---|---|---|---|---|---|---|---|
| | 4 | 3 | 2 | 1 | 4 | 3 | 2 | 1 | 4 | 3 | 2 | 1 | $X^2$* |
| 1) It is necessary to fight against anti-democratic phenomena. | 68 | 27 | 3 | 2 | 30 | 56 | 12 | 2 | 16 | 15 | 48 | 21 | 218.953 |
| 2) It is necessary to defend the rights of minorities everywhere in the world.** | 45 | 48 | 7 | – | 31 | 52 | 13 | 4 | 29 | 50 | 14 | 8 | 30.927 |
| 3) The world will not allow another Holocaust to happen.*** | 8 | 21 | 46 | 25 | 6 | 17 | 37 | 40 | 16 | 10 | 33 | 41 | 23.901 |
| 4) Human beings are primarily negative in nature. | 2 | 15 | 40 | 43 | 5 | 12 | 23 | 60 | 11 | 13 | 17 | 59 | 36.175 |

* For all the lessons: $p < 0.0001$ $df = 6$

** A number of students from the Ultra-Orthodox sector agreed with the statement, but only after making meaningful changes to it: instead of "… the rights of minorities everywhere in the world," they wrote "the rights of Jews." One student who indicated minimal agreement added: "It depends upon who. In my opinion, we should defend and take care of Jews, but not gentiles."

*** Students frequently added comments, such as: "I hope not, but it is not in our hands"; "There is no answer, as it does not depend on the world but rather in the holy one blessed be he"; and "What does this mean—that it is in our hands? If god wills it, it will be, and if he does not, it will not be. It all depends on our deeds and on the will of god."

| 2008**** | Non-Religious | | | | Traditional | | | | Religious | | | | |
|---|---|---|---|---|---|---|---|---|---|---|---|---|---|
| | 4 | 3 | 2 | 1 | 4 | 3 | 2 | 1 | 4 | 3 | 2 | 1 | $X^2$* |
| 1) It is necessary to fight against anti-democratic phenomena. | 55 | 34 | 9 | 2 | 49 | 42 | 8 | 1 | 34 | 36 | 24 | 6 | 29.065 |
| 2) It is necessary to defend the rights of minorities everywhere in the world. | 50 | 34 | 14 | 2 | 39 | 47 | 13 | 1 | 30 | 34 | 24 | 12 | 45.722 |
| 3) Human beings are primarily negative in nature. | 12 | 21 | 34 | 33 | 6 | 17 | 41 | 36 | 9 | 11 | 30 | 50 | 14.687 |

**** The lesson "the world will not allow another Holocaust to happen" was not offered as an option in the 2008 questionnaire.

* For lessons 1 and 2: $p < 0.0001$, $df = 6$. For lesson 3: $p < 0.05$, $df = 6$.

TABLE 3.5 The Most Important Lesson to Be Learned from the Holocaust,* 1990 (as a percentage)

| | State | State-Religious | Ultra-Orthodox | Total Study Population |
|---|---|---|---|---|
| 1) All Jews in the Diaspora must move to Israel. | 4 | 16 | 15 | 8 |
| 2) The existence of a strong, sovereign, well-established Jewish state is a crucial necessity. | 26 | 38 | 8 | 28 |
| 3) It is not safe in the Diaspora. | 2 | 7 | 23 | 4 |
| 4) There is a necessity for Jewish unity, self-defense, and reliance on ourselves alone. | 6 | 13 | 15 | 9 |
| 5) We need to be aware of all manifestations of anti-Semitism and to fight them as soon as they appear. | 6 | 6 | 15 | 7 |
| 6) The world will not allow another Holocaust to happen. | 8 | 6 | 4 | 7 |
| 7) Israel is the safest place for Jews to live. | 15 | 13 | 12 | 14 |
| 8) It is necessary to fight against anti-democratic phenomena. | 11 | – | – | 7 |
| 9) It is necessary to defend the rights of minorities everywhere in the world. | 20 | 1 | – | 14 |
| 10) Human beings are primarily negative in nature. | – | – | – | – |
| 11) [Invalid (more than one answer)] | 2 | – | 8 | 1 |

* Respondents were asked to select one of the ten lessons listed.

Again, students ranked the Zionist lessons as the most important lessons in their responses to this question as well. And of the Zionist lessons, the students of the State and State-Religious teaching colleges regarded the lesson regarding the "crucial need for the existence of a strong, sovereign, well established Jewish state" to be the most important of all. In the eyes of the students of the Ultra-Orthodox teaching colleges, the most important lesson was that "it is not safe in the Diaspora." The Ultra-Orthodox and State-Religious students also assigned great importance to the lesson "all Jews in the Diaspora must move to Israel," while the state students regarded the lesson "Israel is the safest place for Jews to live" as extremely important. Overall, a large percentage of the Ultra-Orthodox students (31 percent) ranked the Jewish lessons as the most important, as opposed to 19 percent of the State-Religious students and 13 percent of the state students.

The statistical data for the students of the Ultra-Orthodox sector is misleading, as only 23 of the total of 72 students in this group (32 percent) chose one of the possibilities listed in the questionnaire. None of the remaining students in this group selected one particular lesson from among the options. However, a significant number of respondents added their own lessons, such as the need "to get back on the straight and narrow and 'become stronger' [in a religious sense—Y.A.]" or "to become religious and return to God." One student commented: "Nothing listed below is a lesson. We know that the Jewish people is an elevated people, and still it does not annihilate the entire world. No one but the Jews can decide that they are the most superior race."

Some of the ultra-Orthodox students added meaningful comments that shed light on their perspective on the subject. One comment read as follows: "In the Holocaust, we saw miracles and wonders. The entire Jewish people lives and exists on the basis of miracles at every single moment. If god's supervision was not present as we saw during the Holocaust, god forbid, then the Jewish people would not exist at all. We must believe that it is no coincidence that we were brought into the world and born as Jews after such a terrible Holocaust, and that we have an important role to play—to live like true Jews and to raise generations of true Jews. This needs to be well understood."

Elsewhere in the questionnaire, the same student, while expressing complete agreement with the statement "the world will not allow another Holocaust to happen," added: "I very much hope that there will not be another Holocaust, but it does not depend on 'the world.' The Holocaust was the result of transgressions and of envy of the gentiles, not just because this is what happened but because this is how god wanted it to be." Another student, who did not select a most important lesson of the Holocaust, added: "The first lesson is that we should start serving god and practicing Torah and rituals as prescribed, and then there will be no Holocaust and no lessons."

These responses clearly reflect the main elements of the ultra-Orthodox perspective on the Holocaust:

1) The Holocaust was the will of god.
2) The Jews were responsible, or partly responsible, for the Holocaust, due to their transgressions and their throwing off, and rebellion against the burden of the Torah and rituals.

In the 1990 study, I found a relatively high, and in many ways surprising prevalence of universal lessons in the responses of the students of the State teaching colleges. Thirty percent of this group chose either "it is necessary to fight against anti-democratic phenomena" (11 percent) or "it is necessary to defend the rights of minorities everywhere in the world" (20 percent). This stands in striking contrast to the less than 1 percent of the students from the State-Religious and Ultra-Orthodox colleges who chose these lessons. The relative pervasiveness of universal lessons in the State sector may be partially explained by instruction on the Holocaust in some of the state colleges, which also emphasizes universal aspects of the subject. Universal lessons were also supported by non-religious students in the 2008 study, with 89 percent agreeing that "it is necessary to fight against anti-democratic phenomena" and 84 percent agreeing that "it is necessary to defend the rights of minorities everywhere in the world." Similar percentages (91 percent and 86 percent) of traditional students agreed with these lessons as well.

Based on other studies and assessments and on my own experience in teaching and education, it is clear that young Israelis have extremely limited knowledge and awareness of genocides that have befallen other peoples. Young Israelis learn about the Holocaust in a particularistic Jewish context alone and learn virtually nothing about the Gypsy, Armenian, and Rwandan genocides in their high schools and in Israeli institutions of higher education. The dominant approach to Holocaust education in Israel stresses the uniqueness of the Jewish genocide. I argue that this approach, which places the Holocaust in a separate category all its own, is somewhat limiting and decreases the extent to which we can learn from it.

### *Comparison with Other Studies*

The studies of Herman and Farago do not contain detailed data regarding questions relating to the lessons of the Holocaust. In contrast, Yeshayahu (Charles) Liebman's 1975 study of a random sample of Jewish Israelis over the age of 18 does address these questions. In response to the question of what is the most important lesson to be learned from the Holocaust, 58 percent of the respondents answered either that all Jews must move to Israel or that the existence of a strong, sovereign, well established Jewish state is a crucial necessity. Another 9 percent answered that it is not safe in the Diaspora, and 23 percent formulated the lesson of the Holocaust in universal terms (the need to fight against anti-democratic phenomena and to defend the rights of minorities everywhere in the world).[13]

Although there are differences between the lessons addressed by the two studies (my study included more lessons), Liebman's study of the general population appears to be consistent with the general thrust of the responses of the students from the State-Religious and Ultra-Orthodox teaching colleges in my study. However, students from the State sector tended to frame the lessons to be learned from the Holocaust in less all-encompassing Jewish terms, and more universal terms.

Comparing the results of my 1990 study and the study undertaken by the organizers of the March of the Living in the same year illustrates an interesting phenomenon. The March of the Living study presented respondents with possible lessons of the Holocaust that were similar to the lessons presented in my study (their questionnaire was based on my questionnaire).[14] This study provides us with data from questionnaire responses provided by teenage participants between the ages of 16 and 18 from Israel, the United States, and France (198, 264, and

89 participants respectively), prior to their visit to Poland but after registering for the March of the Living.[15]

All the respondents agreed that the Holocaust obligates the existence of a sovereign Jewish state and that it is necessary to fight against all manifestations of anti-Semitism. However, there were differences in their opinions regarding the other lessons that should be learned from the Holocaust. The most prominent finding of the comparison has to do with the different opinions of American teens, in comparison to Israeli and French teens, regarding issues related to Jewish immigration to Israel. Only a relatively small percentage of the American respondents (40 percent) thought that the Holocaust obligates Jewish immigration to Israel, as opposed to a much higher percentage of the Israeli (88 percent) and French (72 percent) youth.[16] In addition, many fewer American teenagers agreed with the lessons "it is not safe in the Diaspora" and "Israel is the safest place for Jews to live" than their French and Israeli counterparts. We can assume that their support for the Zionist lessons increased after the tour of the death camps in Poland and the tours in Israel (the progression "from Holocaust to revival" included in the March of the Living program).

A study I carried out in France in 1977–1980 examined attitudes toward the Holocaust and its implications (in addition to other elements of their Jewish identity) among members of Jewish youth movements.[17] Among other findings, it was determined that the youth usually generated lessons from the Holocaust that were consistent with their values and their worldview. Zionists frequently adopted Zionist lessons, and those planning to immigrate to Israel generated lessons that supported their intention to move to Israel (such as "all Diaspora Jews must move to Israel"). Members of Zionist youth movements generated lessons that were similar to the lessons espoused by Israeli youth, while members of Jewish youth movements based on more universal principles chose primarily universal lessons, few Jewish lessons, and no Zionist lessons whatsoever. Alternatively, it is also possible that their broader worldviews were shaped by the lessons they adopted in light of the Holocaust (and perhaps other factors, such as anti-Semitism). If this is the case, then the Holocaust must be understood as the reason.

The importance of the Zionist lessons of the Holocaust was also illustrated by another question, which focused not on the Holocaust but on the state of Israel. I presented the students in the 1990 study with a number of reasons justifying Israel's right to exist; the reason that received the highest level of support among students from the State teaching colleges was "the suffering of the Jews in the Diaspora as a people without a homeland." This reason was also frequently repeated by students from the State-Religious colleges, although less than god's promise to the fathers of the nation that the Land of Israel would be given to the people of Israel. When asked to chose one reason from all the reasons listed, religious students chose the divine promise as the most important of all reasons

(84 percent of the State-Religious students and 86 percent of the students from the Ultra-Orthodox sector).

After this reason, with significantly less support (7 percent), State-Religious students selected the suffering of the Jewish people in the Diaspora as the most important justification for the state of Israel's right to exist. The same percentage chose the Jew's desire to return to the country throughout all the generations. Among the Ultra-Orthodox students, the number one reason cited was divine promise, followed by the Jewish desire to return to the country, with 12.5 percent.

In accordance with its extremely different worldview, the non-religious students selected completely different reasons to justify of the existence of the state of Israel. When asked to choose one reason from a list of possible reasons, 46 percent chose the suffering of the Jews in the Diaspora as a people without a homeland; 22 percent chose the settlement of the country during the modern period; 12 percent chose international recognition of the idea of a Jewish state; 9 percent chose the Jews' desire throughout the generations to return to the Land of Israel; 6 percent chose the divine promise; and 4 percent chose the people of Israel's settlement in the country during ancient times.

Indeed, whereas the religious students surveyed in the 1990 study justified the existence of the state of Israel based on *religious reasons,* the students of the State teaching colleges cited primarily *historical reasons,* the most prominent of which was the suffering of the Jews in the Diaspora as a people without a homeland. From their perspective, they are undoubtedly referring to the period of the Holocaust, during which Jewish suffering in the Diaspora reached incomprehensible levels. This view is reflected in the education system by the widespread connection between Holocaust and renewal known as "from Holocaust to revival."

The lessons of the Holocaust espoused by the Israeli state education system are first and foremost Zionist, and they have been transmitted and received. We can assume that the very different responses of the State-Religious and Ultra-Orthodox students are also the product of the education provided by their respective education sectors, which are more closed in nature and based on very different values.

In Liebman's sample of the general population, 30 percent chose Jewish suffering in the Diaspora as the most important factor justifying the existence of the state of Israel. In second and third place were the Jews' longing to return to Eretz Israel (24 percent) and the divine promise to the Jewish people (17 percent).[18]

It can be concluded that Israeli society espouses the Zionist lessons and Jewish lessons of the Holocaust. The universal lessons were mentioned much less frequently, perhaps as a result of the Israeli education system, which emphasizes the uniqueness of the Holocaust and which is not open to the idea of teaching about other cases of genocide. The level of support for universal lessons expressed in my 2008 study was even lower than that expressed in my study of 1990.

### *Identification with and Pride for the Jews during the Period of the Holocaust*

A number of the questions I asked in my study were aimed at assessing students' attitudes toward the Jews who lived during the Holocaust. As we have seen, Israeli attitudes toward the Jews from the period of the Holocaust were once characterized by criticism, opposition, distance, and in many cases alienation. With a semi-implicit, semi-explicit air of criticism, and a great lack of empathy and understanding, young Israelis frequently asked: "Why did they go like sheep to the slaughter?"

In recent years, the Israeli education system has attempted to present a different view of the life and behavior of the Jews during the Holocaust. It has tried to emphasize the many expressions of physical heroism in the Jews' struggle, even in comparison to expressions of resistance by others (prisoners of war, soldiers, etc.). At the same time, it has also tried to show that the resistance and struggle against the Nazis was reflected in other forms of resistance as well (such as Jewish martyrdom; faith in god and the maintaining of ritual practice under the most adverse conditions; the maintaining of humanity; the sanctification of life; the operation of welfare and aid institutions, etc.), and not just physical heroism. My findings suggest that the attitude of young Israelis has changed significantly. In instances in which comparisons could be carried out with studies from the past, I will try to illustrate this change.

### *"We Are All Holocaust Survivors"*

I asked respondents the following question: "The term 'Holocaust survivor' can also be used to refer to people who are not physically survivors. For example, some say that in many ways we are all Holocaust survivors. Do you agree with the statement: 'All Jews in the world should see themselves as if they are Holocaust survivors'?" In both my 1990 and 2008 studies, students from all three subgroups expressed extremely high levels of agreement with this statement, and the differences between the groups were not found to be statistically significant.

In the 2008 study, all three sub-groups expressed a significantly lower level of agreement with the statement. Subjects' written explanations for their answer to this question (in response to an open-ended question) can be divided into a number of categories:

**A. Identification with the Fate of the Jews During the Holocaust and with Holocaust Survivors**

"We could have been born back then."

"I am the offspring of those Holocaust survivors, and there is continuity."

"I could have also been in the Holocaust."

**B. The Totality of the Solution**

"If they had not stopped the Holocaust in time, Hitler would have carried out his plot against all of them."

**TABLE 3.6 Understanding Jews Today as Holocaust Survivors: Agreement with the Statement *"All Jews in the world should see themselves as if they are Holocaust survivors"* (as a percentage)**

| 1990 | | | |
|---|---|---|---|
| | State | State-Religious | Ultra-Orthodox |
| (1) Agree with the sentence | 80 | 84 | 90 |
| (2) Agree with the sentence only regarding Jews from Europe | 4 | 6 | – |
| (3) Agree with the sentence only regarding anyone who was present there | 11 | 6 | 8 |
| (4) Do not agree with the sentence | 6 | 5 | 2 |
| | | | |
| **2008** | | | |
| | Religious | Traditional | Non-Religious |
| (1) Agree with the sentence | 69 | 56 | 47 |
| (2) Agree with the sentence only regarding Jews from Europe | 5 | 4 | 5 |
| (3) Agree with the sentence only regarding anyone who was present there | 5 | 24 | 25 |
| (4) Do not agree with the sentence | 21 | 16 | 23 |
| $p < 0.0001$ $df = 6$ $X^2 = 26.656$ | | | |

"Hitler was about to annihilate our entire people and to reach all countries."

**C. The Impact of the Holocaust on Our Lives Today**

"Those who did not physically experience the Holocaust were injured psychologically, and this injury is reflected in us."

"This event overshadows our lives and influences our opinions."

**D. The Holocaust and the Revival**

"Because of this fact [that Holocaust survivors remained alive], there was a need for a state for the people and the state of Israel was established."

"It is only because of them that we are in the Land of Israel."

**E. The Unity of Jewish Destiny**

"All Israel is responsible for one another."

**F. Responsibility for the Jewish Future**

"The number of Jews decreased, and in any case we bear responsibility for the future of the Jewish people."

"With the decrease in the number of Jews, the great responsibility to increase the study of the Torah and strengthen it in the future fell upon our shoulders."

G. **The Danger of Another Holocaust and Fears of Anti-Semitism**
"Theoretically, every Jew living abroad could get hurt in the same way." "The Holocaust is a symptom of a general phenomenon which could have been—and still could be—perpetrated in any place and at any time against the Jewish people."

Agreement with the sentence reflects an understanding of the Holocaust not only as "an event from the Jewish historic past that is getting increasingly farther away," but as something that "continues to touch the present and future of the Jewish people."[19] Interestingly, my findings reflect much greater agreement with the sentence than the studies of Herman and Farago, despite the fact that, based on an analysis of their findings, Farago believed that, at the time, support for the idea that all Jews should feel like they are Holocaust survivors had decreased in recent years.[20]

If I am correct in this interpretation of the sentence, which is based on an analogy with the Passover Haggadah, the relevancy and presence of the Holocaust as an event with meaning for the present and future of the Jewish people has remained strong for young Israelis through the years, although it appeared significantly weaker in the 2008 study than in the 1990 study.

## *Identification*

In all sub-groups, I found a high level of identification with the Jews who suffered during the Holocaust. In the 1990 study, the intensity of identification was lowest among the state students, higher among the State-Religious students, and highest among the students from the Ultra-Orthodox sector. In the 2008 study, it increased from the non-religious, to the traditional, to the religious. This direction of increasing identification is consistent with the responses to the rest of the questions pertaining to the Jews during the Holocaust.

According to Farago: "Over the years, students' overall identification with the victims of the Holocaust has increased. This finding is indicative both of the atmosphere in Israeli society and the success of the education system in creating such a norm among the students, even if only on a declarative level."[21] I agree with this assessment, and it is possible to identify an intensification of this trend over the years. My 1990 data indicates even greater identification than the levels expressed in the studies of Herman and Farago in 1965, 1974, and 1985, which were also very high.[22] The level of identification expressed in my 2008 study, while still very high, was lower than that expressed in the 1990 study. It would be interesting to follow the changes and see whether we are witnessing a change in the trend of increasing identification with the victims of the Holocaust: the beginning of a decline in the extent to which Jews today are regarded as Holocaust survivors, and in Jewish Israelis' identification with their suffering. However, if such a decline is

**TABLE 3.7 Identification with the Suffering of the Jews during the Holocaust (as a percentage)**

| 1990 | | | |
|---|---|---|---|
| | State | State-Religious | Ultra-Orthodox |
| Yes, to a Great Extent | 68 | 85 | 93 |
| Yes | 29 | 14 | 7 |
| To a Minimal Extent | 3 | 1 | – |
| No | – | 1 | – |
| | | | |
| 2008 | | | |
| | Religious | Traditional | Non-Religious |
| Yes, to a Great Extent | 70 | 52 | 49 |
| Yes | 24 | 36 | 40 |
| To a Minimal Extent | 5 | 10 | 9 |
| No | 1 | 2 | 1 |
| $X^2 = 13.39$ | $df = 6$ | $p < 0.05$ | |

in fact taking place, it is not necessarily related to the Holocaust. Rather, it may be due to a growing lack of sympathy for the suffering of others in general and a decline of social values overall, which has also been reflected in the alienating and often unsympathetic treatment of Holocaust survivors living in Israel.

## *Pride*

As part of a series of questions dealing with their attitudes toward various periods in Jewish history, I also presented students with a question on their attitudes toward the behavior of the Jews during the Holocaust. Particularly in the case of the secular Jews, the prevalent attitude toward other periods of the history of Diaspora Jewry, such as the Shtetl period or Jewish life in Mediterranean countries, was one of indifference ("I have no particular feeling about it") or lack of knowledge ("I do not know enough about the period"). To a much lesser extent, respondents also expressed a sense of pride.

In the 2008 study, I found that 50 percent of the religious students were proud of the Shtetl period, while 41 percent had no particular feeling, 1 percent were ashamed, and 8 percent did not know enough about the period. The situation was different in the traditional sub-group, in which 12 percent expressed pride, 46 percent indicated that they had no particular feeling, 2 percent were ashamed, and 41 percent did not know enough about the period. The level of pride expressed was much lower among the non-religious, with 10 percent expressing pride, 60 percent indicating that they had no particular feeling, 2 percent indicating that they were ashamed, and 28 percent not knowing enough about the period.

A totally different picture emerges when we assess students' attitudes toward the period of the Holocaust. In the past, many young Israelis saw the Holocaust as the extreme, clear-cut expression of the period of exile. As we have seen, they were frequently critical of the Jews alive during the period for going "like lambs to the slaughter." However, my findings show that the vast majority of students in both the 1990 study and the 2008 study were proud of the behavior of the Jews during the Holocaust.

The following table reflects their responses (as a percentage):

**Table 3.8 Attitudes toward the Behavior of Jews during the Holocaust (as a percentage)**

| 1990 | | | |
|---|---|---|---|
| | **Ultra-Orthodox** | **State-Religious** | **State** |
| 1) I am proud of the behavior of the Jews during the Holocaust. | 97 | 77 | 89 |
| 2) I have no particular feeling toward the behavior of the Jews during this period. | 3 | 10 | 1 |
| 3) I am ashamed of the behavior of the Jews during this period. | – | 5 | 3 |
| 4) I do not have sufficient knowledge about the behavior of the Jews during this period. | – | 6 | 6 |
| 5) [Added responses at their own initiative] | – | 1 | 2 |
| | The test is invalid due to the limitations of the sample size. | | |
| | | | |
| **2008** | | | |
| | **Religious** | **Traditional** | **Non-Religious** |
| 1) I am proud of the behavior of the Jews during the Holocaust. | 76 | 70 | 65 |
| 2) I have no particular feeling toward the behavior of the Jews during this period. | 21 | 21 | 25 |
| 3) I am ashamed of the behavior of the Jews during this period. | 3 | 4 | 7 |
| 4) I do not have sufficient knowledge about the behavior of the Jews during this period. | 1 | 5 | 3 |
| 5) [Added responses at their own initiative] | | | |
| It was not possible to determine whether a significant difference existed between the different sectors due to the insufficient number of responses in some of the cells. | | | |

The level of pride expressed by the subjects (future teachers) in the 1990 study is even significantly higher than that reflected in the responses of the Israeli high school students in 1965, 1974, and 1985. However, this difference might also stem from the differences between the study populations, which I regard as extremely significant. This response is consistent with other responses, which allow me to conclude that the Holocaust is becoming an even more meaningful aspect of Jewish Israeli identity (see more on this below). The fact that my sample consisted of a defined group within the country's young population also helps to explain the greater sense of pride expressed. As I explained earlier, increased pride regarding the behavior of Jews during the Holocaust was not accompanied by increased pride, interest, or knowledge regarding Jewish life prior to the Holocaust. At the same time, the 2008 study revealed a slight decrease in pride in the behavior of the Jews during the Holocaust, as well as an increase in the number of respondents with no particular feeling about the period. This may be an indication of a reversal in the trend of increasing pride in the course of time, which may now be declining.

The great majority of respondents in the 1990 study (83 percent) were proud of the behavior of the Jews during this period, and I found no significant difference stemming from extraction. In fact, Jews from Middle Eastern extraction tended to express slightly more pride than the other groups (86 percent). Thus, the different attitudes regarding the behavior of the Jews during the Holocaust that apparently once existed among Jews from different countries of origins could not be detected in the response of these subjects. I believe that this reflects the Holocaust's role as a central component of the Zionist-nationalist ethos and as a main component of the so-called "civil religion" of Israeli society.

The future Israeli teachers surveyed in the 1990 study were proud of the behavior of the Jews during the Holocaust, identified with the sentence "all Jews in the world should see themselves as if they are Holocaust survivors," and identified with the suffering of the Jews during the period of the Holocaust much more than young Israelis from twenty-five, fifteen, or even five years earlier. With regard to these questions, I identified a trend of increasing pride as one moves from students of the state colleges, to students of the State-Religious colleges, to students of the Ultra-Orthodox colleges.

Herman argues that pride regarding the behavior of Jews during the Holocaust is linked to strong Jewish identity and a sense of shame regarding weak Jewish identity.[23] If this is correct, the intensification of the Jewish feelings that has taken place over the years may help explain the increased sense of pride and identification, and the feeling that all Jews should all see themselves as if they are Holocaust survivors.

As I have noted, the results of the 2008 study indicate a change in direction, and we are now witnessing a trend of decreasing pride, identification, and the feeling that we should all see ourselves as if we were Holocaust survivors.

### *The Perspective of Time—The Prominence of the Holocaust in Historical Consciousness*

We have seen that non-religious young Israelis tend to regard only events from later periods of Jewish history in general, and the twentieth century in particular, as events with special importance for the destiny of the Jewish people or special personal relevance. And of the events they listed (the question was an open-ended question) as having the most influence on both a general Jewish and a personal level, three appeared with great frequency: the Holocaust, the establishment of the state of Israel, and the wars fought by Israel. It is interesting to note that while the first two events are related to the national, Zionist, and Israeli aspects of Jewish history, the Holocaust is clearly a different type of event. Nonetheless, many young Israelis tended to regard it more (and perhaps primarily) from a Zionist and Israeli perspective than from a Jewish or universal perspective.

**Table 3.9 Frequently Listed Historical Events that Influenced Personal Destiny and the Destiny of the Jewish People, 1990 (as a percentage)**

| Ultra-Orthodox Sector | | | | | | | | |
|---|---|---|---|---|---|---|---|---|
| | Historical Events that Influenced the Destiny of the Jewish People | | | | Historical Events with Relevance for You and Your Destiny | | | |
| Event | 1 | 2 | 3 | Total | 1 | 2 | 3 | Total |
| The Holocaust | 19 | 15 | 33 | 67 | 45 | 8 | 20 | 73 |
| Establishment of the State | 0 | 3 | 9 | 12 | 4 | 10 | 7 | 21 |
| The Exile | 8 | 7 | 9 | 24 | 4 | 10 | 3 | 17 |
| The Giving of the Torah | 28 | 16 | 6 | 50 | 21 | 10 | 17 | 48 |
| | | | | | | | | |
| State Sector | | | | | | | | |
| Event | 1 | 2 | 3 | Total | 1 | 2 | 3 | Total |
| The Holocaust | 54 | 28 | 9 | 91 | 42 | 14 | 8 | 64 |
| Establishment of the State | 5 | 33 | 30 | 68 | 22 | 24 | 10 | 56 |
| World War II | 6 | 4 | 1 | 11 | 3 | 2 | 1 | 6 |
| | | | | | | | | |
| State-Religious Sector | | | | | | | | |
| Event | 1 | 2 | 3 | Total | 1 | 2 | 3 | Total |
| The Holocaust | 20 | 34 | 28 | 82 | 18 | 27 | 6 | 51 |
| Establishment of the State | 2 | 17 | 45 | 64 | 20 | 22 | 35 | 76 |
| The Giving of the Torah | 23 | 12 | 1 | 36 | 26 | 7 | 7 | 40 |

TABLE 3.10 Frequently Listed Historical Events that Influenced Personal Destiny and the Destiny of the Jewish People (partial list), 2008 (as a percentage)[24]

| Religious | | | | | | | | |
|---|---|---|---|---|---|---|---|---|
| | Historical Events that Influenced the Destiny of the Jewish People | | | | Historical Events with Relevance for You and Your Destiny | | | |
| Event | 1 | 2 | 3 | Total | 1 | 2 | 3 | Total |
| The Holocaust | 12 | 26 | 16 | 50 | 33 | 12 | 3 | 41 |
| Establishment of the State | 7 | 6 | 35 | 43 | 6 | 22 | 23 | 40 |
| Biblical Events | 55 | 22 | 11 | 83 | 25 | 6 | 5 | 31 |
| | | | | | | | | |
| Traditional | | | | | | | | |
| Event | 1 | 2 | 3 | Total | 1 | 2 | 3 | Total |
| The Holocaust | 52 | 25 | 8 | 77 | 34 | 14 | 7 | 45 |
| Establishment of the State | 11 | 28 | 21 | 51 | 18 | 28 | 4 | 40 |
| Biblical Events | 8 | 5 | 3 | 24 | – | – | – | – |
| | | | | | | | | |
| Non-Religious | | | | | | | | |
| Event | 1 | 2 | 3 | Total | 1 | 2 | 3 | Total |
| The Holocaust | 48 | 27 | 12 | 80 | 42 | 11 | 4 | 44 |
| Establishment of the State | 8 | 34 | 25 | 59 | 13 | 24 | 11 | 36 |
| Biblical Events | 10 | 4 | 3 | 16 | 1 | 2 | 1 | 3 |

This table above reflects the fact that the Holocaust was the most frequently listed event in all three sectors, both as an event that influenced the destiny of the Jewish people (an event with objective historical significance) and as an event that is "especially relevant to you and your destiny" (an event with subjective historical significance). There were two exceptions to this generalization: In the 1990 study, students of the State-Religious colleges cited the establishment of the state more frequently (76 percent) than the Holocaust (51 percent) as a historical event influencing their personal destinies. Similarly, in the 2008 study, religious students listed different biblical events more frequently (83 percent) than the Holocaust. In the 1990 study, however, all but a few of the respondents from the State sector, and almost all respondents from the religious sectors, listed the Holocaust (or, much less frequently, World War II).[25]

Students from the State-Religious teaching colleges in the 1990 study listed the Holocaust much more frequently (77 percent) as an event that impacted the destiny of the Jewish people and less as an event with special personal relevance. In contrast, the establishment of the state was listed less as an event that impacted the destiny of the Jewish people (63 percent) and more as an event with special personal relevance (76 percent). In the State sector, the Holocaust and the establishment of the state are listed frequently, in that order, as the historical events that most influenced the destiny of the Jewish people, and in the same order, though less frequently, as historical events with the greatest personal relevance.

The students from the Ultra-Orthodox sector surveyed in the 1990 study also listed the Holocaust more frequently than any other event, albeit more as an event with special personal relevance (72 percent) than as an event that influenced the destiny of the Jewish people (66 percent). The establishment of the state of Israel was regarded as much less important on both the Jewish national level and the personal level, and it was listed less frequently than the giving of the Torah and the exile as an event that influenced the destiny of the Jewish people.

Responses to this question also reflected the change in trend from previous studies, in which students listed the Holocaust much less frequently. In Farago's 1985 study, which reflects a change from the studies that preceded it, 44 percent of the students surveyed selected the Holocaust as the historical event with the greatest influence on their destiny, more than any other event. In the earlier studies (1965 and 1974), the Holocaust emerged as the third most influential historical event, after the establishment of the state of Israel and the War of Independence, which were ranked first, and whatever happened to be the most recent war at the time (in Farago's 1968 study it was the Six Days War, and in his 1974 study it was the Yom Kippur War), which was ranked second.[26]

Until the 1970s, the Holocaust was generally regarded as something that happened to "them" (the exilic Jews), "there" (in Europe). Since then, it has come to be understood as something that happened to us, here. In the eyes of young Israelis, it has moved into first place as the most prominent event in Jewish history, even more prominent—in all three education sectors—than the establishment of the state. In the State and Ultra-Orthodox sectors, it is also seen as a historical event with great personal influence despite the many years that have passed since then, which might also have been expected to decrease in personal influence over time. In 1990, my study population consisted of members of the second and third generation. In my 2008 study, I noted a decline in the frequency with which the Holocaust was cited, although it still remained the most frequently cited event with subjective relevance (to them or their destiny). The Holocaust was listed by 40 to 45 percent, more than any other event but far less than the percentage of students who listed it in the study of 1990. Much larger percentages listed the Holocaust as an event that influenced the destiny of the Jewish people, with 80 percent among the non-religious students, 77 percent among the traditional students, and 50 percent among the religious students.

While I do not know if this indicates a change in the trend, the increasing prominence of the Holocaust in the historical consciousness of young Israelis appears to have declined in the findings of the 2008 study. According to the findings of the 1990 study, the prominence of the Holocaust was still increasing at the time. In my opinion, this is evidence of the important place occupied by the Holocaust in Israeli national consciousness today.[27]

I believe that these results reflect the efforts made by the state socialization system–the political leadership, the state media, and the Israeli education system–to transform the Holocaust into a cornerstone of the Israeli "civil religion." It also reflects the prevalent tendency to regard the Holocaust as a unifying force and a point of consensus within Israeli society.

Some circles within Israeli society– most prominently within the secular sector and the State-Religious sector, among others–believe that the Holocaust should constitute a central element of the Jewish and Zionist education of young Israelis. From their perspective, the fact that the Holocaust occupies a major place in Israeli national consciousness (the "Israeliness" of the Holocaust) and Jewish-Zionist education may help decrease Jewish emigration from Israel and to rectify the lack of clarity surrounding the issue of Zionist education and its results. I believe that the Holocaust provides the content (perhaps the *only* content) accompanying the move from "Israeliness to Jewishness" discussed earlier.

There is no doubt that the attitudes of young Israelis toward the Holocaust have undergone significant changes. While I do not know if these changes have been internalized, there has clearly been a change at least on the declarative level. I am also not certain whether these changes are also indicative of a fundamental change in attitude toward the Jewish people and "exilic" Jewish history.

I find the claim that "everyone was a hero," which is often voiced in the context of the behavior of the Jews during the Holocaust, extremely problematic—just as problematic, lacking in understanding, and alienating as the critical question: "why did they go like lambs to the slaughter?" This claim is indicative of an ahistorical view of the Holocaust, as is the discrepancy between attitudes toward the Holocaust and attitudes toward other periods in Jewish history.

Sociologist Yeshayahu Liebman holds that "Israel is no longer detached from the Diaspora as it once was."[28] I agree that Israel is in fact no longer detached from the Holocaust, because the Holocaust has become a major part of what Liebman refers to as the "civil religion" of the state of Israel. However, young Israelis do remain largely detached from the pre-Holocaust and pre-state Diaspora, and from the history of the Jewish communities around the world during the period following the establishment of the state. Liebman argues that "according to the new civil religion, Israel is the continuation of Jewish history and is directly linked to the hardships of Diaspora Jewry."[29] I argue that young Israelis are "directly linked" to the Holocaust, which they regard as the essence of the overall experience of Jews living among the gentiles. They are not directly linked to Jewish history and the Jewish people of before and after the Holocaust.

The role played by the Holocaust in Israeli consciousness and the consciousness of young Israelis and students continues to grow in scope and intensity and appears to be stable, despite the changes that indicate somewhat of a decline in this trend in the study of 2008. This is also clearly reflected in my studies. At the same time, the phenomenon in itself is indicative of neither a comprehensive and balanced historical consciousness of the many different aspects of the Holocaust, nor an accurate understanding of the event itself. In many ways, it too offers only a partial approach to understanding the Holocaust.

### *Differences in Opinions according to the Variable of Extraction*

I broke down responses to the questions pertaining to the Holocaust, to Jews during the Holocaust period, and to the implications of the Holocaust by extraction. To this end, I delineated three distinctive extraction-based groups:

1) Israeli Extraction—Both parents born in Israel.
2) Eastern Extraction—Both parents born in countries in Asia and Africa.
3) Western Extraction—Both parents born in either Europe or the United States.

My assumption was that any extraction-based differences would emerge primarily along these lines, which together accounted for 71 percent of the 1990 study population. Children of "mixed marriages," which constituted 29 percent of the study population, were not considered in the comparison.[30]

In the 1990 study, no extraction-based differences were found in students' responses to questions relating to the Holocaust. Moreover, students of Eastern extraction actually expressed slightly greater, but statistically insignificant, agreement with the statement "All Jews in the world should see themselves as if they are Holocaust survivors." Eighty-three percent agreed with the statement, in contrast to 80 percent of the students of Western extraction and 78 percent of the students of Israeli extraction.

I also found a small, yet again statistically insignificant difference in the expression of pride. Eighty-six percent of the students from Eastern extraction said they were proud of the behavior of the Jews during the Holocaust, in contrast to 80 percent of the students of Western extraction, and 83 percent of the students of Israeli extraction.

I only found one small, and again statistically insignificant difference indicating otherwise. Seventy-five percent of the subjects of Eastern extraction said they identified with the Jews who suffered during the Holocaust, in contrast to 77 percent of the students of Western extraction and 79 percent of the students of Israeli extraction.

In the 2008 study, I divided respondents into four groups: mixed extraction (one parent of Eastern extraction and one parent of Western extraction); Israeli extraction (both parents born in Israel, regardless of their extraction); Eastern extraction (both parents from Middle Eastern countries); and Western extraction (both parents from Western countries).

When asked to what extent they identified with the Jews who suffered during the Holocaust, respondents' answers could be broken down as follows (differences were found not to be statistically significant):

**TABLE 3.11 Responses to the Question, *"To what extent do you identify with the Jews who suffered during the Holocaust?"* 2008 (as a percentage)**

| | Not At All | Little | Large | Great |
|---|---|---|---|---|
| Mixed Extraction | 2 | 8 | 34 | 56 |
| Israeli Extraction | 1 | 12 | 39 | 48 |
| Eastern Extraction | – | 4 | 45 | 51 |
| Western Extraction | 2 | 7 | 37 | 54 |
| Due to an insufficient number of answers in some of the cells, I was unable to determine whether there was a statistically significant difference. | | | | |

The extraction-based distribution of responses to the statement "all Jews should see themselves as if they are Holocaust survivors" was found to be statistically significant, and it was actually the students of Eastern extraction who expressed the highest level of agreement.

**TABLE 3.12 Agreement with the Statement, *"All Jews should see themselves as if they are Holocaust survivors,"* 2008 (as a percentage)**

| | Do Not Agree | Agree Minimally | Agree | Strongly Agree |
|---|---|---|---|---|
| Mixed Extraction | 26 | 18 | 6 | 50 |
| Israeli Extraction | 19 | 24 | 4 | 53 |
| Eastern Extraction | 14 | 21 | 2 | 63 |
| Western Extraction | 21 | 28 | 8 | 43 |
| $X^2 = 20.36$ | $df = 9$ | | $p > 0.016$ | |

Pride regarding the behavior of the Jews during the period of the Holocaust is widespread throughout all extraction-based groups, with 62 percent among respondents of mixed extraction, 69 percent among respondents of Israeli extraction, 68 percent among respondents of Eastern extraction, and 72 percent among respondents of Western extraction. Although responses to the question of whether the Holocaust constitutes a major aspect of identity were not found to be statistically significant, a large number of respondents indicated that that they think it does. Seventy-one percent of respondents of mixed extraction responded in this manner (45 percent agreed and 26 percent strongly agreed), as did 64 percent of respondents of Israeli extraction (43 percent agreed, and 21 percent strongly agreed), 63 percent of the respondents of Eastern extraction (42 percent agreed, and 21 percent strongly agreed), and 61 percent of respondents of Western extraction (35 percent agreed, and 26 percent strongly agreed).

These findings also confirm my assertion that the Holocaust has in fact become a major component of the Jewish identity of Israelis, regardless of extraction—a component which at the moment serves to unify Israeli society around the idea that "we are Jews because of our suffering" or "we are Jews because of our Holocaust." Identification with victims of the Holocaust has become an accepted norm among Jewish-Israeli high school and university and college students, apparently due, among other things, to the influence of the education system. Nonetheless, differences certainly still exist among opinions on the Holocaust, stemming from the variable of extraction, and I also have no research-based understanding of the opinions of Jewish Israelis coming from lower socioeconomic backgrounds or possessing lower levels of education. These subjects could be explored by means of studies that undertake a more thorough examination of the variable of extraction.

### *Learning and Assessing Knowledge about the Holocaust*

As noted above, I refrained from asking questions assessing the knowledge of respondents based on the premise that knowledge-assessing questions should not be intermingled with questions aimed at assessing attitude. I also did not attempt to examine the manner in which the Holocaust is being taught in the Israeli education system. I did, however, ask respondents to provide information regarding their studies and their own assessment of their personal knowledge about various subjects related to this study. Although the information I received can certainly not be regarded as objectively accurate, it may provide an indication of the degree to which high-schools and institutions of higher education (colleges and universities) have been addressing the subject, as well as how the students assess their own knowledge.

The subjects related to nineteenth- and twentieth-century Jewish history before and after the Holocaust, Zionism, the Arab-Israeli conflict, Israeli society, and Diaspora Jewry are taught much more frequently on the high school level than in colleges and universities. In fact, they are hardly ever taught in institutions of higher education, with some exceptions.[31]

According to the students' responses in the 1990 study, the most commonly taught subjects were Zionism and the Holocaust, followed by the Arab-Israeli conflict (in high schools), which was taught much less frequently. The subject studied least in institutions of higher education was nineteenth-century Jewish history and Diaspora Jewry. Student responses in the 2008 study also indicated that as in 1990, the most widely studied subjects remained the Holocaust and

Zionism, in that order. The Arab-Israeli conflict and Israeli society were taught much less frequently.

Below are findings relating to the extent to which the two most common subjects (the Holocaust and Zionism) are taught, according to responses of the subjects.

**TABLE 3.13 Extent of Instruction on the Holocaust and Zionism at the High School Level, 1990 and 2008 (as a percentage)**

| *"During your high school studies, to what extent did you study the following subjects?"* | | | | |
|---|---|---|---|---|
| **1990** | | | | |
| **The Holocaust** | | | | |
| | 4<br>A Very Large Extent | 3<br>A Large Extent | 2<br>A Small Extent | 1<br>None At All |
| State | 48 | 40 | 10 | 2 |
| State-Religious | 67 | 28 | 4 | – |
| Ultra-Orthodox | 86 | 12 | – | 2 |
| | | | | |
| **Zionism** | | | | |
| | 4<br>A Very Large Extent | 3<br>A Large Extent | 2<br>A Small Extent | 1<br>None At All |
| State | 36 | 48 | 15 | 2 |
| State-Religious | 55 | 31 | 13 | 1 |
| Ultra-Orthodox | 26 | 35 | 35 | 4 |
| | | | | |
| **2008** | | | | |
| **The Holocaust** | | | | |
| | 4<br>A Very Large Extent | 3<br>A Large Extent | 2<br>A Small Extent | 1<br>None At All |
| Religious | 34 | 35 | 22 | 9 |
| Traditional | 54 | 32 | 13 | 1 |
| Non-Religious | 36 | 42 | 21 | 2 |
| | | | | |
| **Zionism** | | | | |
| | 4<br>A Very Large Extent | 3<br>A Large Extent | 2<br>A Small Extent | 1<br>None At All |
| Religious | 31 | 35 | 19 | 15 |
| Traditional | 45 | 34 | 20 | 1 |
| Non-Religious | 28 | 45 | 23 | 3.5 |

It is important to note that the students surveyed in the 1990 study usually attended high schools of the same education sector as the institution of higher education they were attending during the study. According to the responses of the students, the Holocaust was the most widely taught subject of all the subjects I checked in all three education sectors. I also found that the Holocaust and Zionism were taught more in State-Religious high schools than in state high schools. In fact, all the subjects I checked were taught more in State-Religious high schools than in state high schools (with the exception of the Arab-Israeli conflict, which was taught with similar frequency in both sectors).

The data provided by the Ultra-Orthodox sector was particularly interesting. According to student responses, the Holocaust was taught more in the Ultra-Orthodox sector than in the other two sectors, where it is also the most widely studied subject. Although content and methodology for teaching the Holocaust and its implications differed substantially from sector to sector, this was not an issue I studied. nineteenth- and twentieth-century Jewish history before and after the Holocaust and Diaspora Jewry were also taught more frequently in the Ultra-Orthodox sector than in the other two sectors, while Zionism, the Arab-Israeli conflict, and Israeli society were taught much less frequently.[32]

In the 2008 study, the traditional students reported having studied the Holocaust and Zionism more frequently than the religious and non-religious students, and the same picture emerged with regard to the other subjects of study as well.

When I examined the extent to which these subjects were taught within the teacher-training programs, I found that they were taught in the ultra-orthodox sector (albeit to a lesser degree than on the high school level) and that they were hardly taught in the State and State-Religious sectors. Again, the more widely studied subjects in the teaching colleges were Zionism and the Holocaust. My study of students of the Open University also revealed that the students were hardly taught the subjects in question, with the exception of students for whom the subjects constituted their main area of study. According to student responses, the subjects taught—and again, to a minimal extent—were Zionism and the Holocaust.

**TABLE 3.14 Extent of Instruction on the Holocaust and Zionism in Teacher-Training Institutions, 1990 (as a percentage)**

| *"During your post-secondary education, to what extent did you study the following subjects?"* | | | | |
|---|---|---|---|---|
| 1990 | | | | |
| **The Holocaust** | | | | |
| | 4<br>A Very Large Extent | 3<br>A Large Extent | 2<br>A Small Extent | 1<br>None At All |
| State | 17 | 24 | 31 | 28 |
| State-Religious | 5 | 5 | 37 | 53 |
| Ultra-Orthodox | 41 | 5 | 21 | 33 |

| Zionism | | | | |
|---|---|---|---|---|
| | 4<br>A Very Large Extent | 3<br>A Large Extent | 2<br>A Small Extent | 1<br>None At All |
| State | 10 | 22 | 29 | 39 |
| State-Religious | 10 | 10 | 27 | 53 |
| Ultra-Orthodox | 10 | 18 | 18 | 55 |

I also found that the Holocaust and Zionism were taught more frequently in State teaching colleges than in State-Religious teaching colleges. In some colleges of this kind, students cannot receive a teaching certificate without first passing a special seminar on the Holocaust. In both State and Ultra-Orthodox teaching colleges, the Holocaust was the most widely taught subject of all the subjects I checked, while Zionism was the most widely taught subject in the State-Religious teaching colleges.

Within the framework of this study, I was unable to determine the correlation between extent of study and level of knowledge with regard to the subjects in question. In any case, the Holocaust clearly emerges from both studies as the most widely taught subject on both the high school and post-secondary levels. In all three sectors, the Holocaust was also the subject in which students felt they had a very high level of knowledge, in contrast to all the other subjects.

**TABLE 3.15 Knowledge about the Holocaust, According to Respondents' Assessment of Their Level of Knowledge (as a percentage)**

| 1990 | | | | |
|---|---|---|---|---|
| | 4<br>Very Extensive Knowledge | 3<br>Extensive Knowledge | 2<br>Little Knowledge | 1<br>No Knowledge |
| State | 35 | 59 | 6 | 1 |
| State-Religious | 39 | 54 | 7 | – |
| Ultra-Orthodox | 72 | 23 | 5 | – |
| | | | | |
| **2008** | | | | |
| | 4<br>Very Extensive Knowledge | 3<br>Extensive Knowledge | 2<br>Little Knowledge | 1<br>No Knowledge |
| Religious | 36 | 47 | 17 | – |
| Traditional | 28 | 56 | 15 | 1 |
| Non-Religious | 28 | 54 | 18 | – |

TABLE 3.16 Knowledge about Zionism, According to Respondents' Assessment of Their Level of Knowledge (as a percentage)

| 1990 | | | | |
|---|---|---|---|---|
| | 4<br>Very Extensive Knowledge | 3<br>Extensive Knowledge | 2<br>Little Knowledge | 1<br>No Knowledge |
| State | 25 | 49 | 26 | – |
| State-Religious | 29 | 51 | 19 | 1 |
| Ultra-Orthodox | 30 | 36 | 30 | 4.5 |
| | | | | |
| 2008 | | | | |
| | 4<br>Very Extensive Knowledge | 3<br>Extensive Knowledge | 2<br>Little Knowledge | 1<br>No Knowledge |
| Religious | 31 | 47 | 22 | – |
| Traditional | 15 | 50 | 32 | 3 |
| Non-Religious | 14 | 46 | 37 | 3 |

As I have noted, the students' assessment of their own knowledge should not be regarded as an objective criterion. In fact, I strongly believe that their actual level of knowledge is lower than they think it is, and sometimes significantly so. It is also important to consider the great significance of what it means to "know" about the Holocaust. When students say that they know something about the Holocaust, what do they mean? In any event, it is clear that the students in both studies regard the Holocaust as the subject in which they are most knowledgeable.

My intention here is not to say that the Holocaust is taught too much, but rather to draw attention to the imbalance between the extent to which the Holocaust is taught (and perhaps the resulting level of knowledge) and the study of other subject areas and events in pre- and post-Holocaust modern and contemporary Jewish history, which are not taught and about which students know much less.

There may be a correlation between teaching and knowledge and between knowledge and opinions and attitudes, although establishing this would require further research. Lack of knowledge and lack of opinion (for example, regarding Jewish life in the Shtetl, as discussed in the previous chapter) may place the Holocaust outside of historical, Jewish, and general contexts, and this may result in incorrect generalizations, stereotypes, and emphases in young Israelis' attitudes toward the Holocaust and its implications.

It is precisely because of its centrality in Jewish identity that this lack of balance is so important. The substance of Holocaust instruction should also be considered—something I did not do within the framework of the present study. For example, do we and should we be teaching about the extermination of "the other victims" of the Holocaust (this is problematic terminology from a number of perspectives—"other" with reference to whom?): the non-Jewish victims of the Nazi regime such as Gypsies, homosexuals, political prisoners, Russian prisoners of war, the mentally ill, and Jehovah's Witnesses? Based on my assessments, we can assume that these cases of mass murders are hardly taught.

Finally, most subjects related to modern Jewish history are hardly taught in colleges and universities, except within the framework of specific academic departments. They are taught much more frequently on the high school level. This fact enables me to conclude that Israeli teachers—at least those trained in colleges—and the vast majority of university students acquired the little knowledge they have about subjects related to modern Jewish history and Jewish identity when they were in high school. I believe that what they learned in high school a number of years ago does not constitute sufficient training for teachers who will soon be shaping the consciousness and identity of the Israeli students of the future.

Students reported having learned about the Holocaust primarily in the following frameworks: history lessons in school; programs for Holocaust and Heroism Memorial Days; and visits to Holocaust memorial museums. They learned much less during conferences, individual lectures, and their university and college studies (trips to Poland were not offered as an option in this context).

Of the total 2008 study population, 73 percent believed (46 percent agreed, and 27 percent strongly agreed) that the Holocaust should influence the political decisions of the state of Israel. Sixty-nine percent, a slightly lower percentage, believed (40 percent agreed, and 29 percent strongly agreed) that the Holocaust should play a larger role in the life of the state. Seventy percent of the religious respondents agreed with this position, as did 80 percent of the traditional respondents and 66 percent of the non-religious respondents.

Eighty-one percent, an even higher percentage (37 percent agreed, and 44 percent strongly agreed), believed that as many teens as possible should visit the death camps in Poland. Interestingly, the religious students were less supportive of the trips to Poland (64 percent) than the non-religious (82 percent) and traditional students (89 percent). The students believed that the Holocaust should be a major component—*the* major component—of the identity of the state (and of young Israelis). It appears that few of them have encountered Yehuda Elkana's short, controversial and ever so important article "The Need to Forget," from which I again quote: "Symbolically speaking, two people left Auschwitz: a minority, insisting that 'it would never happen again' and a frightened majority insisting that 'it would never happen to us again.'" (Haaretz, 2 March 1988). Israeli society moves between the universal and Jewish memories of the Holocaust, and the particularist Jewish approach appears to be gaining strength. The attitudes toward the role of the Holocaust in the life of the state and the Jewish identity of its citizens expressed by most of the students surveyed in both studies reflect the positions of the educational and political establishment.

## The *Nakba* and Me

### *Introduction*

Palestinians both inside and outside Israel sometimes relate to their tragedy, the *Nakba,* in similar, though not identical terms to those they use when discussing the Jewish Holocaust. They typically use the term "Nakba," meaning "tragedy" or "catastrophe," to refer to what happened to them in 1948 (they refer to the Jewish Holocaust as "al-Karisa"). Many Palestinians object to the fact that the Nakba is hardly taught in schools in Israel. While emphasizing the fundamental difference between the Holocaust and the Nakba, it is nonetheless important to remember that a great sense of victimization plays a major role in both Arab Israeli and Jewish Israeli society. Beyond the very real pain and memory related to these two events, both societies make manipulative political use of the tragedies that befell them.

The fundamental question we need to ask ourselves in this context with regard to Israel's Arab citizens is whether it is important that young Arabs growing up and being educated in Israel learn about the Holocaust, and if so, why? Is it important that they learn about the Nakba? At the same time, we must ask ourselves whether young Jewish Israelis who are already studying the Holocaust should also learn about the Nakba.

In practice, Arab schools in Israel teach the Holocaust, and they do so from a primarily Jewish-Zionist perspective. So far, there have been no studies that can help us assess how this manner of instruction has impacted young Arabs and their attitude toward Jews. As I have said, we do not even know for certain how the teaching of the Holocaust influences the way members of Jewish society in Israel see themselves. We also have no research-based understanding of how the Holocaust influences these societies' attitudes toward one another, or how the Holocaust influences the way in which both societies view the Arab-Israeli conflict. In the same way, we do not understand the practical significance (for either society) of the fact that, as we will see, the Palestinians living inside and outside of Israel relate to their tragedy as an event with formative influence.

Ilan Gur-Zeev and Ilan Pappe discuss each nationality's attitude toward the national memory of the "other" in their article "Palestinian Control of the Memories of the Holocaust and the Nakba."[33] Gur-Zeev and Pappe argue that the central streams in Zionism continued denying the Nakba and systematically denying Israel's role in Palestinian suffering. In their opinion, this affected the Palestinian perception of the Holocaust as well as of the Nakba. The Palestinian response incorporates differing and at times contradictory positions on the Holocaust, including complete denial; indifference; recognition that it took place but minimization of its scope and moral significance; and complete recognition of the event and its moral and universal implications as a unique phase in the history of human evil. The authors of the article hope it will be possible to conduct a critical Israeli-Palestinian dialogue that is free of ethnocentricity and that can address the unique memory of each group, as well as that of the "other."

For years, both Jews and Arabs have incorrectly contextualized the subject of the Holocaust within the ongoing debate surrounding the Jewish-Palestinian conflict. This has usually resulted in the distortion of historical facts on both sides. This dangerous combination of national issues better illustrates the need for serious, in-depth research on the subject, and perhaps on those aspects related to teaching.

In any event, this sense of victimization constitutes an important component of the identity of both Palestinians (living inside and outside the state of Israel) and Israeli and non-Israeli Jews. This fact must be recognized by all those working on the question of Arab attitudes toward the Holocaust who aim to encourage the evolution of new attitudes on the subject.

As of today, students in the upper grades of Arab high schools in Israel are obligated to study a one-half unit course on the history of the Jewish people in the modern era (approximately 45 hours of instruction), approximately half of which deals with the Holocaust. Arab students are also exposed to the subject during their studies on twentieth-century Europe, and can opt for an expanded, five-unit program in history and choose the Holocaust as an elective, although few actually do so. This may stem in part from the absence of a suitable Arab language textbook on the subject. The lack of interest in the Holocaust as a subject of study among Arab high school students might also have to do with the currently deteriorating relations between Jews and Arabs. As administered today, we have no way of knowing if instruction on the Holocaust in Arab schools draws young Arabs closer to the subject and to Jewish Israelis, or if it actually increases the distance and exacerbates the tension.

In her book *Consistent Violence, 1947–1950,* Ariella Azoulay observes that despite the changes that have taken place in recent years, the Nakba is still perceived by Jewish Israelis as something that happened in 1948 to "them," while the Jews have their own story.[34]

The chapter titled "Arabs and the Holocaust" in David Grossman's book *Present Absentees* also offers a depressing picture.[35] Grossman asked Arab students if they feel that Jews in Israel treat them as the Germans treated the Jews:

> The youngsters did not hesitate. Voices of agreement could be heard from all directions. When I pointed out that Israel is not trying to exterminate the Palestinian people, not for racist reasons and not for other reasons, a boy named Naim shouted at me: "It's exactly the same thing

> here and there. The same thing—Israel wants to get rid of the Palestinians, to exterminate us."
>
> He thought for a moment, and then continued: "O.K., maybe not us physically, but our spirit. It wants to exterminate our history and our literature, and to prevent us from studying our national poets! They are exterminating us morally." He continued in a harsh tone: "They want us to assimilate into society, to be Israelis, to detach ourselves from the other Arab peoples and to forget the meaning of Palestinian! You don't see that as extermination?"[36]

We must hope that any future curriculum will deal seriously with these accusations and account for the unique needs of the Arab population in Israel. Since Grossman wrote the above words in 1992, the Ministry of Education has done nothing to change the situation. Unfortunately, not even the welcome program initiated by the Greek Catholic Priest Father Shufani and the Palestinians was continued, and the chances of any significant change in Israeli government policy in the foreseeable future are extremely slim.

In 1948, more than 400 Arab villages were destroyed, and their hundreds of thousands of Palestinian inhabitants became refugees. The same was true for the majority of the Arab population of 11 cities and towns, which were also mostly or completely depopulated of their Palestinian Arab population. Not only did these villages disappear from the landscape, but they were relegated to the margins of Israeli discourse as well. This was accomplished in part by the erasure or Hebraization of their names and their removal or obfuscation on official maps. At the same time, information disseminated at nearby tourist sites simply ignored their existence and the circumstances surrounding their depopulation, and the Jewish settlements established in their place accepted their dispossession. Underlying this act of erasure, there is almost certainly a unique ideology impacting civil consciousness, among other things.[37] Recent years have witnessed what appears to be the beginnings of an alternative discourse regarding the shaping of memory and space in Israel and the events of the Nakba.[38]

There are numerous estimates regarding the actual number of Palestinian Arabs who became refugees in 1948. According to Noga Kadman, Israeli sources refer to 520,000, while Arab sources place the number at 900,000. Benny Morris speaks of a range of 600,000 to 760,000.[39] I intend to return to this subject in the future.

I asked Jewish students only one question on the Nakba, and I asked Arab students only two. Without a doubt, my study is severely underdeveloped from this perspective. At the same time, however, I asked both the Jewish and Arab students a large number of questions dealing with the Holocaust. My conclusion is that, regardless of the historical facts of the two events, which are certainly not identical, the two rival national groups have turned the Holocaust on the one hand, and the Nakba on the other hand, into primary formative events. Still, I emphasize that, although the Nakba may have involved elements of ethnic cleansing in different parts of the country, it certainly was not an instance of genocide.[40]

I believe that the Palestinians are partially responsible for their tragedy and may even be somewhat to blame for what befell them in 1948. However, we, the Jewish Israelis, were the instigators. I believe that until Jews and Palestinians recognize and respect each other's tragedy, there can be no chance of reconciliation between the two peoples. Certainly, mutual recognition of each group's tragedy is not the only condition for reconciliation, but it is a necessary precondition. It is also important to acknowledge the fact that Jewish Israelis currently have a much greater ability to change the present situation. As the majority group, the power is in their hands.

### *Arab Students' Opinions on the Holocaust*

This sub-section discusses my findings regarding Arab students' opinions on the Holocaust, and I begin with the lessons of the Holocaust as they perceive them. I presented the Arab students with the same ten lessons which I presented to the Jewish students. These lessons were divided into three categories: Zionist lessons, Jewish lessons, and universal lessons. The Arab students expressed a low level of agreement with the Zionist lessons and some of the Jewish lessons. Most did not agree (strongly disagree and agree minimally combined) with the Zionist lessons: "the existence of a strong, sovereign, well established Jewish state is a crucial necessity" (84 percent disagreed), and "it is not safe in the Diaspora" (73 percent disagreed). The Zionist lessons enjoyed a high level of agreement among the Jewish students, with the lesson regarding the necessity of a strong sovereign Jewish state enjoying the highest level of all.

The Arab students rejected the Jewish lessons of the Holocaust as well. They opposed the statement "there is a necessity for Jewish unity, self-defense, and reliance on ourselves alone" (83 percent) more than the statement "we need to be aware of all manifestations of anti-Semitism and to fight them as soon as they appear" (only 35 percent opposed the statement, in contrast to 65 percent who supported it).

It should be noted, however, that Arab students expressed an extremely high level of *agreement* with the universal lessons of the Holocaust. Seventy-nine percent of the Arab students surveyed agreed with the lesson "it is necessary to fight against anti-democratic phenomenon." This was slightly less than the percentage of Jewish students who agreed with the same statement. Students expressed a particularly high level of agreement with the lesson "it is necessary to defend the rights of minorities everywhere in the world," with 85 percent expressing strong agreement (the most unequivocal response), and 97 percent expressing agreement in general. This was higher than the level of agreement expressed by Jewish students (84 percent of the non-religious students agreed with the statement, as did 86 percent of the traditional students and 64 percent of the religious students). In this way, Arab students rejected the Zionist lessons and some of the

Jewish lessons of the Holocaust and agreed with the universal lessons. It seems possible that their unequivocal support for defending minority rights throughout the world is related to their own, ongoing experience. In any event, the level of overall Arab agreement with this statement was higher than the level expressed in each of the Jewish student sub-groups.

For some of the statements, the differences between the Arab sub-groups were not statistically significant, while for others, they were ($P < 0.05$). Table 3.17 reflects the responses of the Arab students.

**TABLE 3.17 Level of Agreement with Lessons of the Holocaust among Arab Students, 2008 (as a percentage)**

| | Disagree | Agree Slightly | Agree | Strongly Agree |
|---|---|---|---|---|
| 1) All Jews in the Diaspora must move to Israel. | 51 | 33 | 14 | 2 |
| 2) The existence of a strong, sovereign, well established Jewish state is a crucial necessity. | 34 | 26 | 31 | 9 |
| 3) It is not safe in the Diaspora. | 40 | 33 | 18 | 9 |
| 4) There is a necessity for Jewish unity, self-defense, and reliance on ourselves alone. | 63 | 20 | 12 | 5 |
| 5) We need to be aware of all manifestations of anti-Semitism and to fight them as soon as they appear. | 10 | 25 | 33 | 32 |
| 6) It is necessary to fight against anti-Democratic phenomena. | 9 | 12 | 25 | 54 |
| 7) It is necessary to defend the rights of minorities everywhere in the world. | 1 | 2 | 12 | 85 |
| 8) Human beings are primarily negative in nature. | 35 | 32 | 17 | 16 |

I also asked the Arab students if they agreed with the sentence: "All Jews in the world should see themselves as if they are Holocaust survivors." Their responses were as follows:

**TABLE 3.18 Agreement with the Statement, *"All Jews in the world should see themselves as if they are Holocaust survivors,"* 2008 (as a percentage)**

| Yes, I agree with the sentence. | I agree with the sentence in the case of Jews who came from Europe. | I agree with the sentence only in the case of people who were there. | No, I do not agree with the sentence. |
|---|---|---|---|
| 10 | 8 | 39 | 43 |

Although the level of agreement with the sentence expressed by the Jewish students surveyed in the 2008 study was lower than in the 1990 study, it was nonetheless considerably higher than the agreement expressed by the Arab students. This was a finding that I anticipated.

My research did not investigate the issue of Holocaust denial directly, and in retrospect it appears that this is an issue about which I should have inquired. However, based on the Arab students' responses to the various questions, their high level of agreement with the universal lessons of the Holocaust, and their identification with Jews who suffered during the Holocaust, this phenomenon did not appear to be widespread.

However, in May 2009, Sammy Smooha published his index of Jewish-Arab relations for 2008, which found, among other things, that 40.5 percent of the Arab citizens of Israel claim that the Holocaust never happened. This finding, which represented an increase in the percentage of denial from 28 percent in 2006, was widely covered by the Israeli media. According to Smooha, Holocaust denial cuts across sectors within the Arab population and is espoused by 37.1 percent of those with high school educations and 56.4 percent of the Negev Bedouin.

Smooha's research question regarding the Holocaust read as follows: "I believe that there was a Holocaust in which the Nazis murdered millions of Jews." Possible responses included: disagree; inclined to disagree; inclined to agree; and agree. This phrasing was translated into Arabic, and 40.5 percent of the Arab citizens of Israel disagreed or were inclined to disagree. Prof. Smooha does not interpret the responses as Holocaust denial in the Western sense of the phenomenon, but rather as a form of opposition or protest.

If Holocaust denial is widespread among Arab Israelis, this also reflects a failure of the Israeli education system, which has never paid sufficient attention to this important issue. Instead of trying to teach Arab students about the Holocaust from a Jewish-Zionist perspective, it would have been more effective to teach them the subject from a universal perspective.

I also asked Arab students if they thought "we should aspire to send as many Arab teens from Israel as possible to visit the death camps in Poland." As we have seen, thousands of Jewish Israeli teens travel to Poland each year to visit the death camps, and there is a great deal of debate surrounding this issue. A small number of Arab teens have also visited the camps in Poland, including some attending Jewish schools and others participating in joint trips. A small majority of the religious and traditional Arab students did not agree that Arab teens should participate in such trips, but most of the non-religious students agreed with the statement (75 percent). A considerable portion of Arab students support participation in such trips.

**TABLE 3.19 Responses of Arab Students to the Statement, *"We should aspire to send as many Arab teens from Israel as possible to visit the death camps in Poland,"* 2008 (as a percentage)**

| | Disagree | Slightly Agree | Agree | Strongly Agree |
|---|---|---|---|---|
| Religious | 30 | 27 | 36 | 7 |
| Traditional | 24 | 21 | 26 | 29 |
| Non-Religious | 12 | 13 | 56 | 19 |
| I could not determine whether there was a statistically significant difference due to the insufficient number of responses in some of the cells. | | | | |

In addition to the above questions, I asked Arab students a number of other questions about the Holocaust and one more question about the Nakba. Both Jewish and Arab students were asked: "To what extend do you identify with the Jews who suffered during the Holocaust?"

**TABLE 3.20 Responses of Arab Students to the Question, *"To what extent do you identify with the Jews who suffered during the Holocaust?"* 2008 (as a percentage)**

| | No | Slightly | Yes | Extremely |
|---|---|---|---|---|
| Religious | 9 | 29 | 41 | 21 |
| Traditional | 5 | 20 | 25 | 50 |
| Non-Religious | 6 | 16 | 39 | 39 |
| I could not determine whether there was a statistically significant difference due to the insufficient number of responses in some of the cells. | | | | |

As we can see, most of the Arab students identified with the suffering of the Jews during the Holocaust, with the non-religious and traditional students expressing greater identification than the religious.

Both Jewish and Arab students were asked two questions about the role of the Holocaust in Israeli public life, and whether the holocaust should influence the decisions of the state of Israel (see table 3.21).

**TABLE 3.21 Responses of Arab students to the Statement, *"The Holocaust plays an excessively major role in the public life of the state of Israel,"* 2008 (as a percentage)**

| | Definitely Not | No | Yes | Yes, Definitely |
|---|---|---|---|---|
| Religious | – | 21 | 45 | 33 |
| Traditional | 8 | 23 | 31 | 38 |
| Non-Religious | – | 18 | 59 | 23 |
| It was not possible to determine whether there was a statistically significant difference due to the insufficient number of responses in some of the cells. | | | | |

In this context, I also asked Arab students whether, in their opinion, "the Holocaust should influence the political decisions of the state of Israel."

**TABLE 3.22 Responses of Arab students to the Statement, *"The Holocaust should influence the political decisions of the state of Israel,"* 2008 (as a percentage)**

| | Definitely Not | No | Yes | Yes, Definitely |
|---|---|---|---|---|
| Religious | 21 | 49 | 18 | 12 |
| Traditional | 23 | 54 | 8 | 15 |
| Non-Religious | 12 | 59 | 6 | 23 |
| It was not possible to determine whether there was a statistically significant difference due to the insufficient number of responses in some of the cells. | | | | |

This question suffered from a degree of ambiguity for both Arab and Jewish students. After all, if the Holocaust can serve to generate different types of lessons, then it can also influence political decisions in different directions, encouraging intensification of Zionist, Jewish, and national values on the one hand, and the strengthening of universal principles on the other hand.

**TABLE 3.23 Extent of Instruction of the Listed Subjects in High Schools, Responses of Arab Students, 2008 (as a percentage)**

| | A Great Deal | A Small Amount |
|---|---|---|
| History of the Arab Nation | 56 | 44 |
| History of Islam | 67 | 33 |
| The Holocaust | 39 | 61 |
| Zionism | 43 | 57 |
| The Nakba | 27 | 73 |
| Arab-Israeli Conflict | 46 | 54 |
| Israeli Society | 54 | 46 |
| Palestinian History | 29 | 71 |

These tables reflect the fact that the Arab students learned more about the Holocaust and Zionism than about the Nakba. According to their own assessments, they learned about the Holocaust a great deal (response 3 and 4 [a large amount and a very large amount] combined) during history classes (47 percent), memorial day programs (29 percent [a large amount]), various university lectures (30 percent), visits to museums (23 percent), and conferences and individual lectures (18 percent).

**TABLE 3.24 Extent that Arab students Learned about the Holocaust in High School, 2008 (as a percentage)**

| | No | A Small Amount | A Large Amount | A Very Large Amount |
|---|---|---|---|---|
| Religious | 18 | 38 | 29 | 15 |
| Traditional | 12 | 49 | 19 | 20 |
| Non-Religious | 11 | 61 | 6 | 22 |
| It was not possible to determine whether there was a statistically significant difference due to the insufficient number of responses in some of the cells. | | | | |

**TABLE 3.25 Extent that Arab students Learned about the Nakba in High School, 2008 (as a percentage)**

| | No | A Small Amount | A Large Amount | A Very Large Amount |
|---|---|---|---|---|
| Religious | 18 | 49 | 24 | 9 |
| Traditional | 33 | 41 | 10 | 16 |
| Non-Religious | 47 | 35 | 6 | 12 |
| It was not possible to determine whether there was a statistically significant difference due to the insufficient number of responses in some of the cells. | | | | |

These findings are not surprising for anyone familiar with the educational realities within Arab schools in Israel. According to the Arab students, they were not taught Palestinian history (71 percent studied it minimally or not at all) and the Nakba (73 percent studied it minimally or not at all).

### *Opinions of Arab and Jewish Students on Teaching the Nakba*

> "Lies, my guts shouted. Khirbet Khizeh is not ours. The Spandau gun never gave us any rights. Oh, my guts screamed. What hadn't they told us about refugees. Everything, everything was for the refugees, their welfare, their rescue—our refugees, naturally. Those we were driving out—that was a totally different matter. Wait. Two thousand years of exile. The whole story. Jews being killed. Europe. We were masters now."
>
> —S. Yizhar, *Khirbet Khizeh*, May 1949

Yizhar's cry was too painful for a society emerging in the midst of war. The television broadcast of Ram Levy's 1978 film adaptation of Yizhar's novella also aroused public and political controversy. Today, it seems that many young Israelis have no idea what it is all about.

**TABLE 3.26 Level of Agreement that Jewish and Arab Citizens of Israel Should Learn and Know the History of the Nakba, Arab Students, 2008** (as a percentage)

| | Disagree | Slightly Agree | Strongly Agree | Very Strongly Agree |
|---|---|---|---|---|
| Religious | – | 3 | 40 | 57 |
| Traditional | 5 | 16 | 16 | 63 |
| Non-Religious | – | 22 | 45 | 33 |
| It was not possible to determine whether there was a statistically significant difference due to the insufficient number of responses in some of the cells. | | | | |

A large percentage of traditional and non-religious Jewish students (79 percent of each group) agreed that the Nakba should be studied. However, the percentage of agreement was much lower among religious Jewish students (38 percent). The high level of agreement expressed by the Jewish students was surprising. The belief that Jews and Arabs should learn and know the history of the Nakba was of course higher among the Arab students, 86 percent of whom expressed agreement (31 percent holding that it is very important, and 55 percent that it is important). Agreement with this point was high within all Arab sub-groups.

Although I asked Arab students a significant number of questions pertaining to the Holocaust and only two questions pertaining to the Nakba, I asked Jewish students only one question regarding the Nakba: "To what extent do you think it is important that Jewish and Arab citizens of Israel learn about the history of the Nakba?"

As we know, the Nakba is not taught within the Jewish education sectors in Israel and is taught only minimally within the Arab education sector. In the fall of 2009, the Zalman Shazar Center published a history textbook titled *Building a State in the Middle East* that was intended for eleventh and twelfth graders. In October 2009, the Ministry of Education ordered that all copies of the book be removed from bookstores because, among other things, it explains the meaning of Nakba, and uses the term "ethnic cleansing." The book was the first to present the Palestinian and the Jewish-Israeli narratives side-by-side. The book was collected from the stores and will be redistributed only after they are revised.[41] Although I have not investigated this point, it is nonetheless reasonable to assume that young Israelis and Israeli students know extremely little about the Nakba. I was therefore surprised by the high percentage of positive responses I received from non-religious and traditional Jewish students regarding learning about the Nakba.

**TABLE 3.27 Level of Agreement that Jewish and Arab Citizens of Israel Should Learn and Know the History of the Nakba, Jewish Students, 2008** (as a percentage)

| | Extremely Unimportant | Unimportant | Important | Very Important |
|---|---|---|---|---|
| Religious | 38 | 24 | 30 | 8 |
| Traditional | 8 | 13 | 45 | 34 |
| Non-Religious | 6 | 15 | 53 | 26 |
| $X^2 = 82.46$ | $df = 6$ | | $P < 0.0001$ | |

As we see, traditional and non-religious Jews expressed a high level of support for teaching about the Nakba (79 percent and 78 percent respectively), while religious students expressed a much lower level of support (38 percent). The vast majority of the Arab students indicated that they believe that it is either important or very important for Jewish and Arab citizens of Israel to learn about the history of the Nakba. They also reported (with no sector-based differences) that, while they learned about the Holocaust in high school, they learned almost nothing about the Nakba (see table 3.27).

The differences between the religion-based sub-groups were not found to be statistically significant. While in high school, the Arab students learned very little, and, in some cases, nothing at all about the Nakba.

In this context, the "Haifa Declaration" of May 15, 2007 is of extreme importance. The Haifa Declaration is one of three documents issued by Palestinian citizens of Israel in recent years (the other two are the "Future Vision of the Palestinian Arabs in Israel" and the "Democratic Constitution"). The Haifa Declaration makes explicit reference to both the Nakba and the Holocaust. It opens by recalling the Nakba and casting it as a "formative event" and a "historic injustice." Later, it explains: "Our citizenship and our relationship to the State of Israel are defined, to a great extent, by a formative event, the Nakba . … This was the event through which we—who remained from among the original inhabitants of our homeland[42]—were made citizens without the genuine constituents of citizenship, especially equality."

The Declaration emphasizes that reconciliation between the Palestinian population and Jewish population of the state of Israel "requires the state of Israel to recognize the historical injustice that it committed against the Palestinian people through its establishment, to accept responsibility for the Nakba, which befell all parts of the Palestinian people, and also for the war crimes and crimes of occupation that it has committed in the Occupied Territories." The Declaration recognizes the right of the Jewish people of Israel to self-determination and to live in peace, security, and dignity alongside the Palestinian people and the other peoples in the region.

The Declaration also speaks explicitly about the Holocaust:

> We are aware of the tragic history of the Jews in Europe, which reached its peak in one of the most horrific human crimes, in the Holocaust perpetrated by the Nazis against the Jews, and we are fully cognizant of the tragedies that the survivors have lived through. We sympathize with the victims of the Holocaust, those who perished and those who survived.
>
> We believe that exploiting this tragedy and its consequences in order to legitimize the right of the Jews to establish a state at the expense of the Palestinian people serves to belittle universal, human, and moral lessons to be learned from this catastrophic event, which concerns the whole of humanity.

I conclude this section by stating that the Holocaust constitutes a major component, and in many ways *the* major component, of Jewish students' identity in general and Jewish identity in particular, and that the Nakba constitutes a major component, and in many ways *the* major component, of the identity of the Palestinian students.

The variable of religiosity was found to have a greater impact on the responses of the Jewish students than the variable of extraction. At the same time, however, my study population cannot be regarded as representative of Israeli society as a whole, as the fact that they are students appears to have significantly influenced their opinions. It is also clearly necessary to assess the influence of the Poland trips and the Israeli education system in this context, though I was unable to do so due to the already large size of the questionnaire.

In any event, it seems clear that reconciliation cannot take place until both peoples recognize the intensity of the tragedy experienced by the other, alongside the trauma that they have suffered themselves. In the meantime, however, reconciliation appears to be as far away as ever, and we are doing painfully little to move forward in the process.

Unfortunately, Israeli textbooks on the history of the twentieth century and the history of nations in the modern era (and almost all books that explore Holocaust instruction in depth) make little or no mention of the Gypsy genocide. In fact, all the non-Jewish victims of the Nazi regime—Gypsies, homosexuals, political prisoners, the mentally ill and physically handicapped, Jehovah's Witnesses, Poles, and Russian prisoners of war—who are sometimes referred to collectively as "the other victims," are mentioned only in passing and sometimes not at all. The Armenian genocide is also barely mentioned, despite the fact that the historical context of the genocide—World War I—is covered in detail. We should therefore not be surprised by my findings which indicate a frighteningly high level of ignorance in Israel regarding instances of genocide perpetrated against other peoples. For instance, in a survey conducted in 1996 among more than

800 B.A. students in seven colleges and universities throughout Israel, students reported knowing virtually nothing about the Armenian and Gypsy genocides. This finding obligates us to dedicate serious thought to this matter.

## *On the Equal Value of Human Life*

In 1997, Jean-Michel Chaumont published a book in France entitled *La Concurrence de Victimes—Génocide, Identité, Reconnaissance* (The Concurrence of Victims: Genocide, Identity, Recognition). The book has three sections: "the time of shame" (1945–1967), "the time of pride" (1967 and onward), and "dilemmas of recognition" (of the crime and tragedy that befell a person or his group of belonging).[43] The book, which sparked substantial debate across Europe, analyzes the role of the Holocaust in defining Jewish self-identity in Europe, Israel, and the United States. In the introduction, Chaumont writes:

> As to the victims of the Nazis, nothing is managed properly. Under an external veil of consensus, slogans such as "never again," "the sacred obligation to remember," and "the struggle against anti-Semitism and racial intolerance," strong differences divide the groups of victims of the Third Reich on the issue of memory: Jewish deportees against underground fighters, Jews against Gypsies, homosexuals against political prisoners, antifascist Jews against Zionists. The lists of confrontations and counterarguments is long and goes beyond the crimes of the National Socialists, especially in the United States where it involves a myriad of groups such as Jews against Armenians, Jews against blacks, Jews against native-Americans, and even Jews against Tutsis, and others ...[44]

Chaumont's words help us better understand the pointed debates that have gone on for more than thirty years, both in Israel and throughout the Jewish world, regarding cases of genocide that have befallen other peoples. At the center of these debates lies the controversial assertion that the Holocaust was a completely unique event, despite the fact that the Holocaust's special importance for the Jews is actually unrelated to its uniqueness as a genocide which did indeed differ in nature from other genocides: The Holocaust was an industry of death based on racist theory and ideology, which sought to exterminate all members of the Jewish people, wherever they may have been. Its special importance is found in its problematic role in the Jewish historical consciousness in which it is supposed to play a decisive role, as it goes without saying that a crime perpetrated against a person or a group always constitutes an important, and usually primary, component of the victim's personal consciousness and worldview. In some cases, lack of recognition emerges as a decisive aspect of efforts to deal with the tragedy and to bring about rehabilitation, which may continue for long periods of time or indefinitely. In this context, we recall Primo Levy's account of camp prisoners who had nightmares of returning home to relatives who did not believe their story.

In this context, it is incumbent upon us to consider the following challenging questions: How do we relate to the just demands of other victims that the murderers, or the heirs of the murderers, acknowledge the crimes committed? How do we relate to the victims' demand that the world recognize the acts of genocide perpetrated against them? How do we relate to their demand that the state of Israel recognize the crimes committed against them? One current example is our response to the semi-justified claim that Israel is providing the Turks with direct and/or indirect assistance in their efforts to deny the genocide they committed against the Armenians.[45]

Clearly, young Israelis should have greater knowledge about the Holocaust than about the tragedies that have befallen other peoples. After all, the Holocaust happened to their people, to them. Nonetheless, the fact that Israel is a nation of survivors and that the Holocaust plays such a major role in Israeli national identity should also make us more sensitive to the tragedies of other peoples.

Some people are opposed to exposing young Israelis to other cases of genocide, as this could ostensibly detract from the uniqueness of the Holocaust in their consciousness and encourage a relativistic approach to the subject—that is, a view that sees the Holocaust as one of many genocides, thus reducing its significance in human history. In contrast, others argue that the Israeli education system places excessive, inaccurate, extreme, and almost exclusive focus on the Jewish victims, while ignoring (whether consciously or subconsciously, or intentionally or unintentionally) prominent and lesser known genocides that have taken place in the course of human history in general and during the twentieth century in particular.

Student awareness of the Nakba and students' attitudes toward learning about the subject are important. I again emphasize that I do not think that the Nakba was a Holocaust or a genocide, but rather a terrible tragedy and formative event for the Palestinians. The Nakba is not taught in the Israeli education system and, as far as I know (although I did not assess the issue directly), remains a relatively unknown subject among its Jewish graduates. My study also shows that the Nakba is taught very little in Arab schools. In this context, it is encouraging to note the responses of Jewish students, who expressed broad support for teaching Jewish and Arab citizens of Israel about the history of the Nakba (79 percent of the traditional and non-religious students surveyed). Nonetheless, it appears highly unlikely that either the Israeli political system or the education ministers of the state of Israel will agree to such a project at any time in the near future.

As we cope with the Nakba, we return to the terrible moment at which the victim of injustice becomes either the perpetrator of injustice or someone who looks on and does nothing. For Jewish Israelis, whose identity is based to such a large degree on a sense of victimization, this is a difficult but extremely important process. Individuals and nations can be both perpetrators and victims, and this duality is in no way exclusive. It should be remembered that in July 2007, the Israeli Ministry of Education authorized use of the concept *Nakba,* which until that point had been prohibited (although this prohibition had not been enforced). As part of the intellectual change within the Education Ministry, Arab schools were authorized to use a book containing the word *Nakba* and a summary of the Palestinian version of the establishment of Israel, alongside the official Israeli version, which emphasizes that it was the Arabs who rejected the UN partition plan.

After the elections and the transfer of power to the Netanyahu government in 2009, things began to move in the opposite direction. The current government supports the "Prohibition of Commemorating Independence Day as a Day of Mourning Bill," which at the time of this writing in February 2010, was still in the process of legislation in the Knesset. The aim of this bill was to prohibit the commemoration of the Nakba on May 14, the day on which Israeli statehood was declared. The amended version of the bill aims to prevent organizations that commemorate the Nakba from receiving state funds. I regard this as a crude attempt to use the law to control individual and collective memory and to shape it in a tendentious manner. Education Minister Gideon Saar also instructed that all mention of the word *Nakba* (which is minimal as it is) be removed from textbooks.

However, the Palestinians too must abandon sweeping, one-sided accusations and reassess their own role in the Nakba. At the same time, they must try to understand the very real and ongoing significance of the Holocaust for Jewish society in Israel and Jewish communities around the world.[46]

In order to overcome the problems arising from these two approaches, some suggest emphasizing the uniqueness of the Holocaust by comparing it to other instances of genocide, thus ensuring that students learn more about the Holocaust while at the same time compelling their historical consciousness to consider other cases of genocide. Incorporating this missing aspect, they argue, will help us explore "our" Holocaust from a broader, more comprehensive, and more accurate perspective, with regard to the Jewish experience in particular and the overall human experience in general.

An important force in the shaping of the historical consciousness of all societies is each society's approach to what it can know and what it wants to know about its own history and the history of others. Acknowledging and addressing the marked absence of other instances of genocide from our collective consciousness is important to us as Jews and Israelis. There is no contradiction between what happened "to us" and what happened "to them." Rather, understanding both aspects completes our knowledge and yields the required synthesis between the particular and the universal. Learning about the Nakba is also necessary in this context, and here I again emphasize that the Nakba was neither a Holocaust nor a genocide, but rather a terrible tragedy that befell the Palestinians. This combination will endow the memory of the Holocaust, and our just demand that the world never forget, with moral significance and universal power. This combination will diminish neither the "value" of the Holocaust nor its uniquely Jewish element. In fact, the opposite is true: It will reinforce universal recognition of its meaning.

The fundamental principle underlying the moral and educational approach expressed in this book and in my other works is the equal value of human life, wherever it may be found.

## Notes

1. Salem Jubran, "The Arabs and the Holocaust: A Historic and Current Perspective," *Bishvil Hazikaron* 17 (1996): 15–18 [Hebrew].
2. Among other sources, see Eric Cohen, ed., *Jewish Identity, Values, and Social Pursuits: The World of Israeli Students in State High Schools* (Tel Aviv, 2008) [Hebrew]; and Yair Auron, "The Holocaust—A Main Factor in Jewish Israeli Identity," in *Jewish Identity, Values, and Social Pursuits,* ed. Eric Cohen, [(PLACE, YEAR) PLEASE ADD THIS INFORMATION] 153–260 [Hebrew].
3. In this context, see, among other sources Tova Tzur, "The Trip to Poland as the High Point of an Educational Process," *Bishvil Hazikaron* 7 (1995): 5–7 [Hebrew]; Jackie Feldman, *Above the Death Pits, Beneath the Flag: Youth Voyages to Poland and the Performance of Israeli National Identity* (New York, 2008), 86; Adi Ophir, "On Feelings that Cannot Be Explained in Words and On Lessons that Cannot Be Questioned," *Bishvil Hazikaron* 7 (1995): 11–15 [Hebrew]; and Yair Auron, *The Pain of Knowledge* (Raanana, 2003) [Hebrew].
4. Uriel Simon, *Seek Peace and Pursue It* (Tel Aviv, 2004), 35–37 [Hebrew].
5. Meir Litvak and Esther Webman, *The Representation of the Holocaust in the Arab World—Facilitator of or Obstacle to the Peace Process* (Tel Aviv, 2006) [Hebrew]. See also Jean Mouttapa, *Un Arabe Face à Auschwitz* (Paris, 2006).
6. Moran Zelikovitz, "A Jewish-Arab Trip to Poland: Pain as a Common Denominator," www.ynet.co.il, 23 April 2006 [Hebrew].
7. Roi Mandel, "A Photo Exhibition on the Holocaust at Na'alin: So That Everyone Can Understand the Suffering," www.ynet.co.il, 27 January 2009 [Hebrew].
8. Benedict Anderson, *Imagined Communities* (New York, 1983), 205.
9. See Firer, *Agents of the Holocaust Lesson,* 149.
10. Ibid., 152; see also 106, which addresses the distinction between "lesson" and "significance."
11. Yad Vashem, Survey on the Holocaust and its Significance for the Jewish People (conducted by Rachel Israeli) (Jerusalem, November 1999) [Hebrew]. Over the years, a large number of studies have examined the differing Israeli attitudes toward the Holocaust and the student trips to Poland. The following is a list of those studies not yet cited in this book: Michal Lev Shlomo Romi, "Israeli Youth and the Holocaust: Knowledge, Emotions and Attitudes following a Journey to Poland," *Megamot* 42, no. 2 (2003): 219–39 [Hebrew]; Shraga Fisherman and Shlomo Kaniel, "Changes in Identity after a Visit to

Poland," *Dapim* 37 (2004): 182–202 [Hebrew]; Dan Bar-On et al., "A Journey to the Holocaust: Modes of Understanding among Israeli Adolescents Who Visited Poland," *Educational Review* (2004): 13–31; Dan Bar-On et al., "Jewish Israeli Teenagers National Identity, and the Lessons of the Holocaust," *Holocaust and Genocide Studies* 18, no. 2 (2004): 188–204; Jackie Feldman, "Marking the Boundaries of the Enclave: Defining the Israeli Collective Through the Poland 'Experience'," *Israel Studies* 7, no. 2 (2002): 84–114.

12. The question was phrased as follows: "Below is a list of possible lessons that must be learned from the Holocaust. Indicate the extent to which you agree with each one."
13. Liebman, "The Holocaust Myth in Israeli Society," 110.
14. Gila Zelikovich and Tzipi Liebman, ["A Comparison of the Opinions of Youth from Israel, the United State, and France," Report, Tel Aviv, 1990.
15. This fact holds great significant for the analysis of my findings, and by no means should the opinions of respondents be seen as representative of the overall population of Jewish youth in these countries. The participants constituted a select group within Diaspora Jewish youth that was assembled under very specific circumstances. This appears to be especially true of the participants from France.
16. Percentages of agreement reflect responses 4 (strongly agree) and 3 (agree) combined.
17. Yair Auron, "The Attitude of the Organized Jewish Youth in France to the Holocaust and anti-Semitism," *Yahadut Zmaneinu* 2 (1984–85): 209–35 [Hebrew].
18. Liebman did not ask respondents to relate to each reason individually. See Liebman, "The Holocaust Myth in Israeli Society," 109.
19. Herman, *Jewish Identity,* 81 [Hebrew].
20. Farago, "The Jewish Identity of Israeli Youth," 274.
21. Ibid., 273.
22. See Herman, *Jewish Identity,* 211 [Hebrew]; and Farago, "The Jewish Identity of Israeli Youth," 273.
23. Herman, *Jewish Identity,* 81 [Hebrew].
24. The table provides only a partial list of events. Students in the 'State sector also frequently cited the wars fought by Israel. For a more detailed analysis, see table 2.11 in chapter 2. Respondents were asked to list three events for each question. The order in which they listed the events was also significant. For this reason, the events listed are presented as percentages in the order listed from left to right (first event listed, second event listed, etc.). The last column reflects the number of times the event was listed out of the total number of respondents as a percentage. The last cell in this column reflects a percentage greater than 100 percent because respondents were able to list more than one event. For this reason, the total number of responses in each table totals more than 100 percent.
25. Out of 360 subjects from the State sector in the 1990 study, the Holocaust and World War II were mentioned 354 times (combined). Overall, the Holocaust and World War II were listed slightly more than 100 percent, because a small number of students did not answer the question. Percentages are out of the total number of responses, and a small number of students listed both the Holocaust and World War II.
26. See Farago, "The Jewish Identity of Israeli Youth," 274; and Herman, *Jewish Identity,* 84 [Hebrew].
27. In contrast, we can also identify a downward trend in the prominence of the wars fought by Israel, and, at least in the case of some students, a more ambivalent attitude toward

Israeliness, the Lebanon war, and events related to the state of Israel (for example, the Intifada).

28. Liebman, "The Holocaust Myth in Israeli Society," 110–11.
29. Ibid.
30. See table 2.2 in chapter 2.
31. Also see table 2.21 in chapter 2.
32. Next to the question on the extent to which Zionism was taught, a number of respondents from the Ultra-Orthodox sector added the word "against," meaning that at times they learned a great deal about Zionism, but from an oppositional perspective.
33. Ilan Gur-Zeev and Ilan Pappe, "Palestinian Control of the Memories of the Holocaust and the Nakba," in *Philosophy, Politics, and Education in Israel*, ed. Ilan Gur-Zeev (Haifa, 2000): 99–123 [Hebrew].
34. Ariella Azoulay, *Consistent Violence, 1947–1950: A Genealogy of a Regime and "The Catastrophe from Their Point of View"* (Tel Aviv, 2009), 11 [Hebrew].
35. David Grossman, *Present Absentees* (Tel Aviv, 1992) [Hebrew].
36. Ibid., 131–32. Also see Gilbert Achcar, *The Arabs and the Holocaust—The Arab-Israeli War of Narratives* (New York, 2010).
37. Noga Kadman, *On the Side of the Road and in the Margins of Consciousness—Depopulated Palestinian Villages of 1948 in the Israeli Discourse* (Jerusalem, 2008) [Hebrew]. Some refer to the higher number of 531 destroyed villages.
38. Ibid., 15.
39. Benny Morris, *The Birth of the Palestinian Refugee Problem, 1947–1949* (Cambridge, 1987), 1.
40. Ilan Pappe, *The Ethnic Cleaning of Palestine* (Oxford: Oneworld, 2006).
41. Or Kashti, "Israel Pulls Textbook with Chapter on Nakba," *Haaretz*, October 16, 2009. In February 2010, in a similar move reflecting government policy on the Palestinian Arab narrative, the Israeli Education Ministry opted not to publish an academic paper recommending that high school students study both Jewish and Palestinian poems about Jerusalem in their literature classes. Or Kashti, "Israel Turns Down Bid to Teach Palestinian Poems in School," *Haaretz*, February 15, 2010.
42. It is interesting to note the Hebrew version's use of the term "*she'erit ha-pleta*," which has typically been used within the Zionist-Israeli literature to refer to the displaced Jewish survivors of the Holocaust. Here, it is used to refer to those Palestinians "who remained from among the original inhabitants of our homeland."
43. Jean-Michel Chaumont, *La Concurrence de Victimes—Génocide, Identité, Reconnaissance* (Paris, 1997).
44. Ibid., 9.
45. Yair Auron, *The Banality of Indifference: Zionism and the Armenian Genocide* (New Brunswick, 2000).
46. Rabah Halabi, "The Palestinians as the Scapegoat of the Holocaust," in *Neve Shalom School for Peace Annual Report for 1998-1999* (1999), 41–43 [Hebrew]. Also see the debate between Azmi Bishara and Dan Michman on "The Arabs and the Holocaust" in the Hebrew language journal *Zmanim* during 1995–99; and Litvak and Webman, *Representation of the Holocaust in the Arab World.*

# CHAPTER 4
# "THE OTHER" AND ME

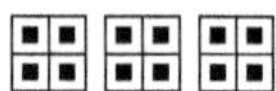

## Mutual Opinions and Social Distance between Jews and Arabs

In October 1944, just months after Paris was liberated from German occupation, French Philosopher Jean-Paul Sartre wrote an important essay titled "Thoughts on the Jewish Question." This text has since then emerged as one of the most significant pieces ever written on racism and the hatred of strangers in general and anti-Semitism in particular, and its power remains as strong today as it was 65 years ago. Its main focus was not "the Jewish question" but rather the French problem: How did it come to pass that France's democratic (republican) majority surrendered to its anti-Semitic minority, and France collaborated with the German Nazis in their efforts to exterminate the Jews?

The issue of racism and hatred of strangers is relevant to Israeli society in a number of ways. Sartre's analysis explores the universal dimensions of the hatred of strangers and of the "other,": "A Jew is a person whom others consider to be a Jew: this is the simple truth that must be accepted as a point of departure. From this perspective, the democrat is correct in his debate with the anti-Semite: the anti-Semite *makes* the Jew."[1] In those days, Sartre believed that Jews were capable of complete assimilation within modern nations, but were nonetheless classified as people whom the nations did not want to assimilate.

According to Sartre's book, Jewish authenticity was only a Jewish approach toward a negative, anti-Semitic force. Such Jews, who ostensibly regarded themselves as Jewish only because of anti-Semitism, were referred to as "Jews against their will," "Jews in the Sartrean sense," or "existential Jews."

Theoretically, Israeli Jews are completely different from the French Jews of the 1930s and 1940s. Indeed, the Israeli, or "the new Jew," aspired to be as different as possible from the "old" Jew of the exile. Nonetheless, this raises two seemingly surprising questions:

1) Has the Jewish identity that has been evolving in Israel over the years assumed traits that are similar—though not identical—to the Sartrean definition of the Jew?

2) If such a process is in fact underway, how and why is it happening? What are the processes that brought it about?

As I have shown, the Holocaust constitutes a major force shaping the identity of Jewish-Israelis, which over the years has become less Israeli and more Jewish. The Holocaust—which is the embodiment of total and supreme evil according to a number of problematic definitions—has become one of the few identity-shaping factors shared by all parts of Jewish-Israeli society. This trend has been reinforced by the youth trips to Poland.

As I will attempt to show, the wars fought throughout the history of Israel also constitute an extremely significant factor in the identity of young Israelis. The influence of the ongoing conflict with the Arabs on Jewish-Israeli identity has yet to be sufficiently explored. However, there is no doubt that the Arabs play a major negative role in shaping Jewish-Israeli identity. Perceived existential threats constitute negative factors of identity which result in the development of a united front to the outside, but not in the development of internal aspects of identity in the positive sense.[2] The fact that our conflict with the Palestinians is a conflict over very real material matters, in contrast to many expressions of racism which often do not involve such matters, also intensifies its influence on the identity of young Israelis. Furthermore, negating factors are also reflected in Jewish-Israeli attitudes toward parts of Israeli society and toward Diaspora Jewry. For the first few years after a Jew either chooses or is forced to immigrate to Israel, he or she is also treated as an "other," as someone who is different and at times foreign, until he or she becomes Israeli in our eyes.

In this way, the decades that have passed since the establishment of the state of Israel have witnessed the evolution of an "oppositional identity" that developed in opposition to the terrible Holocaust; in opposition to the Arabs, who attempt to undermine our very existence; and in opposition to the world, which is allegedly entirely against us.

This perception has far-reaching implications for the worldview and inner-world of the significant number of young Jewish-Israelis who hold it. This chapter will examine Jewish-Israelis' attitudes toward Arab-Israelis (or Palestinian-Israelis), and vice-versa. The fact that some of the questions asked in my study were asked in previous studies enables me to examine attitudinal changes that have taken place over time.

The Nakba and the wars (which for the Palestinians and the Arabs undoubtedly serve as negative factors) are primary components of the identity of Israel's Palestinian Arabs. After all, they are citizens of a country that is locked in conflict with them, that discriminates against them, and that defines itself as a Jewish state. At the same time, Arab-Israeli identity possesses strong religious and national components.

On the eve of Israel's 61st Independence Day (2009), the country's population of 7,411,000 was 75.5 percent Jewish and 20.2 percent Arab (1,4998,000), with an additional 4.3 percent (320,000) made up of immigrants and their offspring who are not registered as Jews. Moshe Lissak, who has examined the major divisions in Israeli society, divides the interaction between Arabs and Jews since the establishment of the state into four main phases:[3]

**Phase I (1948–1966):** The period of military rule, characterized by forced separation between Jews and Arabs.

**Phase II (1967–1992):** The opening up of the Arab sector to Jewish society and to the Palestinians in the occupied territories. This resulted in the Palestinization of Arab-Israelis and the intensification of their national consciousness.

**Phase III (1993–1996):** After the elections of 1992 and the political reversal that brought Yitzhak Rabin back into the prime minister's office, the Israeli government demonstrated a degree of openness toward the Arab population and a willingness to increase the budgets dedicated to this sector of the population. There was also an increased tendency among Arab-Israelis to organize themselves into independent Arab parties. Indeed, Rabin succeeded in getting the Oslo Accords approved by the Knesset to a large degree because of the votes of Arab Knesset members, who during this period took a more active rolein Israeli political decision-making (the voting patterns of Arab-Israelis and the mass abstention from prime ministerial elections resulted in the defeat of Shimon Peres in the 1996 elections, which took place shortly after the assassination of Yitzhak Rabin).

**Phase IV (1996 and onward):** The period of right-wing rule in Israel, with the exception of the government of Ehud Barak, who won the elections of 1999 but was removed from office in the elections of 2001.

After Rabin's assassination, the new spirit of cooperation between the Israeli authorities and the country's Arab population that characterized the period of Rabin's government began to dissipate. Ariel Sharon defeated Ehud Barak in the elections of 2001, and all Israeli governments since then have been presided over by prime ministers from the political right. Israel's relations with the Palestinians in the occupied territories were transformed, and the "spirit of Oslo" became a thing of the past.

The first Intifada broke out in 1987, during the period of national unity government (when Yitzhak Shamir was prime minister and Yitzhak Rabin was minister of defense), and the second Intifada—*Intifadat al-Aqsa*—broke out in September 2000. The onset of the second Intifada was accompanied, in early October 2000, by Arab demonstrations within the borders of the state (the green line) that quickly evolved into violent clashes with the Israeli police, in which twelve Arab-Israelis were killed. "The events of October 2000," as they are commonly referred to in Israel, undoubtedly mark an important milestone in Jewish-Arab relations in the country.

There was no slowing in the process of Palestinization during this period. However, concurrent with it was a process of Israelization: Alongside the demand for autonomy voiced by some Arab-Israelis, a growing number of the began calling for equality and for the transformation of Israeli into "a state of all its citizens" (instead of a "Jewish state," as it is currently defined).

## Opinions of Jewish and Arab Youth on Coexistence and Democracy in Israel during the 1980s and 1990s (1988 and 1994)

The various studies that have explored the opinions of Jewish-Israeli and Arab-Israeli youth on issues of democracy and Jewish-Arab coexistence in Israel during the 1980s and 1990s reveal an atmosphere of intolerance, stereotyping, refusal to accept others and people who are different, and, in some cases, attitudes that can only be described as blatantly racist. Studies and surveys clearly indicated that this was the direction in which Israeli society was headed. Below, I briefly summarize the main findings of some of these assessments in order to effectively convey the severity of the situation, in which negative, generalizing, and racist attitudes have been expressed over a period of many years. For some reason, however, Israeli society chooses not to recognize this reality, and only recently have scholars started to explore racism in Israel as a subject of academic research and discussion.

In 1986, Sammy Smooha found that 58 percent of Israel's Jewish population did not trust Arab-Israelis; 42 percent believed that the state should take advantage of every opportunity to encourage Arab-Israelis to leave the country in order to decrease their population; 22 percent regarded expulsion of the Arab minority as a solution to Jewish-Arab relations in the country; and 24 percent believed that the state should revoke the rights of Arab-Israelis to participate in parliamentary elections.[4] A survey carried out in 1985 by the Van Leer Institute among Israeli high school students found that 42 percent of the study population supported the ideas of Meir Kahane, and that his support among religious respondents reached 59 percent. Sixty percent thought that Arab citizens of the state of Israel did not have a right to full equality, while 47 percent were willing to curtail their rights in practice. In contrast, the students surveyed demonstrated excessive tolerance toward groups working against tolerance (specifically, Kach), and 46 percent supported the freedom of Jews to organize themselves in frameworks aimed at harming Arab citizens.[5]

The 1985 findings received wide coverage in the media. *Maariv* wrote: "The portrait of the Israeli high school student that emerges from the recent studies is one of a teenager who is nationalist and hates Arabs, full of fears regarding the future and saturated with preconceptions, intolerant, in search of simple and easy solutions, and lacking respect for human dignity and civil rights."[6] The same week, *Yediot Aharonot* ran a long article under the headline "The Youth is Being Swept into Kahanism," with the following secondary headlines: "Surveys reveal that the generation born during the Six Days War is surging after the ideology represented by Rabbi Kahane and that their support for him has reached astonishing levels"; "A student in Jerusalem: There was a Holocaust for the Jews in Europe—there should be a Holocaust for the Arabs as well"; and "Students of the Nakhalim Yeshiva: We should encourage Arab emigration from our country."[7] It was relatively easy to counter Kahane. It is much more difficult to acknowledge that the positions he articulated are espoused by a significant number of people in Israeli society. The man is gone, but the phenomenon with which his name is associated is alive and well, and runs deep within Israeli society. It also appears that in the mid 1980s, there was a greater awareness of the power and severity of expressions of racism in Israeli society than there is today.

Subsequent studies also revealed a clear and unequivocal picture. For example, a study of high school students undertaken by the Carmel Institute in 1988 revealed troubling data: Forty percent of students in the state education sector and 50 percent of students in the state-religious sector indicated that they hated Arabs, while in vocational schools of the state-religious sector the figure was 71 percent. Sixty percent of students in the state education sector and 71 percent of students in the state-religious sector expressed a desire for revenge against the Arabs. In the vocational schools of the state-religious sector, 85 percent expressed such a desire.[8]

In 1990, Zeev Ben-Sira carried out a broad study on 1,840 Jewish-Israeli ninth, tenth, and eleventh graders from 24 high schools. According to his findings, 53 percent of the students were in favor of curtailing the human rights of people who had not fulfilled their national duties, and 63 percent were in favor of curtailing the human rights of people who did not recognize Israel's right to exist. Sixty-six percent supported banning public criticism of the authorities on security-related issues; 41 percent supported banning public expression of opinions on issues critical of fundamental values; and 67 percent supported encouraging the Arab inhabitants of the occupied territories to emigrate out of the country.

Ben-Sira concluded his study by stating that although Israeli youth on the whole understand the essence of democracy in the liberal sense of the term, their support for it is relatively low and they have a strong tendency to place limitations and restrictions on it. In statistical terms, although 71 percent of the teens surveyed held that it was very important that Israel be a democracy, when faced with the need to decide between maintaining democratic values or state security, only 13 percent preferred democracy. Ben-Sira also noted that schools played an extremely limited role in the reinforcement of democracy and tolerance.[9]

In 1994, Kalman Binyamini conducted a survey of 642 eights, ninth, and tenth graders in twenty-six classes in nine state schools and seven state-religious schools in Jerusalem, and reported the following findings:

1) 77 percent agreed that it would be acceptable to cause most of the Arabs to leave the territory of the Land of Israel.
2) 47 percent agreed that during periods of aggravated security situations, it is permissible to sacrifice a few principles of democracy.
3) 24 percent held that a non-democratic government implementing policies consistent with their own views would be preferable to a democratic government with policies that are inconsistent with their own views.
4) 52 percent thought that the principles of the Jewish religion were more important than the principles of democratic government.
5) 59 percent thought that it was permissible to limit freedom of the press for the sake of national morale.
6) 48 percent believed that members of the public who opposed the agreement with the P.L.O. were permitted to break the law by means of civil disobedience.[10]

In 1994, the Carmel Institute conducted a broad attitude study among Jewish, Arab, and Druze high school students. The study was a repeat of an abovementioned study that had been conducted in 1988, and its findings were extremely similar.[11] Students were provided with five possible responses to the question: "In your opinion, how loyal are Arab-Israelis to the state of Israel?" The five options ranged from "almost all are loyal" to "almost all are disloyal."

**TABLE 4.1 Responses to the Question, *"Are Arab-Israelis loyal to the state?"* according to Nationality (Carmel Institute, 1994) (as a percentage)**

| | Almost All or Most are Loyal | About Half are Loyal | The Minority or Almost All are Not Loyal |
|---|---|---|---|
| Jews | 20 | 22 | 58 |
| Druze | 18 | 28 | 54 |
| Arabs | 62 | 27 | 11 |

The data indicates that only approximately one-fifth of the Jewish and Druze students believed that either most or almost all Arab-Israelis are loyal to the state, in comparison to 62 percent of the Arab students surveyed. In the state-religious sector, only 11 percent believed that Arab-Israelis are loyal to the state, and in vocational schools and Jewish schools in the occupied territories, the number dropped to 7 and 8 percent respectively. On the subject of equal rights for Arabs,

36 percent of the Jews and 43 percent of the Druze responded that it was either justified or completely justified for Arabs to enjoy full equal rights in Israel, in comparison to (only) 57 percent in the Arab sector.

The data clearly indicates that students from the state education sector had more positive opinions of Arab-Israelis than students from the state-religious education sector. Students from the kibbutz sector within the state system expressed opinions that were much more positive than students from similar schools outside the kibbutz sector. The data also indicates a low variance in the state-religious sector regarding Arab-Israelis' loyalty to the state.

**TABLE 4.2 Responses to the Questions, *"Is it justified for the Arabs to receive equal rights?"* and *"Are Arab-Israelis loyal to the state?"* according to High School Education Sector (as a percentage) (Carmel Institute, 1994)**

| | | Total | Academic | Vocational | Kibbutz | Moshav | Yeshiva | Occupied Terr. | Ext.* |
|---|---|---|---|---|---|---|---|---|---|
| 1) It is justified for Arabs to be granted full rights. | State | 40 | 39 | 40 | 58 | 35 | – | – | 43 |
| | State-Religious | 11 | 12 | 8 | 15 | 16 | 11 | 7 | – |
| 2) Arab-Israelis are loyal to the state. | State | 23 | 23 | 17 | 56 | 36 | – | – | 16 |
| | State-Religious | 11 | 12 | 8 | 15 | 16 | 11 | 7 | – |

1) 1. Completely Justified; 2. Justified; 3. Unjustified; 4. Completely Unjustified
The percentages appearing in the above table represent responses 1 and 2 combined.
2) 1. Almost All Are Disloyal; 2. Only a Small Portion Are Loyal; 3. Half Are Loyal; 4. Most Are Loyal; 5. Almost All Are Loyal
The percentages appearing in the above table represent responses 1 and 2 combined.
* External Schools not included in the State school average.

The 1994 study found that these positions were related to social distance and the degree of hatred between the two sides.

## Hatred for "the Other Side"

The studies conducted by the Carmel Institute in 1988 and 1994 asked Jewish high school students: "Do you hate Arabs?" The 1994 study population also included Arab and Druze high school students. The Arab students were asked the same questions with regard to Jews ("Do you hate Jews?" and "Do you think that the Arabs hate Jews?"), and the Druze students were not asked this type of question.

In the 1988 study, 40 percent of students in the state sector asserted that they hated Arabs (19 percent said that they hated all Arabs, and another 21 percent said that they hated most of them). In the state-religious sector, 50 percent of the respondents asserted that they hated Arabs (26 percent said that they hated all Arabs, and 24 percent said that they hated most Arabs). In the vocational schools of the state-religious sector, the percentage was much higher, with 71 percent of students expressing hatred for Arabs. Sixty percent of students in the state sector and 71 percent of students in the state-religious sector expressed a desire to take revenge against the Arabs (perhaps it would have been helpful to ask what for). Again, in the vocational schools of the state-religious sector, the percentage was higher, at 85 percent.

The findings of the 1994 study reflect a slight decline in the level of hatred for Arabs reported by Jewish students in the state education sector. Nonetheless, 33 percent of the state students and 49 percent of the state-religious students reported great hatred toward Arabs (representing the two most extreme categories out of five: "I hate all Arabs" and "I hate most Arabs"). Students from the state-religious education sector reported greater hatred toward Arabs than those from the state sector. They also expressed greater belief than students in the state sector that Arabs hate Jews. No significant difference was found between male and female respondents. In effect, the percentage of students reporting hatred toward Arabs remained almost unchanged. This was also true of the state-religious subgroup, which expressed particularly strong hatred for Arabs. Among students of the vocational schools, 70 percent reported hatred of Arabs.

The Arab high school students surveyed offered a different picture, with 24 percent reporting hatred toward all or most Jews. In this way, the level of hatred toward the other side appears to be higher in the Jewish sector than in the Arab sector. I do not know if some of the Arab students refrained from reporting hatred toward Jews out of fear of possible repercussions. At the same time, however, a similar percentage of respondents in both sectors believed that the other side hates them (60 percent of the Jewish students and 60 percent of the Arab students). In both cases, the two sides' attribution of hatred to the other side was higher than the hatred actually expressed.

Below are two tables containing data reflecting the mutual hatred of Arabs and Jews, one according to education sector and type of school, and one comparing the data from the studies of 1988 and 1994.

**TABLE 4.3 Mutual Hatred between Arabs and Jews by Education Sector and Type of School in the Jewish Sector Alone (percentage of responses in the two most extreme categories) (Carmel Institute, 1994)**

| | | Total | Academic | Vocational | Kibbutz | Moshav | Yeshiva | Occupied Terr. | Ext.* |
|---|---|---|---|---|---|---|---|---|---|
| Do you hate Arabs? | State | 33 | 27 | 48 | 9 | 26 | – | – | 42 |
| | State-Religious | 49 | 49 | 61 | 22 | 51 | 37 | 38 | – |
| Do the Arabs hate Jews? | State | 55 | 51 | 68 | 22 | 46 | – | – | 64 |
| | State-Religious | 73 | 74 | 70 | 61 | 73 | 74 | 75 | – |

* External Schools not included in the state school average.

The question "Do you hate Arabs?" was also asked in the first survey from 1988. The following table presents comparative data from the two surveys by education sector and type of school. As we have seen, the scale consisted of five levels, with higher numbers reflecting greater hatred toward Arabs.

**TABLE 4.4 Hatred toward Arabs: Comparison over Time By Education Sector and Type of School (Carmel Institute, 1988 and 1994)**

| | | State Sector | | | | State-Religious Sector | | | |
|---|---|---|---|---|---|---|---|---|---|
| | Total | Academic | Vocational | Kibbutz | Moshav | Academic | Vocational | Kibbutz | Moshav |
| 1988 Survey | 3.18 | 2.88 | 3.38 | 2.27 | 3.13 | 3.66 | 4.12 | 2.88 | 3.52 |
| 1994 Survey | 3.07 | 2.76 | 3.46 | 2.14 | 2.73 | 3.33 | 3.71 | 2.78 | 3.37 |

The higher the number, the greater the hatred.

## Social Distance between Jews and Arabs in Israel

The Carmel Institute study measures "social distance" between Jews and Arabs in Israel based on people's opinions of members of the other social grouping, and their willingness to host and be friends with them. In this context as well, no gender-based differences were found.

The findings show that in the Jewish sector, a higher percentage of students was willing to have Arabs as neighbors than were willing to host an Arab in their home or be friends with them. The 1994 study also included a question about behavior in practice: "Do you have an Arab/Jewish friend?" According to the findings, 12 percent of the Jewish students said that they had an Arab friend, in comparison to 46 percent of the Arab students, who said that they had a Jewish friend.

**TABLE 4.5 Arab-Jewish Social Distance by Nationality: Responses to the Statements, *"It would not bother me to have an Arab neighbor," "I am willing to host an Arab in my home,"* and *"I would be pleased if I had an Arab friend"* (percentage of respondents who "agreed" or "strongly agreed") (Carmel Institute, 1988 and 1994)**

| | Jews | Druze | Arabs |
|---|---|---|---|
| It would not bother me if an Arab were my neighbor.* | 47 | ** | 56 |
| I am willing to host Arabs in my home. | 30 | ** | 71 |
| I would be pleased to have an Arab friend. | 23 | 75 | 64 |

1. Strongly Disagree 2. Disagree 3. Agree and Disagree Equally 4. Agree 5. Strongly Agree
* Arabs were asked about Jews (as were Druze, in the case of the one question they were asked).
** Druze were not asked these questions.

The following table presents data regarding the percentage of Jews surveyed in the 1994 Carmel Institute study who either "agreed" or "strongly agreed" to hosting, being neighbors with, or being friends with Arabs, according to school type and education sector.

**TABLE 4.6 Arab-Jewish Social Distance by School Type and Education Sector: Responses to the Statements, *"It would not bother me to have an Arab neighbor," "I am willing to host an Arab in my home,"* and *"I would be pleased if I had an Arab friend"* (percentage of respondents who either agreed or strongly agreed) (Carmel Institute, 1994)**

| | | Total | Aca-demic | Voca-tional | Kib-butz | Moshav | Yeshiva | Occupied Terr. | Ext.* |
|---|---|---|---|---|---|---|---|---|---|
| Having an Arab for a neighbor would not bother me. | State | 51 | 56 | 41 | 70 | 51 | – | – | 42 |
| | State-Religious | 35 | 35 | 36 | 39 | 40 | 30 | 27 | – |
| I am willing to host Arabs in my home. | State | 34 | 39 | 20 | 65 | 44 | – | – | 37 |
| | State-Religious | 17 | 17 | 13 | 34 | 20 | 19 | 15 | – |
| I would be pleased to have an Arab friend. | State | 26 | 29 | 16 | 36 | 40 | – | – | 25 |
| | State-Religious | 15 | 14 | 16 | 21 | 23 | 14 | 12 | – |

1. Strongly Disagree 2. Disagree 3. Agree and Disagree Equally 4. Agree 5. Strongly Agree
* External Schools not included in the state school mean.

The responses of Jewish students within the state-religious sector indicated much greater "social distance" from Arabs than the responses of Jewish students within the state sector. The students from kibbutz schools within the state sector reported much less social distance from Arabs. Arab students in mixed cities reported less social distance from, and more positive attitudes toward Jews. The Arab and Druze expressed a much lower level of social distance toward Jews than the level of social distance expressed by Jews toward Arabs. In this way, it appears that the production of social distance between the two populations relies more on Jews than Arabs. There are two reasons for this. First, because Jews constitute the majority in Israel, decreasing social distance depends more on their intentions and behavior than on that of the minority group. Second, Jewish opinions regarding Arabs reflect greater social distance, rejection, and hatred than Arab opinions regarding Jews.

I also found extremely significant data in my study "Attitudes of Teaching Students in Israel toward Anti-Semitism and Racism," which was concluded in 1996. During this study, teaching students were asked different types of questions regarding Arab citizens of the state of Israel and the provision of proportional representation (that is, in accordance with their relative share of the total population). The study revealed marked differences between teaching students from the state education sector and teaching students from the state-religious education sector.[12]

Here are a number of examples: In response to the statement "Arab-Israelis are citizens of the state of Israel with equal rights," 66 percent of the students of state teaching colleges surveyed either "agreed" or "strongly agreed," while 8 percent indicated that they "strongly disagree." In contrast, 25 percent of the state-religious teaching students either "agreed" or "strongly agreed," while 41 percent indicated strong disagreement. In other words, a much smaller percentage of the students from the state-religious sector regarded Arab-Israelis as citizens with equal rights. In response to the statement "Jews and Arabs can live together in peace," 90 percent of the students in the state sector either agreed or strongly agreed, and 2 percent disagreed. Among the state-religious students, only 64 percent agreed or strongly agreed, and 12 percent disagreed.

The differences are even more pronounced in responses to statements rejecting the idea of equal representation for Arab-Israelis. For example, 32 percent of students from the state sector either agreed or strongly agreed with the statement "equal representation for Arabs will detract from the Jewish character of the state," while 32 percent disagreed. Among the state-religious students surveyed, 63 percent strongly agreed, 24 percent agreed, and 3 percent disagreed. The significant difference between these responses are clear: Students from the state education sector disagreed with the statement ten to eleven times more frequently than the students of state-religious teaching institutions.

There were also great differences between the students' responses to the statement "the state belongs to Jews, and Arabs have no right to take part in political decision-making." Thirty percent of the state students either agreed or strongly agreed with the statement, while 41 percent disagreed. In contrast, 56 percent of the state-religious students strongly agreed with the statement and another 22 percent agreed with it. Only 7 percent disagreed.

Another statement in the survey read as follows: "Arabs of the state of Israel are enemies of the state and want to destroy it." This statement was agreed or strongly agreed with by 30 percent of the of the students from the state sector, and disagreed with by 36 percent. Among the state-religious teaching students, 48 percent strongly agreed and another 22 percent agreed, while only 11 percent disagreed.

These responses reflect the striking fact that 70 percent of the future teachers from the state-religious sector and 30 percent from the state sector regard Arab-Israelis (not West Bank Arabs, as the question explicitly made this distinction) as enemies of the state and as people who want to destroy the state. This is a generalizing, stereotypical, judgmental, and hostile perception of the Arab citizens of the state of Israel.

I would also like to draw attention to two points of interest on the comparative level. First, in comparison to past attitude studies conducted among the adult population, during which Israelis were asked similar or identical questions, the opinions of young Israelis were much more extreme than those of older Israelis. Second, an international youth attitude study published in *Haaretz Weekend Magazine* on 1 November 1996 offers meaningful comparative insight into the positions of Israeli youth as opposed to youth from other countries. According to the article on the study conducted among high school students in 27 European countries, the responses provided by students of Israel's state-religious education sector were the most nationalistic and most aggressive.[13]

Overall, the state of Jewish-Arab relations in Israel and the positions of each side vis-à-vis the other as revealed by the different studies discussed here paint a picture of a dismal, depressing reality. The opinions of members of the Jewish majority toward members of the Arab minority are much more oppositional and rejecting than those espoused by the Arab minority toward the Jews.

Smooha believes that the vast separation between Jews and Arabs that exists today in Israeli society shows that some degree of coercion inevitably lies at the foundation of such separation. In all the surveys, Arabs expressed interest in greater contact with Jews in places of residence, schools, and political parties, and greater openness to the idea of personal friendships with Jews. Jews, in contrast, expressed less interest in close relations with Arabs and were to a great extent opposed to them. For example, 55.3 percent of the Arabs who took part in Smooha's 1995 study expressed a willingness to live in a mixed Arab-Jewish neighborhood, while only 20.4 percent of the Jews who took part in the same study were willing to do so. The present study and other studies I have mentioned revealed comparable attitudes as well. Smooha holds that these asymmetrical opinions reflect Jewish dominance in Israeli society, in which Arabs stand to gain from relations with Jews, who have access to greater resources, more than Jews stand to gain from relations with Arabs. For instance, the probability of a Jew being in a position to help an Arab is much greater than the probability of the reverse being true. One can also conclude that coercion is an essential part of the foundation of this social separation based on the Arab population's support of Arabs moving to live in Jewish towns such as Upper Nazareth and the efforts of a few Arabs to purchase homes and to live in Jewish community settlements such as Katzir. The Arab public does not regard this as a condemnable act of assimilation, but rather as a necessary step in breaking down the discrimination and forced separation, and as a means of acquiring equal opportunity.[14]

These trends also reflect a failure of the Israeli education system in the realm of Jewish-Arab relations, co-existence, and severe expressions of racism. For example, although kibbutz students had no more to gain from their relations with Arabs than students from Jewish high schools in the West Bank and Gaza Strip in the study of 1994, 70 percent of the former indicated that having Arabs as neighbors would not bother them. The percentage dropped to 39 percent among students from religious kibbutzim, to 30 percent among yeshiva students, and to 27 percent among students from yeshivas in the West Bank and Gaza Strip. The significant, often double-digit differences between the various sub-groups (see table 4.6) were reflected in their responses to other questions as well. There were also major differences between the religious and the non-religious. Certain aspects of education, personal values, and ideology also appear to exercise a degree of influence on the production of social distance and attitudes felt by one side toward the other. The studies also clearly reflect that the opinions held by Jewish students of the state-religious sector toward Arab citizens of Israel are particularly harsh.

The assessment of the attitudes of teens over time during the 1980s and 1990s revealed a static situation. On the one hand, attitudes toward Arabs have not grown any more extreme. On the other hand, they have not been moderated in any way. From this perspective, it is as if the peace process that took place during the first half of the 1990s never happened, or at least did not result in a significant change in attitudes toward Arabs in general and Arab citizens of Israel in particular.

The two studies conducted by Seminar Hakibbutzim College in 1996 and 1997 also included a number of questions used by the present study that pertain to Jewish-Arab relations in Israel.[15] The first study was conducted among 1,488 eleventh grade students—1,025 (69 percent) from state schools and 463 (31 percent) from state-religious schools—and focused on attitudes toward anti-Semitism and racism among Israeli high school students. The second study surveyed 429 students—67 percent from six state teaching colleges, and 33 percent from four teaching colleges in the state-religious sector. Most students were between 24 and 26 years of age, and the majority (95 percent) of students from the state sector were women. Although this study focused more on attitudes toward anti-Semitism, it also examined a few aspects of racism in Israel.

In the course of the two studies, which were conducted by the same research team, high school students and teaching students were presented with a series of questions pertaining to equal representation for Arab-Israelis and justifications for denying equal representation. The high school students demonstrated knowledge and understanding of the racist meaning of anti-Semitism and of hatred toward blacks, as well as the significance of behavior toward various minority groups. However, when it came to Jewish-Israelis' opinions toward Arab citizens of the state, attitudes tended to be more complicated. The high school students and teaching students expressed a high level of agreement with statements such as "the state of Israel is a democratic state" and "minorities also must be allowed to express their opinions." However, these democratic, liberal, and somewhat theoretical values did not find expression in their responses to more concrete statements related directly to them—people who are personally and emotionally involved—and to Arab-Israelis.

Close examination of the responses to the different questions revealed a high level of agreement to general, abstract statements such as "the state of Israel is a democratic state," "minorities also must be allowed to express their opinions," and even "Arabs are citizens of the state with equal rights."

The differences that emerge between high school students of the state sector and the state-religious sector are quite significant. The state-religious students expressed less support and greater opposition to the provision of equal rights to Arabs. Among the teaching students, the differences between students from the two education sectors were marked and in some cases almost polar, and extremely significant from a statistical perspective. The mean percentage for state-religious teaching students in favor of providing Arab-Israelis with equal representation was 17 percent lower than that of students in state institutions. In contrast, the mean percentage among state-religious students against the provision of equal representation to Arab-Israelis was 21 percent higher than the students of state institutions. The data also revealed an increase in the opposition expressed toward the provision of equal rights to Arabs in the state-religious sector as students moved from high school to college.

TABLE 4.7 Percentage of Respondents Who Answered "Agreed" and "Strongly Agreed" to the Question, *"To what extent do you agree with each of the justifications for providing Arab-Israelis with equal representation in the Knesset?"* in Each Education Sector (State and State-Religious) among High School Students and Teaching Students, 1996

| Reasons for Provision of Equal Representation | High School Students | | Teaching Students | | Justifications for Deprivation of Equal Representation | High School Students | | Teaching Students | |
|---|---|---|---|---|---|---|---|---|---|
| | State-Religious Sector | State Sector | State-Religious Sector | State Sector | | State-Religious Sector | State Sector | State-Religious Sector | State Sector |
| Minorities must also be allowed to express their opinions. | 74.7 | 71.5 | – | – | They are a minority and are not entitled to such great representation. | 28.5 | 36.8 | – | – |
| Jews and Arabs can live together in peace. | 43.6 | 29.3 | 90 | 64 | Arabs of Israel are enemies of the state and want to destroy it. | 43.3 | 64.3 | 30 | 70 |
| Arab Israelis are citizens with equal rights. | 50.1 | 35.3 | 6 | 25 | They do not fulfill all the obligations of citizens of the state. | 59.0 | 71.9 | – | – |
| Israel is a democratic state. | 87.6 | 82.7 | – | – | Such representation will detract from the Jewish character of the state. | 44.1 | 65.3 | 32 | 82 |

## Student Opinions on Equal Representation for Arabs in 2008

The following table reflects the manner in which students in the 2008 study responded to questions dealing with equal representation for Arab-Israelis.

**TABLE 4.8 Agreement with Reasons Supporting the Provision and/or Deprivation of Equal Representation to Arab-Israelis, according to Religiosity, 2008 (as a percentage)**

| Jewish Student Agreement with Reasons Supporting the Provision of Equal Representation to Arabs | | | | | | |
|---|---|---|---|---|---|---|
| | | 1 Disagree | 2 Agree Slightly | 3 Agree | 4 Strongly Agree | $X^{2*}$ |
| Arab-Israelis are citizens with equal rights. | Religious | 40 | 22 | 19 | 19 | 38.18 |
| | Traditional | 21 | 39 | 29 | 29 | |
| | Non-Religious | 15 | 28 | 34 | 34 | |
| Israel is a democratic state. | Religious | 12 | 25 | 33 | 30 | 19.986 |
| | Traditional | 4 | 14 | 50 | 32 | |
| | Non-Religious | 4 | 14 | 48 | 34 | |
| Jews and Arabs can live together in peace. | Religious | 45 | 30 | 18 | 7 | 42.878 |
| | Traditional | 19 | 33 | 36 | 12 | |
| | Non-Religious | 17 | 29 | 31 | 23 | |
| Minorities must also be allowed to express their opinions. | Religious | 10 | 24 | 37 | 29 | 16.362 |
| | Traditional | 7 | 11 | 47 | 35 | |
| | Non-Religious | 4 | 12 | 45 | 39 | |
| * For all the reasons: $df = 6, p < 0.05$ | | | | | | |
| Jewish Student Agreement with Justifications for the Deprivation of Equal Representation to Arabs | | | | | | |
| $X^{2*}$ | | 1 Disagree | 2 Agree Slightly | 3 Agree | 4 Strongly Agree | $X^{2*}$ |
| Such representation will detract from the security of the state of Israel. | Religious | 12 | 11 | 14 | 63 | 57.24 |
| | Traditional | 3 | 22 | 27 | 48 | |
| | Non-Religious | 13 | 29 | 31 | 27 | |
| Such representation will detract from the Jewish character of the state. | Religious | 13 | 22 | 12 | 53 | 58.759 |
| | Traditional | 7 | 20 | 35 | 38 | |
| | Non-Religious | 21 | 30 | 30 | 19 | |
| They do not fulfill all the obligation of citizens of the state. | Religious | 8 | 15 | 12 | 65 | 40.896 |
| | Traditional | 2 | 15 | 30 | 53 | |
| | Non-Religious | 12 | 22 | 32 | 34 | |

*(continued)*

| | | | | | | |
|---|---|---|---|---|---|---|
| The state belongs to Jews, and Arabs have no right to take part in political decision-making | Religious | 22 | 23 | 12 | 43 | 60.008 |
| | Traditional | 15 | 33 | 23 | 29 | |
| | Non-Religious | 40 | 30 | 16 | 14 | |
| Arabs of the State of Israel are enemies of the state and want to destroy it. | Religious | 13 | 13 | 25 | 48 | 64.011 |
| | Traditional | 18 | 38 | 24 | 20 | |
| | Non-Religious | 34 | 31 | 19 | 16 | |
| * For all the reasons: $df = 6, p < 0.05$ | | | | | | |

As we see, significant religiosity-based differences—between religious students on the one hand and non-religious and traditional students on the other hand—also emerge in the responses of the university students surveyed in my 2008 study, a population that differed in certain ways from the teaching students who answered the same questions twelve years earlier. This was particularly clear in the religious students' widespread agreement with justifications supporting the deprivation of equal rights to Arabs: Seventy-three percent agreed that Arabs of the State of Israel (again, the term "Arabs of the state of Israel" was intentionally used to avoid confusion with the Palestinians of the West Bank) are enemies of the state and want to destroy it, in comparison to 44 percent of the traditional students and 35 percent of the non-religious students. In response to the justification that "such representation will be detrimental to the Jewish character of the state," 65 percent of the religious students agreed, in comparison to 73 percent of the traditional students and 49 percent of the non-religious students. Religious students agreed *less* than others with the reasons supporting the provision of equality: Sixty-three percent agreed that Israel is a democratic state, in comparison to 82 percent of the traditional students and 82 percent of the non-religious students. In contrast, only 25 percent of the religious students surveyed agreed that Jews and Arabs can live together in peace, in comparison to 48 percent of the traditional students and 54 percent of the non-religious students.

We also see that in three studies—the 1996 study of high school students, the 1996 study of teaching students, and the present study—the population that was associated with the religious sector or that classified itself as religious was also typically opposed to equal representation for Arab citizens of the state of Israel, based on their perception that they are enemies of the state who want to destroy it. This opinion was held by 70 percent of the religious-affiliated respondents in the 1996 teaching student study, 64 percent in the 1996 study of high school students, and 73 percent in the 2008 study (in which 48 percent indicated strong agreement).

Such differences between religious and secular respondents are significant and consistent. Kibbutz students also demonstrated greater openness and tolerance in comparison to the secular sector as a whole. Among the non-religious high school students in the 1996 study, the average percentage of those in agreement with reasons for the provisions of equal representation was 71 percent, in comparison to 83 percent among kibbutz students and 66 percent throughout the overall study population. The mean support for justifications depriving proportional representation for secular students as a whole was 61 percent, in contrast to 45 percent among kibbutz students. As we have seen, the mean percentage of the study population in agreement with reasons supporting equal representation was 66 percent. In the case of justifications for deprivation, the mean percentage of agreement was 69 percent. Seventy-seven percent of the kibbutz students surveyed believed that Jews and Arabs can live together in peace, and 37.5 percent believed that Arab-Israelis are enemies of the state and want to destroy it. This amounts to double digit differences between the opinions of kibbutz students and those of other secular sub-groups, not to mention the traditional and religious students. Similar differences, pertaining to openness toward Arabs, mutual hatred, and social distance among kibbutz students were also among the findings of the 1994 study of the Carmel Institute.

These findings most likely reflect the influence of ethical and ideological education toward tolerance and co-existence. This type of education, which is more frequently implemented among kibbutz students, appears to have influenced their opinions, which tend to be more moderate than other sectors of Israelis society.

It should also be noted that the studies on Jewish-Israeli opinions regarding Arabs have found that "the higher one's level of education, the more positive their attitude toward Arabs."[16] We can assume that attitudes toward Arabs among the younger population, including those not acquiring higher education, are even more extreme.

## Positions of Arab Students Regarding Equal Representation for Arabs in the Knesset (2008)

I also asked Arab students a number of questions regarding the provision of equal representation to Arab-Israelis in the Knesset, including: "To what extent do you agree with each of the following reasons supporting the provision of equal rights in the Knesset to Arab-Israelis (in accordance with their relative share of the total population)?" Arab students agreed, although not overwhelmingly, that Arab-Israelis are citizens of the state of Israel with equal rights (53 percent of the religious student, 54 percent of the traditional students, and 50 percent of the non-religious students). However, it appears that the students may not have understood the statement as a prescription of what should be, but rather as a description of the present situation, which would mean that slightly less than half of the Arab students surveyed did not agree that they are citizens with equal rights.

A smaller percentage of Arab students expressed agreement with the statement supporting the provision of equal rights because "the state of Israel is a democratic state" (47 percent of the religious students, 37 percent of the traditional students, and 53 percent of the non-religious students). As appears to have been the case regarding the previous question, I suspect that the low level of support for this reason stems from a lack of clarity regarding the meaning of the words "the state of Israel is a democratic state." That is, it was unclear whether this was intended to mean that Israel is a democratic state in practice, or that it should be a democratic state. As we will see, support for the other two reasons was much higher.

**TABLE 4.9 Responses of Arab Students to the Statement, *"Jews and Arabs can live together in peace,"* 2008 (as a percentage)**

| | | |
|---|---|---|
| Religious | Disagree | 9 |
| | Agree Slightly | 3 |
| | Agree | 47 |
| | Strongly Agree | 41 |
| Traditional | Agree Slightly | 7 |
| | Agree | 39 |
| | Strongly Agree | 54 |
| Non-Religious | Agree Slightly | 12 |
| | Agree | 18 |
| | Strongly Agree | 70 |
| It was not possible to determine whether there was a statistically significant difference due to the insufficient number of responses in some of the cells. | | |

As reflected in the data, the Arab students expressed a greater desire for closer relations with the Jewish majority group than Jews expressed toward Arabs. As we have seen, this is consistent with the pervasive tendency among minority groups to seek closer relations with majority groups. However, we must also keep in mind the particular circumstances of the Israeli context and remember that, despite the realities of significant discrimination, Arabs are nonetheless interested in closer relations with Jews and, as it appears, do not hate them. In the Jewish sector, 25 percent of the religious students, 48 percent of the traditional students, and 54 percent of the non-religious students expressed agreement with the statement "Jews and Arabs can live together in peace." In the Arab sector, the level of agreement was significantly higher.

The statement "minorities must also be allowed to express their opinions" also enjoyed widespread agreement among Arab students, with 100 percent of the traditional and non-religious students and 94 percent of the religious students. These levels are much higher (a double digit difference) than the levels of agreement indicated by Jewish students.

Arab students' responses to the justifications for deprivation of equal representation for Arab-Israelis yielded the opposite picture. The assertion that equal representation would endanger the security of the state of Israel elicited low levels of agreement: 8 percent of the traditional students, 12 percent of the non-religious students, and 18 percent of the religious students. This can be compared to the large majority of Jews who thought that equal representation would be detrimental to state security (77 percent of the religious students, 75 percent of the traditional students, and 58 percent of the non-religious students). A large portion of the Arab students also did not believe that equal representation would be detrimental to the Jewish character of the state: Only 18 percent of the religious students, 24 percent of the non-religious students, and 36 percent of the traditional students agreed with the statement. This can be compared with the Jewish study population, in which the situation was reversed, with 65 percent of religious students, 73 percent of traditional students, and 49 percent of non-religious students expressing belief that equal representation for Arabs would be detrimental to the Jewish character of the state.

Arab students also did not accept the justification that they do not fulfill all the obligations of citizens of the state (referring to the fact that most Arabs do not serve in the Israeli military): Fifteen percent of the religious students, 19 percent of the traditional students, and 35 percent of the non-religious students agreed with this justification, in contrast to 75 percent of the Jewish students. Arab students also rejected the assertion that because the state belongs to Jews, Arab citizens have no right to take part in political decision-making. This justification elicited only 3 percent agreement among the traditional students, and 12 percent agreement among the non-religious and religious students. As we have seen, agreement in the Jewish sector was much higher, with 30 percent among the non-religious students, 52 percent among the traditional students, and 55 percent among the religious students.

Arab students also rejected the last justification for depriving equal representation, which was perhaps the most difficult for the Arabs and which enjoyed a high level agreement among the Jewish students: the assertion that Arabs are enemies of the state and want to destroy it. The data reflecting Arab responses to this justification are presented in table 4.10 below.

**TABLE 4.10 Responses of Arab Students to the Statement, *"Arabs of the State of Israel are enemies of the state and want to destroy it"* (as a percentage)**

| | | |
|---|---|---|
| Religious | Disagree | 88 |
| | Agree Slightly | 9 |
| | Agree | – |
| | Strongly Agree | 3 |
| Traditional | Disagree | 92 |
| | Agree Slightly | 5 |
| | Agree | – |
| | Strongly Agree | 3 |
| Non-Religious | Disagree | 76 |
| | Agree Slightly | 18 |
| | Agree | 6 |
| | Strongly Agree | – |
| It was not possible to determine whether there was a statistically significant difference due to the insufficient number of responses in some of the cells. | | |

In contrast, this was the statement that elicited the highest level of agreement in one sub-group: 73 percent of the religious Jewish students (see table 4.8). Students expressed an extremely high level of agreement with this statement in previous studies as well.

## Social Distance and Mutual Feelings

My questionnaire also included a number of questions assessing social distance and mutual feelings between Jews and Arabs. Although Arab-Israelis are formally equal citizens of the country, there is no doubt that, de facto, they are discriminated against in a significant number of areas. Debates regarding whether Israel is a Jewish state or a democratic state, or, alternatively, a Jewish democratic state or a democratic Jewish state, have been going on in Israel for years. These debates have a significant impact on how Arabs and Jews as groups and as individuals see each other. I explore some of these attitudes below.

Jewish and Arab students were asked the following question: "If you had to choose between two aims—Israel as a Jewish state or Israel as a democratic state—which would you choose?" Students were asked to choose between three responses.

**TABLE 4.11 Responses of Jewish Students to the Question, *"If you had to choose between Israel as a Jewish state and Israel as a democratic state, which would you choose?"* 2008 (as a percentage)**

| | | |
|---|---|---|
| Religious | Jewish | 59 |
| | Both Aspects Important | 31 |
| | Democratic | 10 |
| Traditional | Jewish | 25 |
| | Both Aspects Important | 62 |
| | Democratic | 13 |
| Non-Religious | Jewish | 12 |
| | Both Aspects Important | 45 |
| | Democratic | 43 |
| $X^2$ = 124.36 | *df* = 4 | *P* = 000 |

The above table indicates a significant difference among the religious sub-groups, ranging from an emphasis on Israel's importance as a Jewish state among the religious students, the importance of both aspects among the traditional students, and an emphasis on the importance of Israel as a democratic state among the non-religious students. Again, within the Arab sector, the situation was reversed, with a decisive majority choosing Israel as a democratic state (91 percent of the religious students, 81 percent of the traditional students, and 83 percent of the non-religious students). Only a few respondents chose Israel as a Jewish state, while a slightly larger number indicated that both aspects were of equal importance. When asked if the state of Israel should be a Jewish state or a state of all its citizens, the vast majority agreed and strongly agreed with the latter option, including 100 percent of the religious and traditional students and 94 percent of the non-religious students.

The Arabs and Jewish students were also asked if it was justified to grant Arabs equal rights. Here too, the differences between Arabs and Jews, and the differences among the Jewish sub-groups, were extremely evident, with 62 percent of the religious Jews opposing the provision of equal rights, in comparison to 56 percent of the traditional students and 39 percent of the non-religious students. Again, the reverse was true for the Arab students, a large majority of whom indicated that it was either justified or very justified to provide Arabs with equal rights (77 percent of the religious and non-religious students, and 93 percent of the traditional students).

A number of other questions dealt with related issues. Students were asked whether Israeli Arabs are loyal to the state, and in this context the differences according to religiosity in the Jewish sector were substantial, particularly with regard to the generalizing view expressed by some that cast the Arabs as a whole. Sixty-four percent of the religious students thought that almost all Arabs are not loyal, while only 38 percent of the traditional students and 31 percent of the non-religious students espoused this view.

What is the significance of the fact that the Jewish students consider most Arabs disloyal. Does this include the Arab students as well?

**Table 4.12 Responses of Jewish Students to the Question, *"Are Arab-Israelis Loyal to the State?"* 2008 (as a percentage)**

| | | |
|---|---|---|
| Religious | Almost All Are Not Loyal | 64 |
| | Only Some Are Loyal | 24 |
| | Most Are Loyal | 12 |
| | Almost All Are Loyal | – |
| Traditional | Almost All Are Not Loyal | 38 |
| | Only Some Are Loyal | 50 |
| | Most Are Loyal | 9 |
| | Almost All Are Loyal | 3 |
| Non-Religious | Almost All Are Not Loyal | 31 |
| | Only Some Are Loyal | 52 |
| | Most Are Loyal | 14 |
| | Almost All Are Loyal | 3 |
| $X^2 = 36.886$ | $df = 4$ | $p = 0.000$ |

In contrast to the low percentage of Jewish students who asserted that Arabs are loyal to the state (12 to 15 percent), a large majority of Arabs (approximately 60 percent) believe that most or almost all Arab-Israelis are loyal.

Table 4.13 displays the responses to two questions relating to the manner in which Jewish and Arab students understand their group's attitude toward the other group (the attitude of most Jewish-Israelis toward Arab-Israelis) and the other group's attitude toward their group (the attitude of most Arab-Israelis toward Jews).

I asked Jewish students if they hated Arabs, and I asked Arab students if they hated Jews. The percentage of Jews who said that they hated Arabs was greater than the percentage of Arabs who said they hated Jews. Thirty-six percent of the religious students indicated that they hate either most (24 percent) or all (12 percent) Arabs. In comparison, 29 percent of the traditional students said that they hate most (23 percent) or all (6 percent) Arabs, and 22 percent of the non-

TABLE 4.13 Attitudes of Most Jewish-Israelis toward Arab-Israelis and Attitudes of Most Arab-Israelis Toward Jewish-Israelis—Responses of Jewish and Arab Students, 2008 (as a percentage)

| | | Responses of Jewish Students | | Responses of Arab Students | |
|---|---|---|---|---|---|
| | | Attitude of Most Jews toward Arabs | Attitude of Most Arab-Israelis toward Jews | Attitude of Most Jews toward Arabs | Attitude of Most Arab-Israelis toward Jews |
| Religious | Negative Attitude | 53 | 74 | 26 | 9 |
| | Mixed Attitude | 46 | 24 | 68 | 80 |
| | Positive Attitude | 1 | 2 | 6 | 11 |
| Traditional | Negative Attitude | 37 | 56 | 27 | 10 |
| | Mixed Attitude | 61 | 43 | 73 | 85 |
| | Positive Attitude | 2 | 1 | – | 5 |
| Non-Religious | Negative Attitude | 54 | 58 | 28 | 17 |
| | Mixed Attitude | 44 | 41 | 67 | 66 |
| | Positive Attitude | 2 | 1 | 5 | 17 |

With regard to the responses of both the Jewish students and the Arab students, it was not possible to determine whether there was a statistically significant difference due to the insufficient number of responses in some of the cells.

religious students said that they hate most (16 percent) or all (6 percent) Arabs. The differences between the Jewish sub-groups are clear.

The responses among Arab students varied greatly. Only 3 percent of the religious students and 5 percent of the traditional students attested to hating most Jews, while no one in the non-religious sub-group chose responses indicating hatred (responses 3 and 4). In all three groups, a two-thirds majority chose the unequivocal response: "I do not hate the Jews."

I also included three other statements to assess the degree of social distance between Jews and Arabs. The first statement was: "It would bother me if an Arab was my neighbor." In response to this statement, 63 percent of the religious Jewish students said that it would bother them either a great deal (19 percent) or a very great deal (44 percent). Among the traditional students, the percentage of those it would bother stood at 36 percent, with 13 percent bothered a great deal and 23 percent bothered a very great deal. The percentage of Arab-Israelis who said it would bother them if a Jew was their neighbor was much lower, with 11 percent of the religious students indicating that it would bother them a great deal, and another 3 percent saying it would bother them a very great deal. Among the traditional Arab students, only 5 percent indicated that it would bother them a very great deal, while the remaining 95 percent indicated that it would either not bother them at all or bother them only a small amount. Finally, 100 percent of the non-religious students indicated that they would not be bothered (94 percent not at all, and 6 percent only a small amount). The differences between the responses of Jews and Arabs were found to be statistically significant.

The distribution of responses to the statement "I am willing to host Arabs in my home" is also significant, as the tendency toward great social distance on the part of Jews is reflected here as well. Fifty-nine percent of religious Jewish students were not willing to host Arabs in their home (31 percent were not at all willing, and 28 percent were minimally willing), in comparison to 54 percent among the traditional students (20 percent were not at all willing, and 34 percent were minimally willing) and 44 percent among the non-religious students (16 percent were not at all willing, and 28 percent were minimally willing).

The Arab responses were almost the polar opposite of the Jewish responses, with 6 percent of the religious students expressing unwillingness to host Jews in their homes (3 percent not at all, and 3 percent minimally willing). Among the traditional students, 93 percent were willing to host Jews in their homes, 7 percent expressed minimal willingness, and no one selected the option "not at all." Finally, 100 percent of the non-religious Arab students expressed a willingness to host Jews in their homes, with 78 percent indicating a very great willingness.

Table 4.14 presents the willingness of Jews and Arabs to host members of the other group in their homes, according to the 2008 study.

**TABLE 4.14 Responses to the Statement, *"I am willing to host Arabs/Jews in my home,"* 2008 (as a percentage)**

| | To a Very Great Extent | To a Great Extent | Minimally | Not At All |
|---|---|---|---|---|
| Jewish–Religious | 17 | 24 | 28 | 31 |
| Jewish–Traditional | 16 | 30 | 34 | 20 |
| Jewish–Non-Religious | 28 | 28 | 28 | 15 |
| Arab–Religious | 61 | 33 | 3 | 3 |
| Arab–Traditional | 74 | 19 | 7 | – |
| Arab–Non-Religious | 79 | 22 | – | – |
| Jewish Responses: $X^2 = 19.226$, $df = 6$, $p < 0.005$ | | | | |
| Arab Responses: It was not possible to determine whether there was a statistically significant difference due to the insufficient number of responses in some of the cells. | | | | |

Another statement presented to students was: "I would be pleased to have an Arab/Jewish friend."

When I compare my findings regarding Jewish students to the findings of the Carmel Institute's 1994 study of high school students presented in table 4.5

**TABLE 4.15 Responses by Jewish and Arab Students to the Statement, *"I would be pleased to have an Arab/Jewish friend,"* 2008 (as a percentage)**

| | | Jews | Arabs |
|---|---|---|---|
| Religious | Not At All | 43 | 6 |
| | Slightly | 28 | 3 |
| | Very | 22 | 22 |
| | Extremely | 7 | 69 |
| Traditional | Not At All | 27 | 3 |
| | Slightly | 35 | 14 |
| | Very | 26 | 19 |
| | Extremely | 12 | 64 |
| Non-Religious | Not At All | 21 | – |
| | Slightly | 32 | 11 |
| | Very | 27 | 11 |
| | Extremely | 20 | 78 |
| | | Significant $X^2 = 24.18$ $df = 6, P = 0.000$ | It was not possible to determine whether there was a statistically significant difference due to the insufficient number of responses in some of the cells. |

above, it appears that there was a decrease in overall social distance in the subsequent fifteen years. In 2008, 37 percent of the religious students, 54 percent of the traditional students, and 74 percent of the non-religious students said that it would not bother them to live next door to an Arab neighbor, while in 1994, the mean response among high school students was 47 percent.[17] In 2008, 29 percent of religious students, 38 percent of traditional students, and 47 percent of non-religious students (see table 4.15) indicated that they would be pleased to have an Arab friend. Again, these percentages were higher than the overall mean response in 1994, which was 23 percent. As we recall, the 1994 study also found that the percentage of Arab (64 percent) and Druze (75 percent) teens who indicated that they would be pleased to have a Jewish friend was also higher.

Table 4.6, which reflects Jewish-Arab social distance according to education sector and type of school as assessed by the 1994 study, again indicates that kibbutz students (followed by moshav students) demonstrated the greatest openness to Arabs, particularly in response to the questions regarding Arab neighbors (70 percent) and willingness to host (65 percent), and less with regard to having an Arab friend (40 percent). I have no recent data that would enable me to determine whether Jewish students' attitudes toward Arab citizens of Israel have changed since then, and if so, in what way.

Jewish students were asked if they think that Arabs hate Jews, and most expressed a belief that they do. Arab students were asked if they think Jews hate Arabs. The responses are displayed in table 4.16 below.

**TABLE 4.16 Assessment of the Level of Arab Hatred toward Jews and Jewish Hatred toward Arabs, 2008 (as a percentage)**

| | Jewish Responses Do the Arabs hate Jews? | | Arab Responses Do the Jews hate Arabs? | |
|---|---|---|---|---|
| | Not At All | 7 | Not At All | 3 |
| | Only a Small Number of Jews | 8 | Only a Small Number of Arabs | 31 |
| | Most Jews | 34 | Most Arabs | 52 |
| Religious | All Jews | 51 | All Arabs | 14 |
| | Not At All | 6 | Not At All | – |
| | Only a Small Number of Jews | 22 | Only a Small Number of Arabs | 28 |
| | Most Jews | 50 | Most Arabs | 50 |
| Traditional | All Jews | 22 | All Arabs | 22 |
| | Not At All | 11 | Not At All | 5 |
| | Only a Small Number of Jews | 26 | Only a Small Number of Arabs | 39 |
| | Most Jews | 44 | Most Arabs | 50 |
| Non-Religious | All Jews | 19 | All Arabs | 6 |
| | $X^2 = 45.452$ $df = 6$ $p = 0.000$ Statistically Significant Difference | | It was not possible to determine whether there was a statistically significant difference due to the insufficient number of responses in some of the cells. | |

At this point, I would like to discuss one final aspect of Jewish-Arab relations in Israel. I asked students to indicate the extent to which acts of discrimination occur in Israeli society today. Of the Jewish religious students surveyed, 70 percent said they believed that Arab-Israelis are discriminated against (39 percent indicated a high level of discrimination, and 31 percent indicated a very high level of discrimination). Responses to this question reflected an increase from previous studies: 82 percent of the traditional students surveyed acknowledged the existence of discrimination (51 percent referred to a high level, and 31 percent to a very high level). Among the non-religious students, 86 percent believe that discrimination exists (49 percent on a high level and 37 percent on a very high level). Students also agree that there is slightly more discrimination toward the Arabs in the occupied territories (77 percent of the religious students, 84 percent of the traditional students, and 87 percent of the non-religious students acknowledged such discrimination).

Jewish students regard the level of discrimination against Arabs from within Israel and from the occupied territories as similar to discrimination against new Jewish immigrants from Ethiopia (86 percent of the religious students, 84 percent of the traditional students, and 81 percent of the non-religious students) and against foreign workers (67 percent of the religious students, 81 percent of the traditional students, and 85 percent of the non-religious students).

Arab students also identified a high level of discrimination against Arab-Israelis–higher than the level of discrimination against new Jewish immigrants from Ethiopia and foreign workers. Forty-one percent of the religious students pointed to a high level of discrimination, while another 44 percent pointed to a very high level. Of the traditional students, 83 percent believe that discrimination exists, with 24 percent pointing to a high level, and another 59 percent to a very high level. Seventy-one percent of the non-religious Arab students said they believed there was discrimination, with 53 percent indicating a high level and 18 percent indicating a very high level.

In summary, Jewish-Arab social distance in Israel is great, and to the extent that it is possible to assess its development over time, it appears not only to have not decreased but to have increased. In this context, Arabs are the ones who seek closer relations with Jews, and, as I have said, this phenomenon is consistent with the behavior of minority groups vis-à-vis majority groups. At the same time, it is important to remember that the relationship between Palestinian Israelis (or Arab-Israelis) and Jewish-Israelis is in many ways atypical of most minority groups. One is a dynamic that creates an impossible situation from a Palestinian point of view. This dynamic was once summed up by former Deputy Minister Abdul Aziz Zu`bi, the first Arab deputy minister in Israeli history, as follows: "my country is at war with my people" (or, alternatively, "my people is at war with my country").

In early twentieth century America, women, Jews, and blacks were "others." In Israeli society since the mid twentieth century, the "others" have been Arabs, Jews of Eastern extraction, religious people, and homosexuals. Over the years, the otherness of some of these categories has decreased somewhat. Within the "emotional structure" of Israeli society, Arab-Israelis continue to play the role of the "other," and over the years the "otherness" of this group has actually intensified in some ways.

I believe that continuous, ongoing education regarding the other and those who are different (within Jewish-Israeli society as well) beginning at a young age and continuing throughout all the years of education may serve to help decrease the distance between "us" and the other, or, in some ways, to incorporate the "other" into "us."

## Notes

1. Jean-Paul Sartre, *Thoughts on the Jewish Question* (Tel Aviv, 1978), 41, 42 [Hebrew] (emphasis in original).
2. According to Sartre's analysis, negation of the other, the stranger, the person who is different, and the enemy is an important aspect of the identity of the anti-Semite. For additional reading and thoughts on the other in Judaism and Israeli society, see Haim Deutsch and Menachem Ben-Sasson, eds., *The Other Within and Without* (Tel Aviv, 2001) [Hebrew]; Dan Bar-On, *The Other Within Us: Changes in Israeli Identity from a Psychosocial Perspective* (Beer Sheva, 1999) [Hebrew]; and Yehouda Shenhav and Yossi Yonah, eds., *Racism in Israel* (Jerusalem, 2008) [Hebrew].
3. Moshe Lissak, "Major Cleavages in Israel Society," in *Pluralism in Israel: From Melting Pot To Salad Bowl,* ed. Yaakov Kop (Jerusalem, 2000), 27–54. [ Hebrew].
4. Among other sources, see Sammy Smooha, *Arabs and Jews in Israel: Conflicting and Shared Attitudes in a Divided Society* (Boulder, 1989).
5. See Mina Zemach, *Positions of the Jewish Majority in Israel Toward the Arab Minority* (Jerusalem, 1980) [Hebrew]; and Mina Zemach and Ruth Zin, *Positions of Youth on Democratic Values* (Jerusalem, 1984) [Hebrew].
6. Arieh Bender, *Maariv,* 26 August 1985 [Hebrew].
7. Eli Tavor, Nitza Aviram, and Nechama Duek, *Yediot Aharonot,* 28 June 1985 [Hebrew].
8. Ofra Mayseless, Gal Reuven, and Eli Pishof, *World Views and Attitudes of High School Students on Military Issues and National Security* (Zikhron Yaakov, 1989) [Hebrew].
9. Zeev Ben-Sira, *Democracy and Jewish High School Students: Essence, Support, and Meanings regarding Education and Democracy (A Report)* (Jerusalem, 1990) [Hebrew].
10. Kalman Binyamini, *Political and Civil Standpoints of Israeli Youth in Israel: A Research Report* (Jerusalem, 1994) [Hebrew].
11. Yakov Ezrachi and Gal Reuven, *Opinions and Worldviews of High School Students toward Issues of Society, Security and Peace—Youth Survey No. 2* (Zichron Yaakov, 1995) [Hebrew].
12. Yair Auron, Gila Zelikovitz, and Nili Keren, *Attitudes of Teaching Students in Israel toward Anti-Semitism and Racism* (Tel Aviv, 1996) [Hebrew].
13. Aryeh Caspi, "Peace Through the Sites," *Haaretz Weekend Magazine,* 1 November 1996 [Hebrew]. The study population included some 31,000 high school students between the ages of 14 and 16 from 27 European countries. The participants from Israel included 1,140 Jewish-Israelis, 350 Israeli Arabs, and 1,070 students from the West Bank and the Gaza Strip, and were organized into three groups: State students, State-Religious students, and Arab students. See also: Magne Angvik and Bodo von Borries, eds., *Youth and History—A Comparative European Survey on Historical Consciousness and Political Attitudes among Adolescents* (Hamburg, 1997).
14. Sammy Smooha, "Arab-Jewish Relations in Israel as a Jewish and Democratic State," in *Trends in Israeli Society* (Tel Aviv, 2001): 286–87 [Hebrew].
15. Auron, Zelikovitz, and Keren, *Attitudes of Teaching Students in Israel*; and Nili Keren, Gila Zelikovitz, and Yair Auron, *Anti-Semitism and Racism: An Attitude Study among High School Students in Israel* (Tel Aviv, 1997) [Hebrew].
16. Elihu Katz and Michael Gurvitz, *Leisure Culture in Israel: Patterns in Consumption* (Tel Aviv, 1973), 95–96, 102, 117, 120, 333 [Hebrew].
17. The 1994 Carmel Institute study used a five-level scale. The present study uses a four-level scale.

CHAPTER 5

# THE STATE OF ISRAEL AND ME

## Introduction

From the outset, Zionist ideology articulated a general approach to the problems facing the Jewish people and proposed general directions for solving them. As we have seen, Zionism was based on the concept of a Jewish people and their aspiration to become a sovereign nation. According to Zionism, sovereignty (or the political independence of the Jewish people, which was later explicitly defined as statehood) could only be realized in the Land of Israel.

The establishment of the state of Israel was undoubtedly a victory for Zionism, and some regarded it as the actualization of the ideology. Others, however, regarded the establishment of the state as only one step—albeit, a crucial one—in the redemption of the Jewish people. As we have seen, the Zionist movement was divided regarding whether the state was a critical tool for actualizing Zionism or a goal in itself. Zionism, it should be emphasized, means much more than the support of Israel by Jews in the Diaspora or the national patriotism of Jewish Israelis. Zionism involved much more than pro-Israeli positions.

The ongoing Arab-Israeli conflict continues to be the focus of the country's attention. Along with other factors, this conflict has blurred the ideological debates regarding domestic issues within Israel and Israel's relations with Jewish communities abroad. The Israeli education sectors have placed their emphasis on mobilizing popular identification with the state and have neglected the ideological elements at the heart of Zionism. Moreover, Zionism is taught in a somewhat sterile manner, partly out of concern that ideological clarification may lead to politicization.

In previous chapters, I discussed the fact that Zionism (and Israeliness) is understood primarily in relation to the state of Israel and the Land of Israel. I also discussed the great influence that wars have had on young Israelis, and the fact that they constitute a major component of Jewish-Israeli identity. The majority of my 1990 study population experienced the Yom Kippur war as children and the first Lebanon War as teenagers. Most of the 2008 study population were teenagers or adults during the Second Lebanon War.

My studies, however, do not explore the impact of the Arab-Israeli conflict on the personal and collective dimensions of Jewish-Israeli identity (although this subject is examined a bit more by the 2008 study). Without a doubt, this subject is in need of further study.

Zionism is an ideology that requires interpretation and adaptation to changing realities. Reinterpreting Zionism must involve contending with the realities facing Jewish communities in the free world whose members—despite all their support for Israel (pro-Israeliness) and the important influence of Israel on their identity and consciousness—have no intention of moving to Israel in the foreseeable future. In this context, Israelis' different opinions on Israel-Diaspora relations require clarification. Jewish emigration from Israel should be regarded as a subject in need of thorough discussion by the education system as well.

Young Israelis are less familiar with the ethical and ideological dimensions of Zionism and often regard them as irrelevant. Although Zionism is the focus of this book, Israeli educators have neither attempted nor succeeded in making Zionist ideology and its current meaning relevant to the young Israeli being educated today. We have thus far been unable to present the current realities from the perspective of the goals of Zionism. For this reason, we fail to provide young Israelis within the country's education system the tools necessary to deal with the reality in which they were born and in which they live, and to choose their own path based on ideological and ethical grounds. We also have no authoritative answer regarding the meaning of Zionism in our time.

Within the framework of attitude studies, I presented respondents with a number of groups of questions pertaining to their attitudes toward Zionism (Jewish students) and the state of Israel (Jewish and Arab students). I did not ask questions directly related to definitions of Zionism. Rather, my questions were meant to enable me to better understand the ideological and content-related dimensions of attitudes toward Zionism that transcend the widespread use of phrases such as "I am a Zionist" and "we are all Zionists" (for example, as articulated after the UN's definition of Zionism as racism in 1975), and the futile debates over defining and redefining the meaning of Zionism. I also refrained from including questions with ideological or political implications, although such questions are undoubtedly crucial for a thorough understanding of Israeli attitudes toward Zionism.

The Six Days War fundamentally transformed the character of the state of Israel and the way of life of its inhabitants. As of now, the "seventh day" of the war has lasted for 45 years. Israeli society is divided over how to conclude the war, the future of the occupied territories, and its relations with the Palestinians, some of whom live in Israel. Jewish-Israeli citizens and Arab-Israeli citizens have very different attitudes toward the state of Israel. For the Jewish population, the state was the actualization of the dream of generations. For the Arab population, the establishment of the state in part of the Land of Israel was a tragedy and a defeat.

The second section of Israel's Declaration of Independence, Israel's founding document, includes the proclamation of "the establishment of a Jewish state in the Land of Israel to be known as the State of Israel." The document clearly defines the state of Israel as a Jewish state that "will be open for Jewish immigration and for the ingathering of the exiles." Its democratic character was reflected in the document's section that discusses "development of the country for all its inhabitants"; "complete equality of social and political rights to all its inhabitants irrespective of religion, race, or sex"; "freedom of religion, conscience, language, education and culture"; and "safeguarding of the Holy places of all religions." The declaration also extends a call, "in the very midst of the onslaught launched against us now for months—to the Arab inhabitants of the State of Israel to preserve peace and participate in the upbuilding of the State on the basis of full and equal citizenship and due representation in all its provisional and permanent institutions."

Israel truly did fight against the Palestinian citizens of Israel, who have not enjoyed equal rights, as well as against their fellow Palestinians living outside of Israel. And, as we have seen, Israeli discourse incorporates debates over whether the state should be classified as a Jewish and democratic state, a democratic and Jewish state, or a Jewish-democratic or democratic-Jewish state.

The establishment of Israel was understood as a historic event with great influence on the destiny of the Jewish people in general and on the personal lives and destinies of many of my respondents. A large portion of the student subjects of my study regarded the establishment of the state in this manner, and many ranked it as the second most important event in Jewish history, after the Holocaust.[1] Without a doubt, the establishment of the state of Israel is understood today—in Israel and the Diaspora, and within the international community—as an event that fundamentally changed the destiny of the Jewish people. At the same time, questions also emerge periodically regarding our right to the country and Israel's right to exist, although since the 1980s such questions have been raised much less frequently than they were during the 1970s.

It is also important to remember that there is a statistically significant difference in the relative importance that different students attribute to the influence of the establishment of the state of Israel on the future of the Jewish people. We have seen that in the study of 1990, an 83 percent majority of the students in the State education sector believed that the Jewish people could not survive without the state of Israel (58 percent strongly agreed and 25 percent agreed).[2] In effect, this amounts to the adoption of the Zionist argument that is advanced widely in Israel (in its debate with the Diaspora, among other contexts) in order to justify the state's central and sometimes exclusive role in ensuring the future existence of the Jewish people ("negation of the exile"). However, the percentage of those who believe that the Jewish people cannot survive without the state of Israel dropped to 49 percent (23 percent strongly agree and 26 percent agree) among students from the State-Religious sector, and to 13 percent (79 percent disagree with the statement, and another 8 percent agree slightly) among students from the Ultra-Orthodox sector. The religious students believe (with some differences between the State-Religious and the Ultra-Orthodox sectors) that the Jewish people can survive without the state of Israel because the Jewish religion will ensure its continued existence. The religious believe in god, and without god—without religion, they believe—the Jewish people have no chance of surviving. The religious population does not perceive the state as the force responsible for ensuring the continued existence of the Jewish people in the modern era, as does a large portion of the secular population.

Two of the many comments written in by students from the Ultra-Orthodox sector beside these questions in my 1990 study clearly illustrate this difference. The first student wrote: "Because if there were no Torah, there would be no people. The entire world was created only for the Jewish people, and the fate of those who do not follow the path of Torah and commandments is clear." The second student wrote: "We have seen how the people survives. We have seen many peoples that have ceased to exist, but despite all the exiles, my people has not disappeared."

I presented the Palestinian students with a different statement: "The Palestinian people cannot survive without an independent state."

**TABLE 5.1 Responses of Jewish and Arab Students to the Statements, *"The Jewish people cannot survive without the state of Israel"* and *"The Palestinian people cannot survive without an independent state,"* 2008 (as a percentage)**

| | | Jews | Arabs |
|---|---|---|---|
| | Disagree | 40 | 9 |
| | Agree Slightly | 16 | 19 |
| | Agree | 20 | 31 |
| Religious | Strongly Agree | 24 | 41 |
| | Disagree | 4 | 14 |
| | Agree Slightly | 12 | 19 |
| | Agree | 24 | 35 |
| Traditional | Strongly Agree | 60 | 32 |
| | Disagree | 11 | 17 |
| | Agree Slightly | 17 | 28 |
| | Agree | 25 | 39 |
| Non-Religious | Strongly Agree | 47 | 16 |
| For the Jewish responses: $X^2 = 73.456$, $df = 6$, $p < 0.0001$ | | | |
| For the Arab responses, it was not possible to determine whether there was a statistically significant difference due to the insufficient number of responses in some of the cells. | | | |

The Jewish students expressed a high level of agreement, although the religious students expressed a significantly lower level (44 percent) than the traditional students (84 percent) and the non-religious students (72 percent). As I have said, this can be explained by the different opinions held by the religious, the traditional, and the non-religious populations regarding whether the Jewish people can survive without the Jewish religion. The levels of agreement with this statement were reversed, with 96 percent of the religious students agreeing that the Jewish people cannot survive without the Jewish religion, in comparison to 88 percent of the traditional students and 63 percent of the non-religious.

Of the religious Arab students surveyed, 72 percent agreed with the statement that the Palestinian people cannot survive without an independent state, which is much higher than the level of religious Jewish students who agreed with the statement that the Jewish people cannot survive without an independent state. In comparison, 67 percent of the traditional Arab students and 55 percent of the non-religious Arab students agreed with the statement, reflecting a lower level of agreement than that expressed by the traditional and non-religious Jewish students respectively.

It is important to remember that the Palestinians, in contrast to the Jews, have no independent state for the time being. As we have seen, a decisive majority of Arab students believe that the Palestinians have the right to establish a state that would include parts of the West Bank and the Gaza Strip, and 97 percent said that they are in favor of the establishment of a Palestinian state in the West Bank and the Gaza Strip.

Arab students expressed a relatively low level of agreement (43 percent of the religious students, 59 percent of the traditional students, and 44 percent of the non-religious) with the statement: "The Palestinian people cannot survive without religious belief" (I intentionally did not specify a religion, as Palestinian Arabs belong to different religious groups). In comparison, the percentage of Jewish students who agreed that the Jewish people cannot survive without the Jewish religion was significantly higher.

## Attitudes toward Jewish Emigration from Israel (*Yerida*)

My study asked a number of questions pertaining to Jewish emigration from Israel. Clearly, these questions do not facilitate an in-depth analysis of attitudes toward emigration or its causes. However, they may provide an indication of attitudes toward the phenomenon in general.

We understand Jewish emigration from Israel as a reflection of a basic crisis in the Zionist worldview in its confrontation with the realities of Zionist actualization, at least from the point of view of the emigrants themselves. From the perspective of the goals of the state's Jewish-national education efforts, the qualitative and quantitative scope of this phenomenon undoubtedly attests to a crisis and lack of success, and perhaps even failure.[3]

The issue of Jewish emigration from Israel is without a doubt an educational subject of the utmost importance. Nonetheless, it is a subject that the Israeli education system dares not address. The attitude of tomorrow's teachers is likely to be one of the factors influencing students' attitudes to the subject in the future.

**TABLE 5.2 Attitudes toward Jewish Emigration from Israel according to Religiosity, 1990 and 2008 (as a percentage)**

| 1990 Study | | | | | |
|---|---|---|---|---|---|
| | Extremely Negative | Opposition | Under-standing | Personal Matter | Positive |
| State | 12 | 20 | 45 | 23 | – |
| State-Religious | 39 | 24 | 31 | 5 | 1 |
| Ultra-Orthodox | 28 | 12 | 43 | 18 | – |
| $X^2 = 64.067$ | | $df = 8$ | | $p < 0.001$ | |
| **2008 Study** | | | | | |
| Religious | 11 | 13 | 33 | 43 | – |
| Traditional | 6 | 8 | 39 | 45 | 2 |
| Non-Religious | 4 | 4 | 24 | 64 | 4 |
| $X^2 = 39.746$ | | $df = 8$ | | $p < 0.0001$ | |

An interesting sector-based difference emerges in attitudes toward Jewish emigration from Israel. The most prominent attitude within the State sector is one of understanding and maybe even acceptance. The responses "although I do not agree with this behavior, I might understand it" and "in my opinion, it is a personal matter" together accounted for 68 percent of the responses in the 1990 study. In the 2008 study, agreement with these approaches reached 88 percent among the non-religious students (and another 4 percent who regarded Jewish emigration from Israel in a positive light), which is a very large majority. Among the traditional students, attitudes of acceptance and understanding accounted for 86 percent, while responses such as "my reaction would be extremely negative" or "I would oppose it" accounted for 14 percent. Among the State-Religious students in the 1990 study and the religious students in the 2008 study, negative attitudes and opposition were more widespread.

I believe that attitudes toward Jewish emigration from Israel have been influenced by two factors:

1) The weakening of Israeliness and the crisis and criticism of the state of Israel.
2) A marked strengthening of individualistic values, as opposed to the collective values that were so prevalent in Israeli society in the past.

> Individualistic values are more widespread among the non-religious than in the religious community, which is still a society based on collective values.

Although I did not assess the issue directly, students in both the State and State-Religious sectors attempted to express criticism of the political, social, and ideological realities in their attitudes toward Jewish emigration from Israel. Criticism in the ideological realm might of course be different in the State and State-Religious sectors.

These feelings proved to be particularly significant in the State sector. The weakening of Israeliness that I highlighted in other contexts may result in—and may already be reflected in—a crisis of Israeliness. Israelis have lost the pride they once had in their Israeliness and their country. Because Israeliness is still the prominent component of the identity of young non-religious Israelis today, the crisis of Israeliness holds particular significance for them. In contrast, young religious Israelis have a strong sense of Jewish identity, and the crisis may be working to strengthen the Jewish components of identity of some non-religious Israelis (in order to prevent a vacuum). For others, the decline or crisis of Israeliness may be finding expression in a tolerant, open, understanding, and to a large degree accepting attitude toward Jewish emigration from Israel.

I stress here that, based on their responses, my study population did not appear to be one with a great likelihood of emigration. Still, some differences do exist among the sub-groups (table 5.3). In the 1990 study, the major difference was between the religious students from both sectors (State-Religious and Ultra-Orthodox) on the one hand, and the State students on the other. Specifically, students of the State-Religious and Ultra-Orthodox sectors expressed an unequivocally negative attitude toward emigration, with 89 percent of the Ultra-Orthodox students and 85 percent of the State-Religious students asserting that they had never considered emigrating from the country. This position was shared by only 65 percent of the State students, while 23 percent reported having considered emigration infrequently. The differences among the different sectors in terms of the percentage of students who had considered emigrating from Israel was minimal (6 percent of the State-Religious students, 8 percent of the Ultra-Orthodox students, and 10 percent of the State students).

Responses to the question, "Do you think there is a chance you will emigrate from Israel?" reflected the same general spirit. Although a large majority of the State students in the 1990 study also ruled out emigration, students from the State-Religious and Ultra-Orthodox sectors did so in a more unequivocal manner (see table 5.3).

In the 2008 study, I also found that the percentage of those who actually considered emigrating from Israel was much lower than the percentage of people who expressed understanding or support for emigration, and included 16 percent of the religious students, 21 percent of the traditional students, and 31 percent of the non-religious. These figures are higher than those in the 1990 study. At the same time, when students were asked if there was a chance they would emigrate from Israel in the future, a large percentage responded negatively.

**TABLE 5.3 Chances of Emigration according to Education Sector and Religiosity, 1990 and 2008 (as a percentage)**

| 1990 Study (as a percentage) | | | | |
|---|---|---|---|---|
| | Absolutely Not | Slight Chance | Possibly | Yes |
| State | 36 | 46 | 15 | 3 |
| State-Religious | 65 | 24 | 9 | 2 |
| Ultra-Orthodox | 51 | 26 | 20 | 3 |
| | | | | |
| 2008 Study (as a percentage) | | | | |
| Religious | 36 | 42 | 17 | 15 |
| Traditional | 26 | 49 | 17 | 8 |
| Non-Religious | 19 | 34 | 31 | 16 |
| $X^2 = 36.197$ | $df = 6$ | | $p < 0.0001$ | |

The data reflects a significant increase in the possibility of emigration from Israel, particularly among non-religious students. Thirty-two percent of the religious students surveyed said there was a chance they would emigrate (in the 1990 study, the percentage of State-Religious students who responded in this manner was only 10 percent). Among the traditional students, 25 percent indicated a possibility that they would emigrate from Israel, and among non-religious students the number rose to 47 percent—one out of every two!

Thirty-nine percent of the Palestinian students surveyed opposed Palestinian emigration from Israel, while others accepted emigration in one way or another. In this spirit, 26 percent chose "although I do not agree with this behavior, I might understand it," while another 35 percent either agreed with emigration or supported it (by choosing either "it is a personal matter" or by responding positively).

Two-thirds (66 percent) of the Arab students surveyed have never considered leaving the country, and another 19 percent have only considered it infrequently. In contrast, 2 percent reported considering emigration often, and 13 percent answered "yes," the most unequivocal response. Fifty-seven percent said that emigration for them was not at all a possibility, 14 percent said there was only a slight chance, 22 percent said the emigration was possible, and 9 percent answered "yes."

As we can see, the Arab students indicated a possibility and intention of emigration that was much lower than that expressed by the Jewish students, despite the fact that they lived in a country that is defined as a "Jewish state," and despite the fact that their living conditions were much more complex and challenging than those enjoyed by Jewish students. Fifty-five percent of the Arab students said that they did not know anyone who has emigrated from the country, while the remainder indicated that they knew relatives, close friends, and acquaintance who had done so.

In the 1990 study among future Jewish teachers in the State sector, more respondents said they knew people who emigrated from Israel (including close friends, relatives, and acquaintances). They also knew more people who were considering emigrating from the country at the time they completed the questionnaire, and this often included close friends. Based on my data, it is possible to argue that emigration is more widespread within the social and familial circles within the State sector. I found a similar dynamic in the 2008 study.

Of course, the reasons for emigration differ from population to population. In general, the subjects of my study rarely reported financial reasons, although economic factors are known to play a significant role in encouraging emigration. Based on the analysis of responses of one group of 24 ultra-orthodox students, the reasons offered by students from the Ultra-Orthodox sector in an open question asking them to list reasons for possible emigration can be broken down into three categories:

1) *Reasons of principle, which are actually religious reasons that can result in emigration:* "When it is impossible to live a life based on Torah in Israel"; "when I am unable to live a life based on Torah in Israel and the religious leaders command emigration"; "when my people does not have Torah in Israel, we will follow it." In any event, the reason is not Zionist. For example: "My answer is that I do not oppose it for nationalist reasons but rather for reasons of Jewish law, and if Jewish law permits it, I would regard it positively." Some accused the state, and particularly the education system, of encouraging emigration, with responses such as "because he (the emigrant) simply does not know what the Land of Israel is," and "it is a failure on the part of the state and the flawed education that youth today receive in non-religious schools."
2) *Practical reasons permitting people to leave Israel, sanctioned by Jewish law:* "It is written in the Talmud that a person may leave the land of Israel either to make a livelihood, for marriage, or for medical reasons, and for no other reasons!!"; "Whoever cannot find their place in Israel should emigrate, on the condition that he continues to carry out religious rituals! It is prohibited to emigrate abroad for pleasure—only for health, marriage, and livelihood." Other respondents listed family and/or making a livelihood, or "marriage and the husband's place of study" as possible reasons for emigration.

3) *Reasons related to destiny and god,* such as "I know not where the hand of god will lead me," and "for reasons that god will appoint for me."

Students of the State teaching colleges had different reasons that justified emigration. The three most prevalent of which were[4]:

1) *Reasons related primarily to employment and making a livelihood:* Respondents cited concerns about being unable to find a job and make an adequate income (not standard of living or economic success) as a possible reason for emigration.[5]
2) *Self realization and personal development:* A small number of respondents cited reasons such as "personal development," "to try to live somewhere else where it is possible to live," "I've been there, and it was good," and "when the situation in Israel does not allow me to live happily with my family."
3) *Political-Ideological reasons:* A significant number of those who said that there is chance (usually a "slight chance," which I do not believe reflects the intention to actually emigrate) that they might emigrate or that they once considered emigration offered political-ideological reasons. These included (among others): "for ideological reasons we also emigrated . . . and we returned"; "particularly when it seemed as if the leaders of the country were leading it to destruction"; "when the people who disrespect the value of human life and democratic values grow numerous"; "when the political situation becomes very extreme against my views, I might think about it, but not forever"; "terrorism, Intifada, and wars"; "the Israeli people's policy of occupation"; and "inability to make a difference or lack of belief that the situation can improve." Within this group of non-religious students, I identified Jewish-Israeli identity problems, which, as I noted, found expression primarily in the crisis of Israeliness. At the end of her questionnaire, one of these students commented: "The questionnaire reveals confusion regarding identity (at least in my case), which I attribute to the political realities that blur Jewish-Israeli identity and cause me to feel that I belong less and that I am less willing to make sacrifices." Of the students of the State-Religious colleges, only a few respondents indicated that they might emigrate from Israel.[6]

To the 1990 study, I added two statements aimed at helping to clarify students' attitudes toward Zionism. The great majority of respondents did not agree with the statement that a Jewish person who supports Israel while living in the United States is a Zionist. A few expressed strong agreement with this statement, and approximately 20 percent expressed agreement. In contrast, 50 percent of the students from the State sector and 53 percent from the State-Religious sector agreed with the statement only slightly, and another 22 percent from the State sector and 30 percent from the State-Religious sector disagreed with it.

In addition, a very large majority did not agree with the statement that the role of Zionism came to an end with the establishment of the state. Ninety-one percent of the State-Religious sector and 76 percent of the State sector disagreed with the statement, while virtually all the remaining respondents agreed with it only slightly.

## Zionism: Yes or No?

Finally, in both studies I attempted to address a question which in my opinion is only of limited objective importance to the studies themselves: "Do you see yourself as a Zionist?" As I said, I did not ask respondents for a definition of Zionism. The responses I received were as follows:

**TABLE 5.4 Responses to the Question, *"Do you consider yourself a Zionist (according to your own definition of the term)?"* by Education Sector, 1990 and 2008 (as a percentage)**

| 1990 Study (as a percentage) | | | | |
|---|---|---|---|---|
| | Not At All | To a Minimal Extent | To a Great Extent | Definitely |
| State | 1 | 10 | 41 | 48 |
| State-Religious | 2 | 3 | 19 | 76 |
| Ultra-Orthodox | 63 | 4 | 6 | 27 |
| 2008 Study (as a percentage) | | | | |
| Religious | 7 | 23 | 25 | 45 |
| Traditional | 3 | 24 | 45 | 28 |
| Non-Religious | 7 | 35 | 36 | 22 |

According to the data from the 1990 study, students from the State-Religious teaching colleges not only defined themselves as Zionists much more frequently than students from the other groups, but also chose the most unequivocal response in doing so. It should be noted that some 10 percent of the State students regarded themselves as Zionists to a minimal extent, and a small number did not regard themselves as Zionists at all.

It is also important to note that 63 percent of students from the Ultra-Orthodox sector in the 1990 study asserted that they were not at all Zionists. Here, however, we must pay careful attention to the small print, as those who defined themselves as Zionists also added comments explaining their response. Some of these comments shed interesting light on the opinions of these students. In most cases, the comments, which appear next to the response "I definitely see myself as a Zionist," focused justifiably on the words "according to your definition," and included the following: "My definition of Zionism is very different from the standard definition. I really love the Land of Israel because god commanded us to love it a great deal"; "I am not a nationalist Zionist but rather a Jew who is proud of the Jewish people and not of the Zionist identity card"; "I of course agree with the goals that the Zionists wanted to achieve—when the Messiah comes, the Land of Israel will be a source for my people and for the nations"; "I am a Zionist who is proud of her people's Torah"; "I am a Zionist who is proud of my Judaism and my Torah"; "I love my Land of Israel because god commended [*sic*] me to love it"; "I love the Land of Israel because of Jewish commandment from the heavens." These responses reflect different interpretations of Zionism as a movement and a concept according to the political-ideological meanings given in the late nineteenth century.

The 2008 study reflected a significant decline in the percentage of students who defined themselves as Zionists, with 70 percent of the religious students in comparison to 95 percent of the State-Religious students in the 1990 study (the group of future religious teachers is perhaps a more narrowly defined and "biased" group). Among the traditional and non-religious students, the percentage who classified themselves as Zionists were 73 percent and 58 percent respectively (table 5.4). In any case, respondents' self-definition as Zionists in 2008 was lower than in 1990.

I asked the students three questions regarding their bond with the state of Israel, the Jewish people, and Jewish religion.

**TABLE 5.5 Agreement with the Statements, *"I feel a strong bond to the state of Israel/the Jewish people/the Jewish religion,"* 2008 (as a percentage)**

| | | State of Israel | Jewish People | Jewish Religion |
|---|---|---|---|---|
| Religious | Disagree | 7 | 1 | 1 |
| | Agree Slightly | 15 | – | 2 |
| | Agree | 29 | 9 | 10 |
| | Strongly Agree | 49 | 74 | 86 |
| Traditional | Disagree | 2 | 1 | 1 |
| | Agree Slightly | 7 | 5 | 14 |
| | Agree | 31 | 21 | 39 |
| | Strongly Agree | 60 | 73 | 46 |
| Non-Religious | Disagree | 2 | 4 | 20 |
| | Agree Slightly | 13 | 19 | 44 |
| | Agree | 32 | 38 | 27 |
| | Strongly Agree | 53 | 39 | 9 |
| $X^2$ | | Not statistically significant | $X^2 = 279.958$, $df = 6$, $p < 0.001$ | $X^2 = 97.612$, $df = 6$, $p < 0.001$ |

Among the religious students, the strongest bond expressed was with the Jewish religion (96 percent), followed by the Jewish people (83 percent), and the state of Israel (78 percent). The traditional students also expressed a strong bond with the Jewish people (94 percent), the state of Israel (91 percent), and the Jewish religion (85 percent). In comparison, the non-religious students express slightly weaker connections with the Jewish people (77 percent) and the state (75 percent), and a much weaker connection with Jewish religion (36 percent).

A series of questions, some of which were discussed above, asked Arab students about their identity. The basic structure of these questions was as follows: "To what degree does the fact that you are Palestinian play an important role in your life?" Each question addressed a different aspect of Arab Israeli identity (Palestinian, Israeli, Arab, Muslim/Christian/Druze). Responses indicating a minimal role or no role at all were most prominent with regard to Palestinianess (50 percent), followed by Israeliness (38 percent), Arabness (28 percent), and religious identity (26 percent).

When asked if they felt a strong sense of connection with the Arab nation, the Palestinian people, religion, or the state of Israel, Arab students indicated the following levels of either disagreement or minimal agreement with the following statements: 33 percent with regard to Arabness (meaning that 67 percent did feel a strong connection), 33 percent with regard to Palestinianess, 19 percent with regard to religiosity, and 40 percent with regard to Israeliness. In other words, Arab students' perceived bond with Israeliness was weaker than their sense of connection with all the other components of identity listed.

Four other questions were used to assess the issue of identity, including the connection students feel toward the Arab nation, the Palestinian people, religion, and the state of Israel. Seventy-two percent of the Arab students surveyed indicated a strong bond with the Arab nation; 67 percent indicated a strong bond with the Palestinian people; and 81 percent indicated a strong bond with their respective religion. Students' connection with the state of Israel, which stood as 60 percent (37.5 percent agree, and 22.5 percent strongly agree), was lower than all the other aspects of identity, and their perceived connection to Palestinianess was also not very high.

When asked which aspect of their identity played a more important part in their life, the percentages were similar: Twenty-four percent selected religious identity; 25 percent selected national identity; and 52 percent indicated that religious and national identity were equally important to them. Of course, there were substantial religiosity-based differences: Forty-three percent of the religious students preferred their religious identity (as opposed to 9 percent who preferred their national identity), while 24 percent of the traditional students and 63 percent of the non-religious students preferred their national identities.

The questionnaire contained another question pertaining to emigration from Israel which may hold more significance than the questions that were explicitly focused on the subject itself: "Would you want your children to live in Israel?" Ninety-seven percent of the religious Jewish students answered affirmatively that they would like their children to live in Israel, as did 95 percent of the traditional Jewish students, and 85 percent of the non-religious Jewish students. In fact, the percentage of students who said that they would want their children to live in Israel was higher than the percentage of students who said that they have never considered emigration (85 percent of the religious students, 80 percent of the traditional students, and 69 percent of the non-religious students).

The responses of the Arab students were somewhat different: Eighty-nine percent said they either want (30 percent) or strongly want (59 percent) their children to live in Israel. A decisive majority (89 percent) indicated that they have never considered the possibility of emigrating from Israel (never and rarely combined), and ruled out the possibility of leaving the country in the future (71 percent). In this way, and despite all the difficulties involved, Arab students expressed a clear preference for living in Israel and for having their children live in Israel as well.

Arab citizens of Israel expressed a high level of support for the establishment of a Palestinian state alongside of Israel (this was a finding of my study as well, with 97 to 98 percent of the students responding affirmatively). However, even if such a state were established, most Israeli Arabs said they would rather continue living in Israel.

In a question related to attitudes toward Zionism and the state of Israel, I asked the Arab students whether they agreed with large-scale Jewish immigration to Israel, even if it results in a decline in the standard of living of the veteran citizens of the country. Seventy-seven percent of the religious students did not agree, in comparison to 71 percent of the traditional students and 64 percent of the non-religious students. Interestingly, the level of agreement was higher among the non-religious students. Overall, 24 percent of the Arab students agreed with large-scale Jewish immigration to Israel even if it leads to a decline in the standard of living, while 76 percent opposed it. Finally, when asked how content they were as Israeli citizens, most said they were satisfied, with 14 percent extremely satisfied, 61 percent satisfied, 18 percent unsatisfied, and 7 percent extremely unsatisfied.

Another question, which might be better discussed in a different chapter, asked Arab students whether they would be willing to have their daughter marry a Jew. Seven percent of the respondents indicated that they would be extremely willing and another 17 percent said they would be willing, while 25 percent said they would only be willing to have their daughter marry an Arab, and 51 percent said they were not willing to have her marry a Jew. It should be noted that response distribution according to religiosity was as expected, with 89 percent of the religious students, 78 percent of the traditional students, and 45 percent of the non-religious students unwilling to have their daughters marry a Jew.

The responses of Jewish students on this subject were unequivocal, with the vast majority objecting to such close relations. As we have seen, a large majority also said that they feel closer to Jews from the Diaspora than to Arab Israelis. Arab responses, in contrast, were much less decisive. In fact, most indicated that they felt closer to Israeli Jews (55 percent) than to Palestinians from the Occupied Territories (45 percent), and among the non-religious Palestinians the percentage of students who felt closer to Israeli Jews reached 83 percent.

When asked their feelings about the possibility of their daughter marrying an Arab, Jewish students choose from the three optional responses according to the following breakdown: Ninety-eight percent of the religious students, 90 percent of the traditional students, and 67 percent of the non-religious students selected the unequivocal response: "I am not willing to have her marry an Arab." Ten percent of the traditional students, 25 percent of the non-religious students, and 2 percent of the religious students indicated that they were willing, but that they would prefer her to marry a Jew. Only 1 percent of the traditional students and 9 percent of the non-religious students said that they were definitely willing. In chapter 4, I examined Jews' sense of "social distance" from Arabs and vice versa. Based on the data presented in the present chapter, there is no doubt that Jews' sense of social distance from Arabs is greater than Arabs' sense of social distance from Jews.

In conclusion, the data presented in this chapter highlights three significant phenomena. The first is the fact that the Jewish students surveyed in the 2008 study acknowledged either a possibility that they may emigrate from the country or actual intentions to emigrate that were greater than that of their counterparts from the 1990 study. The second is the fact that Jewish students today are less Zionist than the Jewish students surveyed in 1990. Taken together, these two facts reflect the crisis of Israeliness discussed in previous chapters. The weakening bond of young Jewish Israelis with the state, which I was able to assess, and with the land, which I did not assess but which nonetheless appears clear, helps explain the increase in possible Jewish emigration.

Arab students expressed a sense of connection with the state and a bond with the land which, from certain perspectives, appears surprising in its intensity. A large portion of this population have no plans to move out country and want their children to live in Israel as well.

## Notes

1. See table 2.13 in chapter 2 of this book.
2. See table 2.11 in chapter 2 of this book.
3. On this subject, see chapters 2 and 3 of this book.
4. According to the open-ended responses of one group (34 questionnaires).
5. Responses included: "work"; employment related reasons"; "if I am unable to find employment"; "there is a chance (I will emigrate)"; and again, "I would like to stay here, but with a livelihood and a roof over my head, so that I can live in dignity."
6. According to an analysis of open-ended responses of a group within this sector (41 questionnaires).

# CHAPTER 6
# RELIGION AND ME

## Introduction

Israeli society is a rift ridden society, and one of its deepest rifts is the division between the secular and the religious.[1] In addition to being relevant to questions of Jewish-Israeli identity, this split has social, political, and legal implications as well. Some indicators suggest that the secular-religious divide has intensified since the 1970s and 1980s, at least in some ways. During these decades, one can identify a decreasing level of difference in positions within the religious camp itself, stemming from expressions of religious radicalization in some parts of the national-religious population (which was competing with the ultra-orthodox population).

The decreasing disparities between positions in the religious camp were also the result of the ultra-orthodox's increasing closeness to the political center, as well as its intensive efforts to influence the political center. At the same time, however, it is important to note that the national-religious camp's point of departure is clearly Zionist. The national-religious population tends to attribute religious significance to the state of Israel, often understanding it as the beginning of the redemption. Moreover, the political parties that are either identified with the national-religious stream or that split off from it have emerged as the most right-wing parties on the Israeli political map. In contrast, significant elements of the ultra-orthodox camps continue to deny (with varying levels of intensity) the Zionist ideological foundation of the state of Israel. The various ultra-orthodox institutions do not regard themselves as Zionist, despite their closer relations with the Israeli political center.

Following the Six Days War, portions of the Israeli secular population demonstrated a greater openness to the religious camp's approach of defining nationality in religious terms. Efforts of the religious public to imbue the national ethos with more religious nuances were successful at least to a certain degree. In many ways, this process reflected the theologization of Zionist ideology, including the demand to relate to Jewish law as the guiding force in the case of major national questions, such as the setting of borders or "who is a Jew?"[2] The increasing tendency during this period to define nationality in religious terms was perhaps even better reflected in the Israeli education system. It was during the 1970s and 1980s that the subjects of the 1990 study were socialized. From some perspectives, this process appears to have been somewhat moderated by the mass wave of immigration from the former Soviet Union.

Researchers who have studied the Jewish identity of Jewish Israelis have advanced a number of claims on the subject. Some have argued that the religiosity of students must be considered "extremely relevant to the subject," that "in all studies on this subject, the strong influence of the variable of religiosity was prominent," and that religion influences on a wide variety of opinions."[3] Another scholar defined religiosity as "the decisive variable in determining the intensity of Jewish identity in Israel, like everywhere else."[4] I regard the variable of religiosity as a primary independent variable.

As part of my attitude study on Jewish identity, I also attempted to clarify students' attitudes toward religion. The fact that my sample contained three, and perhaps four sub-groups is likely to generate an interesting assessment of this important subject. Although my study does not address relations between religious Jews and secular Jews, it can shed light on the evolution of the ever increasing tension between the two groups, which is a problem that concerns many Israelis.

This chapter explores the complexities of the relationship between religion and nationality; the role of religion in students' Jewish identity and attitudes toward the various religious groups; the role of religion within Jewish life and its impact on the continued existence of the Jewish people; and attitudes toward mixed-marriages and Jews from abroad, according to religiosity.

## The State, State-Religious, and Ultra-Orthodox Education Sectors

Religiosity was one of the most important independent variables in both of my studies. As I noted earlier, the 1990 study population consisted of 64 percent students from the State education sector, 23 percent from the State-Religious sector, and 13 percent from the Ultra-Orthodox sector.[5] Although the 2008 sample was not constituted in the same manner, the ratio between the groups of students, in accordance with their breakdown into teaching students from different sectors, remained relatively unchanged. The 1990 study population contained 2 to 3 percent more subjects from the State-Religious and Ultra-Orthodox sectors, in comparison to the state-wide population of students in teacher-training programs.[6]

In the early 1990s, Liebman estimated that, at the time, religious Jews made up approximately 20 percent of the Jewish population in Israel, including 5 percent Ultra-Orthodox.[7] It therefore appears that the overall Israeli population in the early 1990s included disproportionally more "non-religious" people than their percentage of students in the state stream in the 1990 sample, which included 25 percent traditional students, and 4 percent religious students. The Guttman Institute studies undertaken with the Avichai Fund ("Beliefs, Observances, and Values among Israeli Jews–2000") broke down the Jewish Israeli population as follows: 5 percent ultra-orthodox; 12 percent religious; 35 percent traditional; 43 percent non-religious; and 5 percent anti-religious. In comparison to the study undertaken in 1991, the relative percentage of traditional Jews in the overall population dropped by 7 percent; the percentage of the non-religious grew by 5 percent; and the percentage of the ultra-orthodox increased by 2 percent. With this, the non-religious replaced the traditional students as the largest group. The breakdown of first through twelfth graders enrolled in Israeli schools during the 2010 academic year was as follows: State sector—58 percent; State-Religious sector—18 percent; and Ultra-Orthodox sector—24 percent.

The first time a group of students from the teaching colleges of the Ultra-Orthodox sector was included in a study appears to have been the study of 1990. This group constituted a sample that was representative of at least one group within the Ultra-Orthodox sector, which is the largest and most important group in terms of the number of students enrolled in its educational institutions.[8] The religious students who took part in previous attitude studies usually came from a national-religious background, as researchers were not permitted to conduct studies on such subjects within ultra-orthodox educational institutions.[9]

My studies also found religiosity to be an extremely influential independent variable. I therefore usually refrained from presenting findings for the entire study population and instead reported responses according to education sector and religiosity (and, very infrequently, according to other variables that were deemed relevant).[10]

I conclude this section by noting a number of important attributes of my study population. In the Ultra-Orthodox sector, a much smaller percentage of the students surveyed were from Eastern extraction than in all the other sample groups. This group was also characterized by a less than average representation of students of Western extraction. That is to say, a high percentage of these students were children of two parents who were born in Israel, and a high percentage of their grandparents were born in Eastern European countries. This data reinforces the claims that some aspects of the Ultra-Orthodox education system come from Eastern Europe. The State-Religious teaching colleges contain a slightly higher than average percentage of students whose parents were born in Eastern countries.[11]

## Religious, Traditional, and Non-Religious Students[12]

Division into sectors does not in itself create the variable of religiosity. A decisive majority of the students, and in fact all the students of the teaching colleges of the

State-Religious and Ultra-Orthodox sectors surveyed in 1990, classified themselves and their parents as religious. In contrast, only 4 percent of the students in the State teaching colleges classified themselves as religious, while 25 percent classified themselves as traditional and the remaining 71 percent as non-religious.

In 1990, Liebman asserts that one-fifth of the adult Jewish population in Israel defines itself as "traditional." He believes that the numbers decreased slightly but steadily during the 1970s and 1980s. Liebman holds that traditional Jews are the most difficult to classify and that this group contains the vast majority of Sephardic Jews. I found this to be true of my study population as well. Liebman also points out the important fact that approximately 45 percent of Israelis defined themselves as secular, and that this number increased slightly during the 1970s and 1980s.[13] This data was also corroborated by the population of my studies.

All subjects in the Ultra-Orthodox sector classified their parents as religious, as did the vast majority (93 percent) of students of the State-Religious teaching colleges. The remainder of the State religious students (except one) classified their parents as traditional. As we have seen, the students who classified themselves as traditional in the 1990 study all belonged to State teaching colleges (25 percent of them). Although this appears to be a high percentage, if it is compared with the information they provided about their parents, we see the process in proper perspective.

Seven percent of the surveyed students from the State sector classified their parents as religious, and another 35 percent classified their parents as traditional. That is to say, the students of the State teaching colleges surveyed during the study of 1990 underwent a process of decreasing religiosity vis-à-vis their parents (and perhaps in comparison to their level of religiosity in previous years).

Within the State-Religious sector, I identified the reverse process: that is, of students becoming more religious. Seven percent of the surveyed students reported being religious, although their parents are not religious (6 percent of the parents were classified as traditional).

I have no way of knowing whether the processes identified during the 1990 study influenced the choice of the college, or whether attending the college sparked the process of becoming either more distant from religion (in the State teaching colleges) or closer to religion (in the State-Religious teaching colleges). It can be assumed that in borderline cases, there was a connection between choice of college and increased or decreased religiosity.

Breakdown of the 2008 study population by religiosity reveals 12 percent religious (more men than women), 23 percent traditional (more women than men), and 65 percent non-religious (more women than men).

The data from the 2008 study reveals that 29 percent of the religious subgroup were more religious than their parents, and that 19 percent were less religious. Among the traditional students, things appear to have moved in the opposite direction: 15 percent were more religious than their parents, and 47 per-

**TABLE 6.1 Religiosity of Respondents versus Religiosity of Their Parents: Responses to the Questions, *"Are you religious, traditional, or non-religious? Are your parents religious, traditional, or non-religious?"* 1990 and 2008 (as a percentage)**

| 1990 | | | |
|---|---|---|---|
| Subject Religiosity / Parent Religosity | Religious | Traditional | Non-Religious |
| Religious | 95 | 11 | 2 |
| Traditional | 5 | 84 | 19 |
| Non-Religious | – | 5 | 79 |
| $p < 0.0001$ | $df = 4$ | $X^2 = 652.160$ | |
| | | | |
| **2008** | | | |
| Subject Religiosity / Parent Religiosity | Religious | Traditional | Non-Religious |
| Religious | 92 | 15 | 4 |
| Traditional | 5 | 74 | 12 |
| Non-Religious | 3 | 11 | 84 |
| $p < 0.0001$ | $df = 4$ | $X^2 = 899.804$ | |

cent were more religious than their parents. Among the non-religious students, 8 percent were more religious than their parents, and 38 percent were less religious. This suggests that, at least among students, the prevalent trend appears to be a move away from religion. It can be assumed that in other circles, this process is proceeding more slowly and, in some, much more slowly. In the traditional sub-group of the 1990 study, 11 percent classified their parents as religious, while 5 percent said that their parents were not religious. Among the non-religious, 19 percent said that their parents are traditional and another 2 percent said that their parents are religious. In other words, the general trend appears to be one of declining religiosity.

Declining religiosity appears to be the most prominent among the traditional students. Within this sub-group, only 35 percent classified themselves as being as religious as their parents. Thirteen percent said they were more religious than their parents, and 52 percent of the students surveyed in the 1990 study reported being less religious than their parents. If, as I have said, the traditional sub-group does in fact constitute the intermediate group between the religious and the non-religious students, my findings enable me to argue that the traditional students tend to be in the midst of a process of moving from religiosity to non-religiosity, and not in the opposite direction.[14] The 2008 study also found that a high percentage of traditional students are less religious than their parents. However, this trend is relevant for the religious as well, as 19 percent of the religious students in the 1990 study said that they were less religious than their parents.

**TABLE 6.2 Religiosity of Respondents in Comparison to Parent Religiosity: Responses to the Question, *"Are you more religious, religious to the same extent, or less religious than your parents?"* (as a percentage)**

| 1990 Study | | | |
|---|---|---|---|
| | Religious | Traditional | Non-Religious |
| More Religious than Parents | 25 | 13 | 3 |
| Same Level of Religiosity | 73 | 35 | 66 |
| Less Religious than Parents | 2 | 52 | 31 |
| $X^2 = 134.706$ | $df = 4$ | $p < 0.0001$ | |
| **2008 Study** | | | |
| | Religious | Traditional | Non-Religious |
| More Religious than Parents | 29 | 15 | 8 |
| Same Level of Religiosity | 52 | 38 | 54 |
| Less Religious than Parents | 19 | 47 | 38 |
| $X^2 = 58.659$ | $df = 4$ | $p < 0.0001$ | |

In subjects' responses to a large number of the questions asked, I did not find the variable of extraction to be statistically significant. That is to say, extraction did not appear to influence students' positions on different subjects. I did, however, identify a correlation between the variable of extraction, or to be more precise, parents' extraction, on the one hand, and religiosity on the other hand (as I have noted, 90 percent of the subjects were born in Israel). Students of Eastern extraction accounted for the largest number of traditional students in the 1990 study population (68 percent). The children of parents of Eastern extraction tended to classify themselves as non-religious less frequently than members of other groups.

The most significant change pertaining to the religiosity of subjects vis-à-vis their parents took place among students of Eastern extraction. Whereas a large majority in the groups of Western extraction and Israeli extraction classified themselves as having the same level of religiosity as their parents, the number dropped to 45 percent among students of Eastern extraction. The direction of change was also clear, with 40 percent reporting that they were less religious than their parents and only 15 percent reporting that they were more religious than their parents.

**TABLE 6.3** Level of Religiosity according to Extraction of Parents, 2008 (as a number)

| Father's Extraction | | | | |
|---|---|---|---|---|
| | Level of Religiosity | | | |
| Extraction | Religious | Traditional | Non-Religious | Total |
| Israeli | 55 | 87 | 257 | 399 |
| Eastern | 23 | 79 | 97 | 199 |
| Western | 28 | 30 | 208 | 266 |
| Unknown | 8 | 11 | 32 | 51 |
| Total | 114 | 207 | 594 | 915 |
| Mother's Extraction | | | | |
| | Level of Religiosity | | | |
| Extraction | Religious | Traditional | Non-Religious | Total |
| Israeli | 53 | 103 | 257 | 399 |
| Eastern | 23 | 68 | 97 | 199 |
| Western | 29 | 26 | 208 | 266 |
| Unknown | 3 | 10 | 32 | 51 |
| Total | 114 | 207 | 594 | 915 |

Most participants in the 2008 study were born in Israel, and I divided them into groups according to the extraction of their parents: 1) students with both parents born in Israel; 2) students with both parents born in Eastern countries; 3) students with both parents born in Western countries; and 4) mixed extraction (parents of different extractions). In this context, I found significant correlation between extraction and religiosity: most students of Israeli extraction classified themselves as non-religious; a high percentage (approximately 40 percent) of students with parents of Eastern extraction were traditional; and more than three-quarters of the students of Western extraction classified themselves as non-religious.

Indeed, the independent variable of religiosity (religious, traditional, and non-religious) emerged as an extremely significant variable. In the case of some questions, this variable enabled me to better understand differences between groups when the variable of sector ceased to be of help.

In the case of many questions related to Jewish identity, traditional students continued to serve as an intermediary group between the religious and non-religious students. For this reason, I will refer to this break-down when discussing responses to certain questions. I argue that in many ways I was dealing with three sub-identities, or profiles of Jewish Israeli identity: religious, traditional, and non-religious (these sub-identities will be discussed further in the conclusion of this book). The national-religious and the Ultra-Orthodox have very little in common when it comes to weighty subjects such as attitudes toward Zionism, Israeliness, and the state of Israel. Or perhaps I am really talking about four sub-groups: secular (non-religious), traditional, national-religious, and ultra-orthodox.

## Attitudes Toward Streams of Judaism

Most Jews in America are affiliated with the non-orthodox streams of Judaism. Israel, however, does not recognize the legitimacy of these streams and does not permit their rabbis to operate in the realm of personal status.

I asked my subjects the extent to which they agreed with the following statement: "The orthodox, conservative, and reform streams are equally legitimate forms of the Jewish religion." In the 1990 study, the vast majority of religious students surveyed disagreed with this statement, and in the State-Religious sector, 95 percent reported disagreement. Within the Ultra-Orthodox sector, opposition was expressed by almost 100 percent of the respondents.

**TABLE 6.4 Attitudes toward Streams of Judaism according to Education Sector Recognition of the Legitimacy of the Non-Orthodox Streams: Agreement with the Statement, *"The orthodox, conservative, and reform streams are equally legitimate forms of Judaism,"* (as a percentage)**

| 1990 Study | | | |
|---|---|---|---|
| | State | State-Religious | Ultra-Orthodox |
| Disagree | 8 | 89 | 98.18 |
| Agree Slightly | 19 | 6 | 1.82 |
| Agree | 32 | 1 | – |
| Strongly Agree | 41 | 4 | – |
| $X^2 = 359.146$ | $df = 6$ | $p < 0.0001$ | |
| **2008 Study** | | | |
| | Religious | Traditional | Non-Religious |
| Disagree | 67 | 16 | 7 |
| Agree Slightly | 15 | 29 | 18 |
| Agree | 10 | 35 | 29 |
| Strongly Agree | 8 | 20 | 46 |
| $X^2 = 199.062$ | $df = 6$ | $p < 0.0001$ | |

The data displayed in table 6.4 indicates an increase in the level of acceptance of the non-orthodox streams of Judaism, particularly within the traditional subgroup, of which 55 percent expressed acceptance, and the non-religious subgroup, of which 75 percent expressed acceptance. This can be compared to the response of the State sector in the 1990 study, which expressed agreement, though not unequivocal agreement, with the statement. No extraction-based differences were identified, but breaking down the study population by religiosity (religious, traditional, and non-religious) again sheds light on the differences. Traditional students again functioned as an intermediate group. The religious students, in contrast, almost decisively denied the legitimacy of the non-orthodox streams, as did 39 percent of the traditional students and 24 percent of the non-religious students.

The non-religious students are not decisive in their opposition to the status quo. In the 1990 study, 41 percent strongly agreed that the orthodox, conservative, and reform streams are equally legitimate forms of Judaism. A study undertaken by the Guttman Institute and the Avichai Fund in 2000 found that two-thirds of respondents agreed with equating the status of the reform and conservative streams with that of the orthodox stream, which is a higher level of agreement than expressed in my study.

This data raises the following question: how much do these students, which include future teachers in Israel, know about the religious streams, and to what extent do they view them from the perspective of the Jewish people as a whole, both in Israel and the Diaspora? As we saw in previous chapters, most of the students lack this perspective, particularly the non-religious students. We can therefore assume that these students and future teachers know very little about the religious streams and therefore see them in extremely general terms.

## Attitudes Toward Intermarriage

The issue of intermarriage terrifies the Jewish people. As we have seen, young Israelis are concerned about two major dangers that in their opinion threaten the well-being of the Jews of the Diaspora: anti-Semitism[15] and assimilation. The most severe expression of this approach emerges in Jewish attitudes toward the subject of intermarriage. Jewish sociologists, demographers, and philosophers are divided on the demographic significance of intermarriage for the future of the Jewish people. In this context, we find differing opinions, some more alarmist than others, regarding the influence of intermarriage on the Jewish identity of the next generation. I assume (I did not assess this issue in my study) that young Israelis know very little about this subject—which is one of the most important subjects relevant to the future of the Jewish people—and that what they know is often generalized knowledge based on stereotypes.

Clearly, asking young Israelis whether there is a chance they might marry a non-Jew does not constitute thorough treatment of the subject, particularly when, in the realities of Israel, the issue at hand is primarily a hypothetical possibility. Nonetheless, responses to this question can provide an indication of attitude on the subject, or a sort of declaration of intentions.

**TABLE 6.5 Responses to the Question, "Is there a possibility that you will marry a non-Jew?" according to Education Sector and Religiosity, 1990 (as a percentage)**

| 1990 Study | | | |
|---|---|---|---|
| | State | State-Religious | Ultra-Orthodox |
| Definitely Not | 57 | 98 | 100.00 |
| Remote Chance | 29 | 2 | – |
| Some Chance | 7 | – | – |
| Yes | 7 | – | – |
| $X^2 = 102.553$ | $df = 6$ | $p < 0.0001$ | |
| **2008 Study** | | | |
| | Religious | Traditional | Non-Religious |
| Definitely Not | 96 | 82 | 29 |
| Remote Chance | 4 | 9 | 33 |
| Some Chance | – | 7 | 23 |
| Yes | – | 2 | 15 |
| $X^2 = 192.681$ | $df = 6$ | $p < 0.001$ | |

Among the religious students in the 1990 study, opposition to the possibility of intermarriage (the response "definitely not") reached 100 percent in the Ultra-Orthodox sector and 98 percent in the State-Religious sector (the remaining 2 percent indicated a remote possibility).[16] Clearly, the unequivocal response of these students stemmed from their religious beliefs.

In the 1990 study, only 14 percent of the students of the State teaching college students thought there was a possibility (7 percent) or some chance (7 percent) that they would marry a non-Jew. Again, the break-down of students by religiosity sheds more light on the subject: the large majority of traditional students in the 1990 study either completely ruled out (71 percent) or indicated that there was only a remote chance (26 percent) of inter-marriage. And although the possibility of intermarriage was somewhat higher, it was nonetheless low. Nine percent believed that there was a possibility they would marry a non-Jew, and another 9 percent believed that there was some chance they would do so. The 2008 study revealed similar attitudes toward intermarriage, with 100 percent of the religious students and 91 percent of the traditional students ruling out the possibility, and a much lower percentage of the non-religious students (38 percent).

Opposition to marrying a *ger* (a primarily religious term used to refer to a convert to Judaism) is also high in all the sectors, although it is of course much lower than the opposition to marrying a non-Jew. When posed with this question, 75 percent of the students in the ultra-orthodox sector chose the response "definitely not." Among students of the State and State-Religious teaching colleges in the 1990 study, one-third of the respondents ruled out the possibility of marrying a convert. It is also interesting to note that the extraction-based and religiosity-based differences in responses to this issue were found to be insignificant. In the 1990 study, 41 percent of the traditional students expressed opposition to the possibility of marrying a convert, which was close to the level of opposition expressed by the religious students (46 percent). In both of these sub-groups, another one-third indicated only a remote chance. Non-religious students expressed a lower level of opposition to marrying a convert than they did to marrying a non-Jew (31 percent), in addition to the other 29 percent who thought there was a remote chance of such a marriage. The 2008 study indicated a substantial increase in the level of agreement with marrying a convert (as opposed to a non-Jew) to 46 percent, which was higher than the level of agreement among the traditional students (44 percent) and non-religious students (25 percent) alike.

In other words, the religious act of conversion is regarded not only by the religious students, but by a significant portion of the secular students as well, as a meaningful act that can influence the decision to marry or not marry someone.

In the 2008 study, I presented students with a statement which is perhaps more relevant to Jewish-Arab relations than to the willingness to marry a non-Jew: "I would be willing for my daughter to marry an Arab." Actually, the statement pertains to both Jewish and Arab nationality and religiosity, which exercised influence on the responses (as we recall, in response to the question "To whom do you feel closer: Arab Israelis or Diaspora Jews?" 99 percent of the religious students, 95 percent of the traditional students, and 86 percent of the non-religious students indicated that the feel closer to Diaspora Jews).

**TABLE 6.6 Responses to the Question, *"Would you be willing to have your daughter marry an Arab?"* 2008 (as a percentage)**

| | | |
|---|---|---|
| **Religious** | Definitely willing | – |
| | Willing, but I would prefer her to marry a Jew | 2 |
| | Not willing | 98 |
| **Traditional** | Definitely willing | 1 |
| | Willing, but I would prefer her to marry a Jew | 10 |
| | Not willing | 89 |
| **Non-Religion** | Definitely willing | 9 |
| | Willing, but I would prefer her to marry a Jew | 25 |
| | Not willing | 66 |
| $X^2 = 56.4$ | $df = 4$ | $p < 0.0001$ |

## Religion and the Future of Jewish Existence

In chapter 2, I discussed respondents' attitudes toward the Jewish people, the Jewish religion, the Land of Israel, and the state of Israel. This section will go into greater depth regarding some of the religiosity-based aspects of these issues.

As we recall, the religious teaching students from both religious sectors indicated in the clearest and most unequivocal terms possible that they feel a close connection with the Jewish religion (100 percent strongly agreed with the statement). However, it is also important to remember that only 25 percent of the students from the State sector described their relationship with religion in this way, in addition to another 46 percent who described their connection with religion as somewhat strong. Overall, 71 percent of the students from the State teaching colleges acknowledged a sense of connection with religion. In contrast, 6 percent described their relationship with religion as "definitely not strong," and another 23 percent described it as "minimally strong."

Religion plays a major role, and to be precise, *the* major role in the Jewish identity of young religious Jews in Israel. As we saw, they also regard religion as the most important factor in maintaining the existence of the Jewish people—more important than the state of Israel. But religion also undoubtedly serves an important function for the traditional population, as well as the non-religious population. Some speak of secular performers of religious rituals, or a substantial number of non-religious Jews who perform religious rituals to some extent. When I examined attitudes toward religion according to religiosity in the 1990 study, I found that 52 percent of the traditional respondents (who are all students of State teaching colleges) felt a very strong bond with religion, and that 43 percent felt a medium bond. Among the students of the State teaching colleges, most respondents who indicated a strong connection with religion were traditional Jews.

However, it should also be noted that 12 percent of the respondents who classified themselves as non-religious feel a very strong bond with religion, and another 49 percent of the non-religious (secular) feel a medium bond with religion. We can therefore conclude that religion plays a meaningful role in the lives of many of the students, including those who do not regard themselves as religious: the traditional students, and some of the non-religious (secular) students.

Chapter 2[17] briefly refers to a series of questions on the Jewish people's chance of survival without the Jewish religion and without the state of Israel. The overwhelming majority of religious students in the 1990 sample either strongly agreed (95 percent) or agreed (4 percent) that the Jewish people cannot survive without the Jewish religion, while students of the state colleges expressed a much more moderate level of agreement. Still, we cannot view this population as one bloc, as it also includes a large number of traditional students who as we have seen constitute an intermediary group. Here too, division along the lines of religiosity provides a clearer picture, as well as statistically significant responses.

**Table 6.7 Agreement with the Statement, *"The Jewish People cannot survive without the Jewish religion,"* according to Religiosity (as a percentage)**

| 1990 Study | | | |
|---|---|---|---|
| | **Religious** | **Traditional** | **Non-Religious** |
| Definitely Agree | 95 | 46 | 24 |
| Agree | 4 | 49 | 42 |
| Agree Minimally | _ | 5 | 27 |
| Disagree | 1 | _ | 7 |
| $X^2 = 250.224$ | $df = 6$ | $p < 0.0001$ | |
| **2008 Study** | | | |
| | **Religious** | **Traditional** | **Non-Religious** |
| Definitely Agree | 86 | 61 | 14 |
| Agree | 10 | 27 | 26 |
| Agree Minimally | 2 | 9 | 33 |
| Disagree | 2 | 3 | 27 |
| $p < 0.0001$ | $df = 6$ | $X^2 = 132.369$ | |

The traditional students in the 1990 study also agreed with the statement, but some less decisively than the religious students. In contrast, approximately one-third of the non-religious students did not agree with the statement, and 7 percent of these disagreed strongly. Here too, in the responses to this question, I saw a lower level of agreement regarding the influence and power of religion. In comparison, I found no significant difference between traditional students and non-religious students regarding the statement, "The Jewish people cannot survive without the state of Israel."[18]

Jewish philosophers in the modern era have debated the role of religion in the past, the present, and the future, and the role of religion in ensuring the continuation of Jewish existence. I asked respondents their opinions regarding the statement, "Jews who perform religious rituals ensure the future existence of the Jewish people more effectively than secular Jews." In the 1990 study, 92 percent of students from the Ultra-Orthodox sector expressed decisive agreement with this statement, in addition to another 3 percent who expressed agreement. Students of the State-Religious teaching colleges agreed, although less decisively (67 percent decisively agreed and 27 percent agreed). In the state colleges, 6 percent agreed with the statement decisively and 17 percent agreed with it. A religiosity-based breakdown of the study population yields a picture reflecting slightly greater polarization between the religious and the non-religious students, with the traditional students again serving as an intermediate group.

TABLE 6.8 Agreement with the Statement, *"Jews who follow the 613 commandments ensure the future existence of the Jewish people more than secular Jews do,"* according to Religiosity (as a percentage)

| 1990 Study | | | |
|---|---|---|---|
| | Religious | Traditional | Non-Religious |
| Definitely Agree | 72 | 18 | 2 |
| Agree | 21 | 25 | 12 |
| Agree Minimally | 5 | 23 | 22 |
| Disagree | 2 | 34 | 64 |
| $X^2 = 323.976$ | $df = 6$ | $p < 0.0001$ | |
| **2008 Study** | | | |
| | Religious | Traditional | Non-Religious |
| Definitely Agree | 58 | 7 | 2 |
| Agree | 13 | 19 | 7 |
| Agree Minimally | 17 | 36 | 17 |
| Disagree | 12 | 38 | 74 |
| $X^2 = 301.158$ | $df = 6$ | $p < 0.0001$ | |

In this context, the religious students' sense of self-importance is clear: they believe, and in fact are completely certain, that they are safeguarding the future of Jewish existence much more than the non-religious. The 2008 study reflected a slight increase in the level of disagreement with the statement expressed by non-religious students.

The chapter "My People and Me" explored attitudes toward the Land of Israel, the State of Israel, and the Jewish religion (comparative data). Below, I offer two important comments regarding the variable of religiosity:

1) Distinguishing between Israel's two religious education sectors—the State-Religious sector and the Ultra-Orthodox sector—is crucial for a proper understanding of students' attitudes toward the state of Israel, as the sense of connection expressed by the State-Religious students was much stronger than that expressed by the students of the Ultra-Orthodox sector.
2) In the case of all the variables, distinguishing between the traditional students and the non-religious students within the study population from State teaching colleges highlights significant and interesting differences.

Traditional students demonstrated the strongest bond with the state of Israel, more than the State-Religious students as a group, and significantly more than the students of the Ultra-Orthodox sector as a group.[19] The same was true with regard to bonds with the Land of Israel, which were strongest among the traditional students, stronger than the non-religious students', and slightly stronger than those of the students from the State-Religious sector).

The opposition of some non-religious and traditional students to the prominent influence of religion was again reflected in the 2008 study. In the 2008 study, the religious students were also not as convinced as they were in the 1990 study that Jews who perform religious rituals (that is, they themselves) are ensuring the future existence of the Jewish people more effectively than secular Jews. In other words, data regarding students from the State teaching colleges pertaining to attitudes toward religion, land, people, and state actually reflect an average between the responses of the traditional students and the non-religious students. This will be demonstrated again with regard to the sense of connection with the Jewish people, a subject which I regard as the most complex, and perhaps the most problematic.[20] It is particularly important with regard to the non-religious students because, in my opinion, their attitude toward the Jewish people should be the main factor shaping the Jewish component of their identity.

**TABLE 6.9 Agreement with the Statement, *"I feel a strong connection with the Jewish people,"* according to Religiosity (as a percentage)**

| | Definitely Not | | Minimal Level | | Medium Level | | Yes, Definitely | |
|---|---|---|---|---|---|---|---|---|
| | 1990 | 2008 | 1990 | 2008 | 1990 | 2008 | 1990 | 2008 |
| Religious | 1 | 1 | – | – | 1 | 11 | 98 | 88 |
| Traditional | – | 1 | – | 5 | 9 | 21 | 14 | 74 |
| Non-Religious | 1 | 4 | 3 | 19 | 36 | 38 | 60 | 39 |
| 1990 | $X^2 = 323.976$ | | | $df = 6$ | | | $p < 0.0001$ | |
| 2008 | $X^2 = 97.612$ | | | $df = 6$ | | | $p < 0.0001$ | |

When I compare the responses in the 1990 study with the responses in the 2008 study, I discover a decline in non-religious students' sense of connection with the Jewish people (from 96 percent to 77 percent), and, to a lesser degree, among traditional and religious students as well.

## Religion in Public and Private Life in Israel and the Diaspora

I asked my subjects a number of questions regarding the role of religion in public and private life in Israel and the Diaspora. In the 1990 study, the religious students in both education sectors thought that religion should play a significant role in public and national life within the state of Israel. Ninety-four percent of the Ultra-Orthodox students and 90 percent of the national-religious students thought that such a role was extremely desirable, and almost all of the remaining students in these categories thought it was important. Within the State-Religious teaching colleges, a smaller but nonetheless high percentage of students thought it was desirable for religion to play a significant role in the personal lives of Jews in Israel (85 percent indicated "extremely desirable"). Overall, almost all the religious students in the sample thought it was either desirable (16 percent) or extremely desirable (83 percent) for religion to play an important role in the personal lives of Jews in Israel.

The responses of religious students to this question in the 2008 study also reflected greater moderation in their attitudes toward the role of religion in public life: 35 percent agreed and 51 percent strongly agreed that religion should play an important role in public life in Israel. Among traditional students, the percentage dropped to 79 percent (56 percent agreed, and 23 percent strongly agreed), and among non-religious students, 32 percent agreed, and only 3 percent strongly agreed, in contrast to 64 percent who did not agree (24 percent disagreed, and 40 percent agreed minimally). In response to the statement, "Religion should play an important role in the personal lives of Jews in Israel," 61 percent of the non-religious students did not agree, in contrast to 19 percent of the traditional students and 1 percent of the religious students.

In the 1990 study, the responses provided by students in the State sector were different, as expected: 38 percent (the large majority) thought it was desirable, and 6 percent thought it was extremely desirable that religion play an important role in public and national life in Israel, as well as in the personal lives of Jews in Israel. Forty-five percent thought that it was undesirable for religion to play an important role in public and national life in Israel, and 17 percent thought it was very undesirable. Fourteen percent thought that it was very undesirable for religion to play an important role in the personal lives of Jews in Israel. This group may consist partly or completely of "ideological secularists," or secular Jews who not only do not perform religious rituals but for whom secularism is a philosophy and a way of life. Some may be what Liebman refers to as "universal secularists."[21]

The responses to the question, "Do you think that religion should play an important role in the lives of Jews outside of Israel?" are interesting. The percentage of religious students who expressed support of such a role remained very high, going relatively unchanged. However, the support expressed by students of the state colleges reflected a significant increase (59 percent said it was desirable, and 10 percent said it was very desirable). Of the remaining students, 27 percent thought it was not desirable, and only 3.5 percent expressed opposition. This data reflects the widespread assumption among some non-religious Israelis that a Jewish existence without religion may be possible in Israel, but not in the Diaspora.

As might have been expected, breaking down the study population by religiosity sheds light on the extreme differences between religious and non-religious students, with the traditional students again serving as an intermediate group. Of the non-religious students in this group, 24 percent thought it would be extremely undesirable for religion to play an important role in public life in Israel and in the personal lives of Jews in Israel (19 percent). However, among the same students, only 5 percent believed that it is extremely undesirable for religion to play an important role in the lives of Jews outside of Israel.

In the 2008 study, I also found that the percentage of students who thought that religion should play an important role in the lives of Jews abroad was higher than those who thought it should play an important role in public and private life in Israel. These students appeared to believe that in Israel it is possible to continue being Jewish without religion, while this is extremely difficult if not impossible to do outside of Israel. Ninety-eight percent of the religious students and 91 percent of the traditional students said they thought that religion should play an important role in the lives of Jews abroad (most of the religious students "strongly support[ed]," while most of the traditional students "support[ed]" this). Of the non-religious Jews, 55 percent supported such a role, and 8 percent strongly supported such a role.

Some young Israelis appeared to be pondering the question of whether Jewish nationality is secular or religious. Some characterized Jewish nationality in the Diaspora—which they regard as religious—differently than they characterizeed Jewish nationality in Israel. If some of the ideological secularists in my sample held fundamental, ideological anti-religious opinions, they clearly constituted an extremely small percentage of the non-religious members of my study population.

A significant number of religious and non-religious students said they understood "Judaism" and "Jewish" more in a religious context ("Jewish," "Christian," "Muslim") than in a national context ("Jewish," "French," "Russian"). The Israeli education system has thus far failed to provide young Israelis with the tools to contend with this subject.

## Notes

1. Horowitz and Lissak, *Trouble in Utopia,* 102–03.
2. Ibid., 98.
3. Farago, "The Jewish Identity of Israeli Youth," 264, 285.
4. Herman, *Jewish Identity,* 173 [Hebrew].
5. See table 2.1 in chapter 2 of this book.
6. Data published by the Israeli Ministry of Education indicates that the population of elementary school children in the country breaks down differently. In 1989–90, the State sector, which has been declining since 1984–85, accounted for 71.3 percent of the students, which was 7.5 percent greater than in my study. The State-Religious sector accounts for 21.3 percent of the students, and the Ultra-Orthodox sector accounts for 7.4 percent of the students, or less than in my sample. Overall, the share of Israel's elementary

school population belonging to the State-Religious and Ultra-Orthodox sectors has increased since 1984–85. As I have noted, the 2010 student population in the Jewish sector consisted of 58 percent studying in the State system, 18 percent in the State-Religious system, and 24 percent in the Ultra-Orthodox system.

7. Liebman, "Some Thoughts on Relations between Religious and Non-Religious Jews," 10–11, 195 [Hebrew].
8. The students of the Beit Rivka College in Kfar Chabad, which is classified as part of the State-Religious sector, also possesses the traits of Ultra-Orthodox sector education. My sample included a small group of 11 students from this institution.
9. Farago, "The Jewish Identity of Israeli Youth," 264.
10. Findings regarding total responses provide little insight due to the great differences among the sectors regarding most of the variables explored.
11. See table 2.2.
12. These were the terms I chose to use in the questionnaire. Note the difference between the term "non-religious" and the term "secular." Among others, see Smilansky, "The Courage to Be a Secular Jew"; and Liebman, *Living Together,* 9–10.
13. See Liebman, *Living Together,* 10–12.
14. As we have seen, Liebman also argues that over the past two decades, there has been a slight but regular decrease in the number of traditional Jews and a slight increase in the percentage of Israelis who classify themselves as secular.
15. Earlier in the book, I discussed a number of questions relating to anti-Semitism that were presented to students. These questions clearly do not facilitate a thorough, comprehensive exploration of the issue. An in-depth study on the attitude of Israeli youth to anti-Semitism is undoubtedly in order.
16. Some students from the Ultra-Orthodox education sector expressed serious reservations regarding such a possibility.
17. On these and other subjects from the perspective of American Jewry, see, among other sources, Uzi Rebhun, *Migration, Community and Identification: Jews in Late 20th Century America* (Jerusalem, 2001) [Hebrew].
18. Chapter 2, table 2.11, which presents responses according to education sectors.
19. The non-religious sub-group and the State-Religious teaching students displayed a similar level of connection to the state of Israel: more than 85 percent chose "an extremely strong connection," and another 10 to 12 percent chose "a medium connection."
20. For a comparison, see table 2.10 in chapter 2 of this book.
21. See Liebman, *Living Together,* 13.

# CONCLUSION

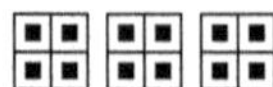

In this book, I have discussed a number of different aspects of Jewish-Israeli identity and Arab-Israeli identity, but certainly not all of them. The fact that it is based primarily on the results of two studies undertaken 18 years apart provides this book with a unique comparative dimension, which is even more enlightening as a result of the additional perspective provided by the participation of Arab students.

Throughout the text, I attempted to present the data in a precise manner, in accordance with the standards of scientific research. However, the empirical data can also be explained and interpreted in ways that differ and may even contradict my approach here. I saw my role as presenting the situation, placing the issues on the educational and ideological agenda, and providing some of the tools necessary to begin discussing them. In this capacity, the study did not aim to propose solutions in the realm of education. I hope that the professionals working in the realm of Jewish and Zionist education, and the many different frameworks working on co-existence and democracy education, will pay close attention to the many interesting findings that have emerged from the material at my disposal.

At the same time, it is important to emphasize that this study did not tackle issues such as attitudes toward anti-Semitism, Diaspora Jewry and Israel-Diaspora relations, the place of Israeli Jews within the Jewish people, religion, intermarriage, Jewish immigration to Israel, Arab Israelis, and democratic values as thoroughly and comprehensively as possible. I hope that intensifying and expanding my research methods and carrying out additional research will enable me to continue gaining a better understanding of the complex questions related to our identity.

It is extremely difficult to talk about Israeli identity, or Israeli *identities* as a single, uniform entity. Tensions between Arab Israelis and Jewish Israelis run extremely high and appear to be getting progressively worse as the Palestinian-Israeli conflict drags on with no solution in sight. It is also difficult to talk about the Jewish-Israeli identity of the Jewish population of the state of Israel in uniform terms. The population's breakdown by education sector and religiosity, which more or less overlaps the division by sectors, reveals significant differences in almost every area of Jewish-Israeli identity.

The identity of Israelis, I emphasize, is not simply Israeli identity alone. Rather, for each sub-group, it is to a large extent a combination of relevant Jewish and Israeli components. Indeed, the variable of religiosity emerges as the factor with the most influence on Jewish-Israeli identity in comparison to all other factors (independent variables), such as country of birth, etc.

In practice, Jewish-Israeli identity can be understood as consisting of four profiles or models of sub-identity:

1) Non-Religious (Secular) Identity
2) Traditional Identity
3) National-Religious Identity
4) Ultra-Orthodox Religious Identity

The Holocaust is the most significant common factor shared by all four sub-identities. However, there are of course differences in the way each sub-identity relates to specific aspects of the subject. Israeli identity also contains a fifth sub-identity: Arab-Israeli, or Palestinian-Israeli identity.

## Non-Religious (Secular) Jewish-Israeli Identity

The majority of the student population of the state education sector possesses this model of identity. People with this identity are more Israeli than Jewish, although this is less true today than it was in the past. The main component of their Jewish identity is the Holocaust.

Non-religious Israelis possess a strong sense of connection with the state and the land—the two Israeli components of Jewish-Israeli identity. Their attitude toward the Jewish components of identity—the Jewish people on the one hand, and the Jewish religion on the other hand—is much weaker and less meaningful, and sometimes one of opposition. The Israeli component of their identity is currently in decline, which reflects the difficulties of Israeliness and perhaps also the crisis (and rupture) in Israeli identity.

From their perspective, the most significant historical events are the Holocaust, the establishment of the state, and the wars fought by Israel.

## Traditional Identity

For Israelis with a traditional identity, Jewishness and Israeliness are very important. The traditional sub-identity is one with an extremely strong, if not the strongest sense of connection to the Land of Israel and the state of Israel, as well as a very strong connection with the Jewish people and the Jewish religion. Most members of this group come from families whose parents are more religious than they are. In many respects, the traditional sub-identity represents an intermediate group with a tendency of decreasing religiosity. A traditional sub-identity is not formed in the opposite direction, from non-religious to religiousness. Jews from Eastern countries constitute a large portion of this group. The historical events that are important to them are the same events that are important to people with a non-religious sub-identity, in addition to events from ancient Jewish history, which they regard as much less significant.

## National-Religious Identity

Judaism and Jewishness are dominant components of this sub-identity. The Jewish identity of Israelis with this sub-identity is based firmly on religion, which is forever bound to the Jewish people, yielding a nationalist religion. Their relationship with the Land of Israel and the state of Israel is also very deep, and their sense of Israeliness is very strong. In their eyes, the most important historical events are the Holocaust, the establishment of the state, and the giving of the Torah.

With regard to issues such as Zionism, Israeliness, and the state of Israel, their approach is similar to that of Israelis who possess a traditional sub-identity. On issues related to religion that I examined (attitudes toward the streams of Judaism, the role of religion in public and private life, and the role of religion in ensuring the future existence of the Jewish people, etc.), their approach is extremely similar to that of Israelis possessing the ultra-orthodox sub-identity (although, clearly, there are also serious differences between these groups regarding many issues of religion).

## Ultra-Orthodox Religious Identity

Israelis who possess this sub-identity see themselves only as Jews. Their attitude toward Israeliness is negative—one of opposition, denial, and repression. Religion provides the content and meaning of their Jewish identity, and on this basis their feelings regarding the Jewish people and the Land of Israel are extremely strong. Their attitude toward Zionism as a political-ideological movement is often negative, and their attitude toward the state of Israel is fairly critical. For them, the most significant events in Jewish history are the Holocaust and the giving of the Torah, followed by other events from ancient Jewish national-religious history. In contrast to the 1990 study, in which they were classified as a separate sub-group, students of ultra-orthodox identity did not participate in the 2008 study as a separate group and were classified as part of the religious sub-group (ultra-orthodox students studied on a number of campuses).

## Arab-Israeli Identity

I treated Arab students as one category, despite the fact that this group contains many different sub-groups, the most prominent of which are based on religious identity. For all of these students, many of whom regard themselves as Palestinians, the Nakba serves as a major force shaping a common identity. In addition to their different levels of religiosity, it is important to remember that Arab Israelis contain a number of different religious groups, such as Muslims, Christians, and Druze, and that even among Muslims there are differing approaches and opinions. There are also differences in attitude toward Arabness and Palestinianess. Israeliness is more than just the citizenship of these students—it is a component of their identity (I do not know the degree to which this is representative of other groups within the Arab-Israeli or Palestinian-Israeli population).

The five sub-identities discussed above share few if any common points, and it is doubtful if any will emerge in the near future. This finding should be regarded as most significant for the educational agenda of all those engaged in Jewish and Zionist education and education toward democracy and co-existence, and should help better enable them to cultivate democratic values in Israeli society.

It is secular Israelis who must contend with the greatest challenges regarding their identity. The questions of identity faced by non-religious young Israelis are more complex than those faced by young religious Israelis, and in some cases they develop into major problems of identity. The Jewish-Israeli identity cultivated by many elements within the non-religious education system often lacks the consistency and clarity necessary to create a harmonious, all encompassing framework. Points of tension tend to evolve around two focal points:

1) The relationship between religion and nationalism, and its impact on Jewish identity.
2) The relationship between Jewishness and Israeliness.

Both points of tension also influence opinions toward and the relationship with Arab-Israelis.

In contrast, the Jewish life and identity of both the national religious and the ultra-orthodox communities is shaped and fueled by a religious worldview. As long as it is not undermined or toppled, this worldview provides young religious Jews with constant, dependable solutions that together constitute a complete whole. Religious students know how to clearly and confidently define their identity. As I have explained, young religious Israelis are Jewish from both a religious and national perspective. This endows them with a deep, meaningful relationship with religion, the people, the land, and the state (with the exception of the ultra-orthodox, and their view of Israeliness and the state of Israel).

The Israeli identity of young national-religious Israelis today is for them strong and meaningful, and strikingly unproblematic. In Israeli society today, young national religious Israelis no longer feel rejected or compelled to defend or justify themselves, as they may have in the past. In fact, they now feel that they have the answers and that the future belongs to them. For example, a large percentage of this population volunteers for elite units within the I.D.F. The major weak point of this subgroup is its weak democratic and humanistic values and its attitude toward "others." In contrast, I posit that the major weak point in the Jewish identity and Jewish education of young non-religious Israelis lies in their Jewish-national identity and their attitude toward the Jewish people in the past and present. The Jewish component of their non-religious identity is fragmented and lacking, and this is reflected in their attitude toward Jewish history, the Holocaust, and particularly the Jewish people in Israel and the Diaspora after the Holocaust. They do not see themselves as part of the Jewish people in any meaningful way. As far as they are concerned, the "People of Israel" refers only to the people living in Israel.

Neither of my two studies directly examined the work and influence of the Israeli education system in the areas discussed throughout this book. However, to some degree, my findings must be understood as the product of the Israeli education system. In my opinion, the major shortcoming of this system is the fact that it fails to cultivate an open, understanding, and well-informed attitude toward the Jewish people that addresses the complexities and that does not disregard others. Without nurturing this component of our identity and understanding ourselves as people who are Jewish as well as Israeli, and without cultivating a positive attitude toward the Jewish people in Israel and the Diaspora in the past and present, we are like a person with two legs trying to get through life by hopping on one foot.

In this way, the current state of affairs is partly the result of education in Israel, which has taken measures to weaken the tolerant, secular national education stream, despite the fact that this stream was supported by people who for many years had worked designing the country's education system. Members of this stream regard the Jewish people as a nation and Judaism not as a religion but rather as a national culture. Initially, this "national secularism" in the form of liberal Zionist socialism, set the dominant ideological tone of spiritualism in Israel. However, the last four decades have witnessed a decline in its status and its ability to present alternatives to the Jewish religion. The Israeli education system, which for years was controlled by this approach, nurtured a distinct sense of Israeliness, strong bonds with the state of Israel and the Land of Israel, and the supremacy of Zionism. This identity was characterized by a strong sense of Israel-centricity and views supporting negation of the Diaspora and the "exilic" Jew.

Young Israelis raised in this educational framework regarded themselves first and foremost as Israeli. As such, the most prominent components of their identity were their relationship with the state and the land. At times, they possessed a limited Zionist approach that highlighted the centrality of the state of Israel, and their attitude toward the Jewish religion and the Jewish people was to some extent hesitant.

This study identified a decline of the Israeli components of Jewish-Israeli identity and an intensification of the Jewish components. This trend, which appears not only to have continued but to have intensified as well, was also recognized by previous identity studies carried out in the 1970s and 1980s. Although I am unable to determine the depth of the processes with any sense of certainty, I am nonetheless able to point out a number of facts:

1) As I have shown in various contexts, the sense of Israeliness in Israeli identity has declined.
2) This decline of Israeliness might explain, or at least help to explain, the intensification of Jewishness. Nonetheless, it is difficult to determine whether there has been a significant change in the way we relate to ourselves as Jews. That is to say, are young Israelis today more Jewish merely because they are less Israeli, or has their Jewishness actually intensified?
3) Without a doubt, the way Israelis perceive the Holocaust has undergone a substantial change. This change, which was also identified by previous studies, was reflected in the 2008 study in unequivocal terms. The Holocaust has become a major force, and at times *the* major force shaping Jewish identity. From this perspective, current attitudes toward the Holocaust do in fact indicate an intensification of Jewishness. At the same time, however, these attitudes also reflect clear Zionist undertones.
4) This significant change in the way we look at the Holocaust—reflected in increased identification with the victims and a greater sense of pride regarding their behavior, among other things—has not involved changes in the way we consider other periods of Jewish history or in our attitudes toward Diaspora Jewry.

Finally, I again emphasize the fact that the population of the 1990 study consisted of future Israeli teachers, a group that until that point had not been studied in this context. The degree to which the education system in general and teachers in particular influence the attitudes of young Israelis is beyond the scope of this book. Still, the 1990 study indicated that the process of attitude change was occurring within the education system as well. This group of professionals is likely to have some kind of impact on the opinions, feelings, and knowledge possessed by the young generation.

Again, my main argument is that we must bring about a fundamental change in our work in this field. If we are truly interested in such a change, we need to begin with institutions that hold formative influence, including institutions engaged in the training of teachers and other educators. It is they who need to initiate the discussion, clarification, and teaching of these issues and introduce them to the different parts of Israeli society, primarily the education system.

We must remember that during the years that elapsed between my two studies, major changes took place in Israel and the world that influenced the identity of young Israelis in various ways. These changes included the rise and fall of the Oslo Accords (1993), the wave of mass immigration from the C.I.S. countries during the 1990s, economic liberalization, increasing socioeconomic disparities, the first Intifada (1987–1991), the al-Aqsa Intifada (2000–2005), globalization, privatization, and the events of 11 September 2001. The influence of these events and processes on Israeli identity has not been sufficiently researched (with the possible exception of the impact of the wave of immigration to Israel from the former Soviet Union).

In general terms, it appears clear that questions of identity in Israeli society have gone virtually unchanged over the years. There has not been a significant change in the relationship among the sub-groups; the Holocaust continues to constitute a major (although slightly weaker) force; there has been little change in how Israeli Jews see the Jews of the Diaspora; and Jewish-Arab relations are still a central issue, although they have been radicalized over the years.

Finally, although this study did not directly address the ongoing influence of the Israeli occupation and control of another people on the bodies and minds of young Israelis, its impact is both undeniable and destructive. In the long term, the occupation also diminishes humanistic values and reinforces attitudes that are undemocratic, generalizing, stereotypical, and in some cases downright racist.

The current attitudes of Israel's young students and future teachers are the product of an existing reality with social, spiritual, ideological, political, and educational aspects. Although in-depth discussion of this reality lies beyond the scope of this book, the introduction addressed some aspects. At this point, it is appropriate to briefly consider some of the educational implications of this situation.

# Epilogue

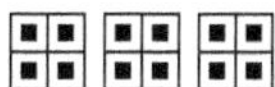

The tensions and struggles among sub-identities in Israeli society continue to go unresolved and will most likely remain unresolved for the foreseeable future. Unresolved also are the fundamental questions regarding Jewish-Israeli identity. Our goal should not be one of forced uniformity or an attempt to do away with the other identities. Rather, we must aspire to recognize and accept the diversity, pluralism, and legitimacy of other expressions of Jewish-Israeli identity.

Historically, it was actually the secular movements in Judaism and Zionism that attempted to negate the profound significance of religion in the Jewish experience, arguing that religion was something of the past and that its disappearance was a necessary condition for social progress. In many ways, the situation has been reversed. The self-image of the religious community, which previously regarded itself as helpless and under siege, has been transformed. The ultra-orthodox have re-established their temporarily weakened authority and are now challenging secular (and religious) Zionism. The same is true of nationalist Zionism, the religious (and secular) expression of which cast doubt upon the validity of the other streams within Judaism and Zionism.

From their perspective, the religious educational frameworks do in fact provide students with the tools to contend with their Jewish reality. Israel's Jewish religious sectors are also more successful in providing such tools because they educate their young members in a world of absolute values. In my opinion, an atmosphere of absolute values cannot and should not exist in the moral and educational realms of the secular sector. The dominance of the religious component in Israel's orthodox religious education sectors typically results in an intentional abstention from addressing issues of pluralism and diversity in the modern Jewish world. Religious education provides no solution for Jewish realities in the midst of change. In some cases, it also fails to provide an answer to the question of sovereign Jewish existence in the state of Israel.

However, it is my contention that the immanent weakness of some (large?) portions of the national-religious sector in recent decades stems from its reliance on messianic-Zionist ideology. In this study, this fundamental ideological weakness is reflected in questions pertaining to attitudes toward the Arab "other" and opinions regarding democratic values. The fact that Israelis who possess a national-religious identity seem to know how to clearly and confidently define their Judaism and Israeliness provides no guarantees for the future. This picture, abounding with faith and self-confidence regarding the steadfastness of the identity of the religious-Zionist students in the study population, which is greatly influenced by messianic ideas, may very well crash and crumble on the rocks of practical reality. The Jewish ultra-orthodox worldview is fueled and shaped solely by religion. Most elements within the ultra-orthodox sector deal neither with the Israeli nor the Zionist components of their identity which underlie the very existence of the state of Israel. At the same time, the responses of the ultra-orthodox students in the 1990 study indicate that their negation of their Israeliness and Zionism is not as complete as the ultra-orthodox worldview would have us believe.

Still, the ability of secular Judaism and humanistic Zionism to stand the test of time will depend first on itself—that is, on its ability to define its principles, to struggle for them, and to successfully pass them down from generation to generation. According to Aba Kovner, "More than ever, the future of the Jewish people is dependent on Jews' attitudes toward themselves, their past, and the terrible tragedy they suffered, as well as on the self examination obligated by this historical consciousness."[1]

As secular Jews, we currently face two major questions:

1) Will we have the courage to be secular Jews? In 1981, Yizhar Smilansky wrote: "There are many religious Jews and even more non-religious Jews. There are, however, few secular Jews. For them, the required steadfastness and courage to understand and assume responsibility is too great."[2] However, I want to emphasize that being a secular Jew does not mean disconnecting from the past, from tradition, and from our heritage—not even our religious heritage. Being a secular Jew means taking a critical approach to this heritage, seeing Judaism not as a source of authority but a source of inspiration, and having the ability to chose from it what is meaningful and relevant.
2) Will we be able to nurture our awareness of and sense of connection to the Jewish people? Consciousness of the homeland, the state, and the land cannot replace consciousness of the people because the state of Israel exists for the sake of the Jewish people. The state has no roots, and its designation for the Jewish people diminishes its importance.[3]

For more than four generations, Jewish education in the Land of Israel was based on the aim of enabling Jews to establish roots in their homeland. Today, however, as Rotenstreich says, "Jews in Israel will have no roots in their country and homeland if they have no roots in the Jewish people." Following this, one can argue dialectically that young Israelis will not be active citizens of their homeland if they do not feel themselves to be members of the Jewish people living their lives in their homeland, with a connection to the Jewish people.[4]

Eliezer Schweid also believes that a connection to the homeland is a function of national identification. In his opinion, the basis of the national connection to the country is neither landscape, nature, fauna, flora, nor archeology, but rather history and culture: individuals' identification with their people and its history and culture. It is from these things alone, Schweid contends, that a connection to the homeland may emerge.[5]

On the relationship between the state of Israel and the Jewish people, Rotenstreich argues as follows: "Change and the obligation to change is the responsibility of the Jews of the state of Israel.... The automatic nature of the connection with the Jewish people is not likely to serve as a guarantee, because this connection does not exist in a vacuum. The natural tendency within the state of Israel is to highlight differences, and this brings with it the possibility of divisiveness."[6]

I propose implementing the ideas suggested by the thinkers quoted above. Since the Six Days War, educational, ideological, and research frameworks that are secular in nature have paid extensive attention to the heritage, tradition, legends, and holidays of Israel. While such activity is to be welcomed, it often seems that it is being done in an apologetic manner, in an attempt to prove that we, who in this context are termed "secular Jews," are also good Jews.

The number of trips to Poland has also increased in recent years. While I do not oppose such trips in themselves, I do think it is mistaken to believe that they alone can provide a solution to the challenges of Jewish and Zionist education by instilling within young Israelis the "Zionist message".

The trips to Poland are in many ways a microcosm of our Jewish and Zionist education. Within the spiritual and emotional boredom and neglect and the quest for the matriculation certificate that typically characterizes the school years of most young Israelis, the trip to Poland constitutes a curious, alluring, and extremely significant experience that sparks a torrential and inspiring storm of emotions. In this context, trips to Poland have the potential to become the most important, meaningful, and influential educational force in the life of young Israelis. Under no circumstances should this be allowed to happen. At Auschwitz, we do not learn about how people live. We learn about how Jews died. Who were the victims? How did they live their lives? What was their reality? What were their religious, cultural, and spiritual values? We know very little about these things. Searching for national identity in the ashes among the furnaces, and in the killing ditches of Poland, is pointless and ultimately fruitless. Extermination camps and military cemeteries cannot be the only common ground between young Israelis and the Jews of the Diaspora. This would mean that we are one people unified only by common tragedy; that we as a people are a function of tragedy, of the continuum of Jewish suffering: that we are eternal victims.

In Israel and abroad, we once hoped and believed that the Holocaust represented a crossroads, a turning point in human history. We believed that the greatest moral failure ever known to human civilization would make us wiser and teach us lessons that can be summed up by the words "never again." Although the world adopted this motto, acts of genocide continue to take place today. We now know that the Holocaust was not, and most likely will not serve as that long awaited crossroads beyond which the world will no longer allow such events to recur. To a certain extent, teaching and education can help change this situation. Knowledge and awareness of genocide as a phenomenon is a necessary precondition (although clearly not the only one) for addressing it and attempting to improve it.

This should be simple, and should boil down to struggling against every act of genocide so that it will not reoccur in the future. "Never again" should mean, among other things, teaching the subject. But the reality of things is different and much more complicated. Israeli students know almost nothing about the different cases of genocide that have taken place around the world.

My experience as an educator has shown me that teaching about genocide provides new perspectives and broadens horizons. Moreover, learning about the subject brings about a change in the level of awareness and involvement. Students are surprised to learn that they knew nothing about the Armenian genocide, the Gypsy genocide, and the genocide of the people in Rwanda that took place before our very own eyes. They are astounded when they realize the significance of the fact that they knew nothing about these events, and even more so, of *why* they knew nothing about them. They are even more shocked when they learn about the positions of the state of Israel. As a result, some become activists on issues related to genocide, for example by helping to provide aid to the refugees of Darfur.

If we had managed to more effectively embrace the universal implications of the Holocaust, the suffering experienced by the Jews and the Palestinians should have motivated us to work toward compromise and reconciliation. This, however, does not reflect the reality of the situation today.[7]

Still, the major shortcoming of Jewish and Zionist education in non-religious frameworks lies less in what it contains and more in what it does not contain. Its weakness lies in the fact that it does virtually nothing to develop a relationship with the Jewish people that is open and aware of the complexities involved, and that does not disregard others.

The situation calls for making a serious change and for dedicating ideological and educational efforts to this "unseen" issue. My proposed area of study, "Contemporary Jewry," can also be referred to as "The Jewish World in Our Times, in Israel and the Diaspora," and should aim to increase knowledge and understanding, and to change opinions. This field of study would focus on the similarities and differences between the Jewish people in Israel and the Diaspora, on what divides and unifies them. This course of study should help young Israelis examine the questions that are important to their Judaism and Israeliness from a broader perspective of time (Jewish existence in the modern era) and space (Jews in Israel and Jews in the Diaspora).

We must venture outside the realities of Israel to the realities of Diaspora Jewry and use the questions that are crucial for the future of Jewish existence in Israel in order to better understand the Jews of the Diaspora. This will make learning and discussing Diaspora Jewry relevant to young Israelis and incorporate the subject into their realm of knowledge and reference. At the same time, it will also enable them to see themselves from another perspective.

In this context, it is also important to note that the approach that holds that educational efforts to address Jewish emigration from Israel should focus on strengthening Israeliness is mistaken. According to this approach, a Jewish person with a Jewish identity can emigrate to anywhere in the world and still remain a Jew, whereas someone with an Israeli identity is only Israeli in Israel. In contrast, I believe that the educational components of emigration are also located in Jewish and not Israeli contexts. It is from these Jewish contexts that Israeliness emerges as a choice of Jewish-Israeli uniqueness, and not vice-versa.

We must aspire to a more appropriate balance of the human, Jewish, and Israeli components of identity than that which exists today. It is as a result of our existence as people and members of human civilization that we are Jews and Israelis. The move from patriotism to nationalism can be extremely quick. Indeed, nationalism is one of the most toxic poisons of the modern era, and within it lies great destructive capacity. Identity constructed even partially on a foundation of negative factors and shaped in the context of ongoing conflict is especially vulnerable to this danger, and we must remain aware of this dynamic. This threat is even more serious for those with religious sub-identities. Their attitudes toward racism and the "other" have not changed over the years. Levels of racism remain extremely high, and on the state level nothing has been done to prevent or reduce the phenomenon.

Failure in democracy education, education toward co-existence, and education against racism is likely to be sizable and to have serious repercussions. We must begin working as intensively as possible on substantial education against racism, and we must acknowledge the racism that is around us. We must also acknowledge that we are not only the object of racism, but that we hold racist views as well, as was demonstrated in this volume.

We must also teach Israeli students about the two great cultures that Jews and Arabs produced throughout history. Arab culture remains completely unknown to young Jewish Israelis, who only extremely rarely meet the young Arabs who live alongside them in the state of Israel.

The question is not whether we should teach about the Jewish present and past, the values of democracy, and the struggle against racism as educated people are obligated to do. The challenging, fundamental question is how do we go about engaging in these subjects through true dialogue with the younger generation. This is a necessary precondition (although there are certainly others) for creating relevance and involvement. How do we develop the emotional dimension alongside the intellectual dimension?

Will we succeed in generating an educational process that brings about true identification with a Judaism that is positive, democratic and respectful of others; that is vivacious and creative, and inextricably linked to the long heritage of Jewish culture; and that young Israelis choose as their own? Here, I again emphasize my belief that Jewishness and Israeliness has neither value nor meaning for young Jewish Israelis unless they choose them.

Some readers will almost certainly disagree with all or some of the ideological and educational guidelines proposed above, and this is a good thing. I believe strongly that we need to encourage discussion on disputed issues as well. Only through teaching, study, clarification, and discussion will we be able to devise the plan or plans necessary to revitalize Jewish and Zionist education and to tackle the issues facing Jewish-Israeli identity today.

## Notes

1. Aba Kovner, "From Generation to Generation," *Moreshet* 50 (1991): 13 [Hebrew].
2. Smilansky, "The Courage to Be Secular."
3. Rotenstreich, *On Jewish Existence in the Present,* 169.
4. Ibid., 167–68.
5. Eliezer Schweid, *Jewish Nationalism* (Jerusalem, 1972), 133.
6. Rotenstreich, *On Jewish Existence in the Present,* 168.
7. For example, see Avihu Ronen, "The Suffering of the Other: Teaching the Holocaust to Jews and Arabs," in *Multiculturalism and Israeli Society,* ed. Ohad Nachtomi (Jerusalem, 2003), 193–302 [Hebrew]. In my opinion, this humanistic approach is also expressed in the ten books published for the course "Genocide" by the Open University, as well as the program *Sensitivity to the World's Suffering: Genocide in the 20th Century* (Tel Aviv, 1994) [Hebrew].

# Selected Bibliography

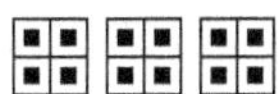


Achcar, Gilbert. *The Arabs and the Holocaust—The Arab-Israeli War of Narratives.* New York: Metropolitan Books, 2010.

Agassi, Joseph. *Between Faith and Nationality: Towards an Israeli National Identity.* Tel Aviv: Papirus, 1984 [Hebrew].

Al-Haj, Majid. "Identity and Orientation Among the Arabs in Israel: A Situation of Double Peripherality." *State, Government and International Relations* 41/42 (1997): 103–22 [Hebrew].

———. "The Impact of The Intifada on the Orientation of the Arabs in Israel: The Case of a Double Periphery." In *Framing the Intifada: Media and People,* ed. Akiva Cohen and Gadi Wolsfeld. Norwood: A Blex Publishing Corporation, 1993.

Almog, Oz. *The Sabra: The Creation of the New Jew.* Berkeley: University of California Press, 2000.

Anderson, Benedict. *Imagined Communities.* New York: Verson, 1983.

Angvik, Magne, and Bodo von Borries, eds. *Youth and History—A Comparative European Survey on Historical Consciousness and Political Attitudes among Adolescents.* Hamburg: Korber-Stiftung, 1997.

Auron, Yair. "The Holocaust—A Main Factor in Jewish Israeli Identity." In *Jewish Identity, Values, and Social Pursuits,* ed. Eric Cohen. Tel Aviv: Kelman Center for Jewish Education, Tel Aviv University, 2008 [Hebrew].

———. *The Pain of Knowledge.* New Brunswick: Transaction Publishers, 2005.

———. *The Banality of Indifference: Zionism and the Armenian Genocide.* New Brunswick: Rutgers University Press, 2000.

Auron, Yair. *The Banality of Denial:Israel and the Armenian Genocide.* New Brunswick: Rutgers University Press, 2007

———. "The Attitude of the Organized Jewish Youth in France to the Holocaust and Anti-Semitism." *Yahadut Zmaneinu* 2 (1984–85): 209–35 [Hebrew].

———. *Jewish-Israeli Identity.* Tel Aviv: Sifriat Poalim, 1983 [Hebrew].

Auron, Yair, Gila Zelikovitz, and Nili Keren. *Attitudes of Teaching Students in Israel toward Anti-Semitism and Racism.* Tel Aviv: Seminar Hakibbutzim College of Education, 1996 [Hebrew].

Avineri, Shlomo. *Varieties of The Zionist Idea.* Tel Aviv: Am Oved, 1980 [Hebrew].

Azoulay, Ariella. *Consistent Violence, 1947–1950: A Genealogy of a Regime and "The Catastrophe from Their Point of View."* Tel Aviv: Resling, 2009 [Hebrew].

Bar-On, Dan. *The Other Within Us: Changes in Israeli Identity from a Psychosocial Perspective.* Beer Sheva: Ben-Gurion University Press, 1999 [Hebrew].

Bar-On, Dan et al. "A Journey to the Holocaust: Modes of Understanding among Israeli Adolescents Who Visited Poland." *Educational Review* (2004): 13–31.

———. "Jewish Israeli Teenagers, National Identity, and the Lessons of the Holocaust." *Holocaust and Genocide Studies* 18, no. 2 (2004): 188–204.

Ben-Sira, Zeev. *Democracy and Jewish High School Students: Essence, Support, and Meanings regarding Education and Democracy (A Report).* Jerusalem: Guttman Institute of Applied Social Research, 1990 [Hebrew].

Binyamini, Kalman. *Political and Civil Standpoints o Israeli Youth in Israel: A Research Report.* Jerusalem: The Hebrew University, NCJW Research Institute for Innovation in Education, 1994 [Hebrew].

Buber, Martin. *Judaism and the Jews.* Jerusalem: Hasifria Hatziyonit, 1959–60 [Hebrew].

Calderon, Nissim. *Pluralists Against Their Will: Multiculturalism versus Pluralism in Israel.* Tel Aviv: Zmora Bitan, 2000 [Hebrew].

Caplan, Kimmy. "The Holocaust in Contemporary Israeli Haredi Popular Religion." *Modern Judaism* 22 (2002): 146–68.

Caspi, Aryeh. "Peace Through the Sites." *Haaretz Weekend Magazine,* 1 November 1996 [Hebrew].

Chaumont, Jean-Michel. *La Concurrence de Victimes—Génocide, Identité, Reconnaissance.* Paris: La Découverte, 1997.

Cohen, Eric, ed. *Jewish Identity, Values, and Social Pursuits: The World of Israeli Students in State High Schools.* Tel Aviv: Kelman Center for Jewish Education, University of Tel Aviv, 2008 [Hebrew].

Deutsch, Haim, and Menachem Ben-Sasson, eds. *The Other Within and Without.* Tel Aviv: Yediot Aharonot, 2001 [Hebrew].

Dubnow, Shimon. *Letters on Ancient and Modern Judaism.* Tel Aviv: Dvir, 1936–37 [Hebrew].

Eilam, Yigal. *Judaism as Status Quo.* Tel Aviv: Am Oved, 2000 [Hebrew].

Elon, Amos. *The Israelis: Founders and Sons.* London: Weidenfeld and Nicolson, 1971.

Ezrachi, Yakov, and Gal Reuven. Opinions and Worldviews of High School Students on Issues of Society, Security and Peace—Youth Survey No. 2. Zichron Yaakov: Carmel Institute for Social Studies, 1995 [Hebrew].

Farago, Uri. "The Jewish Identity of Israeli Youth, 1965–1985." *Yahadut Zmaneinu* 5 (1989): 259–89 [Hebrew].

———. "Holocaust Consciousness among Youth Students in Israel." *Dapim l'Kheker Hashoah* 3 (1984): 159–177 [Hebrew].

———. "The Connection Between Approaches to Zionism and Jewish Identity among Israeli Youth." *Iyunim b'Khinuch* 18 (1978): 30–37 [Hebrew].

———. *Stability and Change in the Jewish Identity of Working Youth in Israel: 1965–1974.* Jerusalem: Hebrew University of Jerusalem, Levi Eshkol Institute, 1977 [Hebrew].

Feldman, Jackie. *Above the Death Pits, Beneath the Flag: Youth Voyages to Poland and the Performance of Israeli National Identity.* New York: Berghahn Books, 2008.

———. "Marking the Boundaries of the Enclave: Defining the Israeli Collective through the Poland 'Experience.'" *Israel Studies* 7, no. 2 (2002): 84–114.

Firer, Ruth. *Agents of the Holocaust Lesson.* Tel Aviv: Hakibbutz Hameuchad, 1989 [Hebrew].

———. *Agents of Zionist Education.* Tel Aviv: Haibbutz Hameuchad and Sifriat Poalim, 1985 [Hebrew].

Fisherman, Shraga, and Shlomo Kaniel. "Changes in Identity after a Visit to Poland." *Dapim* 37 (2004): 182–202 [Hebrew].

Friedman, Menachem. *Haredi Ultra-Orthodox Society: Sources, Trends, and Processes.* Jerusalem: The Jerusalem Institute for Israel Studies, 1991 [Hebrew].

———. "The State of Israel as a Religious Dilemma." *Alapyim* 3 (1990): 24–68 [Hebrew].

———. *Society and Religion: The Non-Zionist Orthodoxy in the Land of Israel, 1918–1936.* Jerusalem: Yad Ben-Zvi, 1978 [Hebrew].

Gorny, Yosef. *In Search of National Identity.* Tel Aviv: Am Oved, 1990 [Hebrew].

———. "The Attitude of the Poale Zion Party in the Land of Israel toward the Diaspora (During the Second Aliyah)," *Hatzionut* 2 (1970–71) [Hebrew].

Grossman, David. *Present Absentees.* Tel Aviv: Hakibbutz Hameuchad, 1992 [Hebrew].

Gur-Zeev, Ilan, and Ilan Pappe. "Palestinian Control of the Memories of the Holocaust and the Nakba." In *Philosophy, Politics, and Education in Israel,* ed. Ilan Gur-Zeev. Haifa: University of Haifa and Zmora Bitan, 2000 [Hebrew].

Ha'am, Ehad. "Three Steps." In *The Collected Writings of Ahad Ha'am.* Tel Aviv: Dvir, 1952–53 [Hebrew] (originally published 1899).

Halabi, Rabah. "The Palestinians as the Scapegoat of the Holocaust." In *Neve Shalom School for Peace Annual Report for 1998-1999* (1999) [Hebrew].

Hazaz, Haim. *The Sermon and Selected Stories (According to the Curriculum of the Ministry of Education).* Tel Aviv: Dvir, 1991 [Hebrew].

———. "The Sermon." In *Modern Hebrew Literature,* ed. Robert Alter. New York: Behrman House, 1975.

Herman, Simon N. *Israelis and Jews: The Continuity of an Identity* (New York: Random House, 1970).

———. *Jewish Identity: A Social Perspective.* Beverly Hills: Sage Publications, 1977.

———. *Jewish Identity: A Social Psychological Perspective.* Jerusalem: Hasifria Hatziyonit, 1980 [Hebrew].

Hermann, Tamar, and David Newman. "The Dove and the Skullcap: Secular and Religious Divergence in the Israeli Peace Camp." In *Living Together: Religious-Secular Relations in Israeli Society,* ed. Yeshayahu (Charles) Liebman. Jerusalem: Keter, 1990 [Hebrew].

Horowitz, Dan, and Moshe Lissak. *Trouble in Utopia.* Tel Aviv: Am Oved, 1990 [Hebrew].

Jubran, Salem. "The Arabs and the Holocaust: A Historic and Current Perspective." *Bishvil Hazikaron* 17 (1996): 15–18 [Hebrew].

Kadman, Noga. *On the Side of the Road and in the Margins of Consciousness—Depopulated Palestinian Villages of 1948 in the Israeli Discourse.* Jerusalem: November Books, 2008 [Hebrew].

Kashti, Or. "Israel Turns Down Bid to Teach Palestinian Poems in School." *Haaretz,* 15 February 2010.

Katz, Elihu, and Michael Gurvitz. *Leisure Culture in Israel: Patterns in Consumption.* Tel Aviv: Am Oved, 1973 [Hebrew].

Katznelson, Berl. "Being Tested (Conversations with Youth Leaders)." In *The Writings of Berl Katznelson,* vol. I. Tel Aviv: Mapai Publications, 1950 [Hebrew].

Keren, Nili, Gila Zelikovitz, and Yair Auron. *Anti-Semitism and Racism: An Attitude Study among High School Students in Israel.* Tel Aviv: Seminar Hakibbutzim College of Education, 1997 [Hebrew].

Kimmerling, Baruch. *The Invention and Decline of Israeliness: State, Society and the Military.* Berkeley: University of California Press, 2001.

Kimmerling, Baruch, and Joel Migdal. *The Palestinian People: A History.* Cambridge, MA: Harvard University Press, 1990.

Kovner, Aba. "From Generation to Generation." *Moreshet* 50 (1991) [Hebrew].

Kurzweil, Baruch. *Our New Literature—Continuity or Revolt?* Jerusalem: Schoken, 1965 [Hebrew].

Leibowitz, Yeshayahu. *Faith, History, and Values.* Jerusalem: Academon Publications, 1983 [Hebrew].

Lev, Michal, and Shlomo Romi. "Israeli Youth and the Holocaust: Knowledge, Emotions, and Attitudes following a Journey to Poland." *Megamot* 42, no.2 (2003): 219–39 [Hebrew].

Levinsohn, Hanna, Elihu Katz, and Majid al-Haj. *Jews and Arabs in Israel—Common Values and Reciprocal Images.* Jerusalem: Sikui, the Association for the Advancement of Equal Opportunity, 1995 [Hebrew].

Levy, Shlomit, Hanna Levinsohn, and Elihu Katz. *A Portrait of Israeli Jewry: Beliefs, Observances, and Values among Israeli Jews 2000.* Jerusalem: The Guttman Center, the Israeli Center for Democracy and the Avichai Fund, 2002 [Hebrew].

———. *Beliefs, Observances, and Social Interaction among Israeli Jews.* Jerusalem: Guttman Institute of Applied Social Research, 1993 [Hebrew].

Levy, Shlomit, and Louis Guttman. *Diaspora Jewry in the Eyes of the Israeli Public.* Jerusalem: Institute of Applied Social Research, 1981 [Hebrew].

Liebman, Yeshayahu (Charles). "Some Thoughts on Relations between Religious and Non-Religious Jews." In *Living Together: Religious-Secular Relations in Israeli Society,* ed. Yeshayau (Charles) Liebman. Jerusalem: Keter, 1990 [Hebrew].

———. "The Holocaust Myth in Israeli Society." *Tefutsot Israel* 19, no. 5 and 6 (Winter 1981) [Hebrew].

Liebman, Yeshayahu (Charles), ed. *Living Together: Religious-Secular Relations in Israeli Society.* Jerusalem: Keter, 1990 [Hebrew].

Liebman, Yeshayahu (Charles), and Eliezer Don-Yehiya. "The Dilemma of Traditional Culture in the Modern State: Changes and Developments in Civil Religion in Israel." *Megamot* 28, no. 4 (1984): 461–486 [Hebrew].

———. *Civil Religion in Israel: Traditional Judaism and the Political Culture in the Jewish State.* Berkeley: University of California Press, 1983.

Lissak, Moshe. "Major Cleavages in Israel Society." In *Pluralism in Israel: From Melting Pot to Salad Bowl,* ed. Yaakov Kop. Jerusalem: The Center for Research of Social Policy in Israel, 2000 [Hebrew].

Litvak, Meir, and Esther Webman. *The Representation of the Holocaust in the Arab World—Facilitator of or Obstacle to the Peace Process.* Tel Aviv: Tami Steinmetz Center for Peace Research, 2006 [Hebrew].

Luz, Ehud. *Parallels Meet.* Tel Aviv: Am Oved, 1985 [Hebrew].

Mandel, Roi. "A Photo Exhibition on the Holocaust at Na'alin: So That Everyone Can Understand the Suffering." www.ynet.co.il, 27 January 2009 [Hebrew].

Mayseless, Ofra, Gal Reuven, and Eli Pishof. *Attitudes and Worldviews of High School Students on Military Issues and National Security.* Zikhron Yaakov: Israeli Institute for Military Studies, 1989 [Hebrew].

Morris, Benny. *The Birth of the Palestinian Refugee Problem, 1947–1949.* Cambridge: Cambridge University Press, 1987.

Mouttapa, Jean. *Un Arabe Face à Auschwitz.* Paris: Albin Michel, 2006.

Nachtomi, Ohad. *Multiculturalism and Israeli Society.* Tel Hai Academic College and Jerusalem: Magnes Publications, 2003 [Hebrew].

Ophir, Adi. "On Feelings that Cannot Be Explained in Words and on Lessons that Cannot Be Questioned." *Bishvil Hazikaron* 7 (1995): 11–15 [Hebrew].

Oz, Amos. "Homeland." *Under This Blazing Light (Essays).* Tel Aviv: Sifriat Poalim, 1979 [Hebrew].

Pappe, Ilan. *The Ethnic Cleaning of Palestine.* Oxford: Oneworld, 2006.

Peled, Yoav, and Gershon Shafir. *Being Israeli: The Dynamics of Multiple Citizenship.* Cambridge: Cambridge University Press, 2002.

Peres, Yochanan, and Eliezer Ben-Rafael. *Cleavages in Israeli Society.* Tel Aviv: Am Oved, 2006 [Hebrew].

Raanan, Zvi. *Gush Emunim.* Tel Aviv: Sifriat Poalim, 1980 [Hebrew].

Rafaeli, Aryeh. *National Conventions of Russian Zionists: A Source on the Zionist Movement in Russia.* Tel Aviv: Katzir, 1963–64 [Hebrew].

Rebhun, Uzi. *Migration, Community and Identification: Jews in Late 20th Century America.* Jerusalem: The Magnes Press, The Hebrew University of Jerusalem, 2001 [Hebrew].

Rotenstreich, Nathan. *On Jewish Existence in the Present.* Tel Aviv: Sifriat Poalim, 1972 [Hebrew].

Rouhana, Nadim. *Palestinian Citizens in an Ethnic Jewish State: Identities in Conflict.* New Haven, CT: Yale University Press, 1997.

Rouhana, Nadim, and Asad Ghanem. "The Crisis in Ethnic State: The Case of the Palestinian Citizens in Israel." *International Journal of Middle East Studies* 30 (1998): 321–46.

Rubinstein, Amnon. *The Zionist Dream Revisited: From Herzl to Gush Emunim and Back.* Tel Aviv: Schoken, 1980 [Hebrew].

———. *To Be a Free Nation in Our Land.* Tel Aviv: Schoken, 1977 [Hebrew].

Rubinstein, Danny. *On the Lord's Side: Gush Emunim.* Tel Aviv: Hakibbutz Hameuchad, 1982 [Hebrew].

Said, Edward. *Orientalism.* New York: Vintage Books, 1979.

Sartre, Jean-Paul. *Thoughts on the Jewish Question.* Tel Aviv: Sifriat Poalim, 1978 [Hebrew]

Scholem, Gershom. "Who Is a Jew?" *Dvarim be-Go.* Tel Aviv: Am Oved, 1976 [Hebrew].

Schweid, Eliezer. "The Justification of Religion and the Test of the Holocaust," *Yahadut Zmanenu* 5 (1988–89) [Hebrew].

———. *Jewish Nationalism.* Jerusalem: S. Zack and Co., 1972 [Hebrew].

Shavit, Yaakov. *From Hebrew to Canaanite.* Tel Aviv: Domino, 1984 [Hebrew].

Shenhav, Yehouda, and Yossi Yonah, eds. *Racism in Israel.* Jerusalem: Van Leer Institute and Hakibbutz Hameuchad, 2008 [Hebrew].

Simon, Ernst. *Are We Still Jews?* Tel Aviv: Sifriat Poalim, 1982 [Hebrew].

Simon, Uriel. *Seek Peace and Pursue It,* revised and expanded 2nd ed. Tel Aviv: Yediot Aharonot, 2004 [Hebrew].

Smilansky, Yizhar. "The Courage to Be a Secular Jew." *Shdemot* 79 (1980–81): 74–80.

Smith, Hanoch. "Israeli Attitudes toward American Jews." *Tfutsot Israel* 1 (1984) [Hebrew].

Smooha, Sammy. "Arab-Jewish Relations in Israel as a Jewish and Democratic State." *Trends in Israeli Society.* Tel Aviv: The Open University, 2001 [Hebrew].

———. "The Regime of the State of Israel: Civil Democracy, Non-Democracy, or Ethnic Democracy?" *Israeli Sociology* 2, no 2 (2000): 565–630 [Hebrew].

———. "Ethnic Democracy: Israel as an Archetype." *Israel Studies* 2 (1997): 198–241.

———. *Autonomy for Arabs in Israel?* Raanana: The Institute for Israeli Arab Studies, 1996 [Hebrew].

———. *Arabs and Jews in Israel: Change and Continuity in Mutual Intolerance.* Boulder: Westview Press, 1992.

———. *Arabs and Jews in Israel: Arabs and Jews in Israel: Conflicting and Shared Attitudes in a Divided Society.* Boulder: Westview Press, 1989.

Talmon, Yaakov. "The Six Days War in Historical Perspective." In *The Era of Violence,* Tel Aviv: Am Oved, 1974 [Hebrew].

Tzur, Tova. "The Trip to Poland as the High Point of an Educational Process." *Bishvil Hazikaron* 7 (1995): 5–7 [Hebrew].

Ya'ar, Ephraim, and Ze'ev Shavit. "Processes and Trends in Collective Identity." In *Trends in Israeli Society,* vol. II, ed. Ephraim Ya'ar and Ze'ev Shavit. Tel Aviv: Open University, 2003 [Hebrew].

Ya'ar, Ephraim, and Ze'ev Shavit, eds. *Trends in Israeli Society.* Tel Aviv: Open University, 2001 [Hebrew].

Yad Tabenkin. *The Attitude of the Youth Movements of the Land of Israel Labor Movement to the Diaspora during the Holocaust (Symposium on Youth Movement Research).* Yad Tabenkin, 1990 [Hebrew].

Yad Vashem. *Survey on the Holocaust and its Significance for the Jewish People* (conducted by Rachel Israeli). Jerusalem: Yad Vashem, November 1999 [Hebrew].

Yaniv, M. *Group Identification, Personal and Collective Self Image, and Deviations in Inter-Group Attribution Among Jews and Arabs in Israel.* Ramat-Gan, Hamul, 1998 [Hebrew].

Yehoshua, A. B. *Toward Normalcy.* Jerusalem: Schoken, 1980 [Hebrew].

Yiftahel, Oren. "The Model of Ethnic Democracy and Jewish-Arab Relations in Israel: Geographic, Historical, and Political Aspects." In *The Jewish-Arab Cleavage: A Reader,* ed. Ruth Gavison and Dafna Hecker. Jerusalem: Israeli Democracy Institute, 2000 [Hebrew].

———. *The Research on the Arab Minority in Israel and its Relations with the Jewish Majority: A Survey and Analysis (Survey 12).* Givat Haviva, Institute for Peace Studies, 1993 [Hebrew].

Yonah, Yossi. "A State of All Its Citizens: A Nation State or Multi-Cultural Democracy? Israel and the Limits of Liberal Democracy." *Alpayim* 16 (1998): 238–63 [Hebrew].

Yonah, Yossi, and Goodman, Yehuda, eds. *Maelstrom of Identities: A Critical Look at Religion and Secularity in Israel.* Jerusalem: Hakibbutz Hameuchad and Van Leer Institute, 2004 [Hebrew].

Yuchtman-Yaar, Ephraim, and Tamar Herman. *The Peace Index, 2002-2003.* Tel Aviv: Tami Steinmetz Center for Peace Research, 2003. http://sprit.tau.ac.il/socant/peace [Hebrew].

Zelikovitz, Moran. "A Jewish-Arab Trip to Poland: Pain as a Common Denominator," 23 April 2006. www.ynet.co.il [Hebrew].

Zemach, Mina. *Through Israeli Eyes: Attitudes toward Judaism, American Jewry, Zionism and the Arab-Israeli Conflict.* New York: The American Jewish Committee, 1987.

———. *Positions of the Jewish Majority in Israel toward the Arab Minority.* Jerusalem: Van Leer Institute, 1980 [Hebrew].

Zemach, Mina, and Ruth Zin. *Positions of Youth on Democratic Values.* Jerusalem: Van Leer Institute, 1984 [Hebrew].

# INDEX

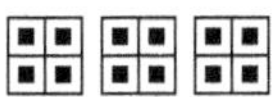

www.ingramcontent.com/pod-product-compliance
Lightning Source LLC
Chambersburg PA
CBHW060032030426
42334CB00019B/2296
*9781782387954*